PORTFOLIO / PENGUIN

THE AGE OF OVERSUPPLY

Daniel Alpert is a founding managing partner of investment bank Westwood Capital, LLC. He is widely quoted in the business media and was featured in the Academy Award—winning documentary *Inside Job*. Alpert is also a fellow in economics of the Century Foundation, the United States' oldest policy think tank. He lives in New York.

THE AGE OF
OVERSUPPLY

OVERCOMING
THE GREATEST CHALLENGE TO
THE GLOBAL ECONOMY

DANIEL ALPERT

Portfolio / Penguin

PORTFOLIO / PENGUIN
Published by the Penguin Group
Penguin Group (USA) LLC
375 Hudson Street
New York, New York 10014

USA | Canada | UK | Ireland | Australia | New Zealand | India | South Africa | China
penguin.com
A Penguin Random House Company

First published in the United States of America by Portfolio / Penguin, a member of
Penguin Group (USA) Inc., 2013
This paperback edition with a new preface published 2014

ISBN 978-1-59184-596-6 (hc.)
ISBN 978-1-59184-701-4 (pbk.)

Printed in the United States of America
10 9 8 7 6 5 4 3 2 1

Designed by Pauline Neuwirth

To Arlene and Gerald Alpert, who taught me what I most needed to know, and to George, Hollis, Owen, and Charles, who will need to know more than I can teach them.

CONTENTS

In September 2012, the U.S. Federal Reserve Bank announced and—shortly thereafter—implemented its third, and by far largest, installment of "quantitative" monetary easing. "QE3," as the initiative is known, has resulted in the Fed acquiring over $1.35 trillion in U.S. government securities through January 2014,[1] and it is expected to generate aggregate purchases of over $1.5 trillion through the anticipated end of the program in mid-2014.

QE3 went well beyond the Fed's two earlier rounds of quantitative easing—QE1, from November 2008 to June 2010, and QE2, from November 2010 to June 2011—and will, when ended, have gone on for longer than even the Fed's initial round of easing during the heart of the global financial crisis and the Great Recession. The rationale behind QE3 can best be described as "shock and awe," an effort to shock the U.S. economy into reflation and growth by flooding it with awe-inspiring amounts of cash while attempting to bring long-term interest rates back near historic lows seen in mid-2012 and perhaps forcing down the value of the dollar to make U.S. exports more competitive and imports less attractive.

However, by those measures, QE3 was less than successful. Inflation in the United States continued to fall during the implementation of the policy, reaching lows unseen since the Great Recession itself. Per capita real disposable income barely budged, falling well off its trajectory from 2010 through the commencement of QE3. Long-term interest rates, while falling back a bit initially, ultimately rose well past their 2012 lows, sending bond markets tumbling even before the announcement of the Fed's tapering back its purchases—which sent long-term interest rates well above levels before QE3 began. Needless to say, for a variety of reasons I address in the book, the dollar did not tank.

What was "successful" about QE3, in the eyes of some, was what happened in the financial economy (as opposed to the real "main street" economy). As I wrote in chapter 6 of this book, in a section entitled "The Limits of the Fed," hyper-easy money policy set off a rush of speculation in risk assets. As is the intent with any extraordinary monetary-easing measures, the Fed's interventions over three rounds of QE flooded the economy with liquidity to avoid lock-up of the financial economy, made it very inexpensive to borrow, and, ultimately, made so-called "risk-free" assets—such as high-quality government debt—very unattractive to own by virtue of the parsimonious returns thereon. Commodities—especially gold, having seriously burned speculators in a spectacular collapse after its run up resulting from QE1 and QE2, and non-monetary metals and oil, having been overvalued by speculators during those prior rounds, relative to end demand—were no longer seen as safe.

So liquidity finally flocked to public equities, especially those easily leveraged with cheap money, which ran up to valuations by the end of 2013 that by some measures (such as the CAPE ratio popularized by 2013 Nobel laureate Robert Shiller) made them more expensive than anytime other than during the market bubbles of 2008, 2000, and 1929. From the announcement of QE3 through the end of 2013, the S&P 500 Index appreciated by over 31 percent.[2]

U.S. housing, which did not reach its post-bubble statistical low valuation until early 2012 (a fact that seems forgotten two years later),[3] took off as well—rising gradually at the start of the historically low bond yields that were reached between QE2 and QE3 and then accelerating greatly during QE3. By the end of 2013, U.S. housing prices had, on average, retraced nearly half the value lost since their bubble-era peak. Prices rose, fueled by the same low interest rates that fueled the stock markets, but were driven higher still by the post-crises anomaly of tight inventories of for-sale housing amid rates of household formation (and thus incremental demand) that continued at levels lower than at any time since the Great Depression (no, that isn't a typo—and that's in nominal, nonpopulation-adjusted terms).

Looking back at the recovery in home prices that occurred simultaneously with QE3, we saw a continuation of the phenomena described in chapter 11 hereof—inventories constrained by homeowners remaining underwater relative to their bubble-era mortgage and thus unable, or unwilling, to sell their homes—combined with those with very low levels of home equity, insufficient to afford a down payment on a new home and therefore de facto non-sellers. We also experienced a large number of investor purchasers of homes able to access low-cost capital to acquire the limited inventory that was available and to pay up for it when necessary. Writing about the third quarter of 2013, Zillow, the real estate database firm, noted:

> ... One in five American homeowners with a mortgage remains underwater, a stubbornly high rate that is contributing to inventory shortages and holding back a full market recovery. The "effective" negative equity rate, which includes those homeowners with a mortgage with 20 percent or less equity in their homes, was 39.2 percent in the third quarter. Listing a home for sale and buying a new one generally requires equity of 20 percent or more to comfortably meet related expenses.[4]

One cannot find a more classic example of a market unable to find a true "clearing" price level because of nonmarket influences (i.e., government policy initiatives).

But in elevating price levels for U.S. housing and sending public equity markets to new historic highs, the Fed's impact on the real economy—demand for goods, services, labor, and new capacity (plants and equipment)—was far less than anyone could have possibly expected from such a massive intervention. Ultimately, the rapid appreciation of financial assets (and both here and throughout the book I, as is generally the practice in economics, include real estate as a financial asset) in 2013 created a "wealth effect" recovery in which the small percentage of Americans owning stocks—and a far more substantial number owning homes—were, and felt, richer and supported a modest recovery in consumption. This, for a while at least, spilled over into the economies of other developed and developing exporting economies, which benefitted from the increased consumption—which some economists refer to as "leakage" of the U.S. monetary stimulus. But as events seem to be demonstrating at this writing, such wealth effect–created demand is proving unsustainable in the age of oversupply.

One of the most obvious reasons why wealth effect–reliant demand is unsustainable is that the price of equities influences the consumption patterns of only a small, but very wealthy, number of consumers. A more disturbing reason is that in an age in which wages are not growing (and are unlikely to, as discussed throughout the book, but particularly in chapter 8), the wealth effect has been transmitting to consumers who were made exuberant by rising home prices, chiefly by means of rising consumer debt, which hit new post-bubble highs in 2013,[5] resulting in the exacerbation of the declining U.S. household savings rate. The ability of households to continue to consume by taking on more debt has rather unpleasant limits, as we saw in 2007. Lastly, in a world of inadequate global demand for labor, production, and capital relative to the supply thereof, there is a tendency for businesses, consumers, and investors to materially misread improvements in one nation's economic results when other competitive nations are showing downwardly trending performance.

In a nearly fully globalized economy for goods, and even some services, strength in the United States that comes with concomitant weakness in China and other emerging producers (or in Germany that comes at the expense of the European periphery *and* emerging producers), as we saw in the second half of 2013, can only be sustained for a very limited time, until the price levels offered by those deprived of demand for their output are lowered to recapture such demand. This would not be the case in an environment in which supply and demand were more evenly matched, but in the age of oversupply what we get instead is the tossing around of the "hot potato" of inadequate demand among nations and regions, yielding disinflationary tendencies around the world.

Thus, financial asset price appreciation, the resulting wealth effect, and short-term rises in business activity fail to result in the advanced economies reaching "escape velocity" where increased consumption produces a virtuous demand for additional *domestic* capacity and labor, which in turn sets wages and prices on a reflationary path. As 2014 dawned and the reality of the Fed's exiting the policy that sustained financial asset appreciation set in (which it is doing precisely because the Fed came to see little sustainable benefit to the real economy from quantitative easing—and potentially problematic distortions therefrom), global stock markets—first in the emerging nations and then in advanced nations—initially reacted with dread.

The failure of QE3 to ignite price and wage reflation was writ large in

2013, during which U.S. goods prices actually deflated from twelve months earlier.[6] While services rose in price, the principal contributor to price inflation in services was, unsurprisingly given the above discussion, inflation in the cost of housing. Housing costs comprise some 41 percent of the U.S. Consumer Price Index, and shelter alone is over 52.5 percent of the services component of the CPI.[7] The peculiar confluence of easy money and structural anomalies in the U.S. housing market resulted not only in price appreciation of owner-occupied homes but also restricted inventories. These factors, together with an enormous rise in the number of households that—since the Great Recession—no longer qualified for mortgages, saw many more families thrust into the conventional rental housing market, causing U.S. rents to rise by 2.9 percent over the course of 2013.[8]

Add inflation in medical services during 2013 (which has since been staunched, for a variety of underlying reasons) and you have the vast majority of 2013's anemic 1.6 percent core U.S. inflation. As further housing price inflation is unlikely to prove sustainable in the absence of wage growth, with healthcare service pricing already declining and with prices of imports (and exports) falling with global oversupply, where is price inflation to come from in 2014? In fact, there are few sectors to look to, and the bias going forward is far more likely to be deflationary.

During the course of 2013, especially after the Fed announced its intention to taper its asset purchases, the conventional bond market wisdom was that interest rates on U.S. treasury securities would rise as a result of the planned change in policy. The benchmark ten-year yield increased by over 1.25 percent from their 2013 low to their high at the end of the year.[9] At year end, expectations were that they would rise further still. But as I wrote in Q2 2013, in chapter 13 of this book, and have reiterated publically numerous times since, with the confluence of ultra-low inflation (tending toward deflation in the absence of the factors previously discussed), a global "oversupply" of demand for high-quality, hard-currency sovereign debt, and with both domestic and global growth data continuing to be unimpressive, there simply is nothing underpinning a more precipitous rise in U.S. sovereign debt yields.

What there was, at year-end 2013, was a collective fear of what financial market participants call a "falling knife."[10] The perception that the Fed's buying of U.S. obligations had been materially influencing the prices at which those bonds were trading (and, perhaps just as importantly, the perception that all market participants shared that notion) overwhelmed the aforementioned underlying economic fundamentals. Sure enough, as the Fed reasserted that it would proceed with QE despite soft economic data at the beginning of 2014, instead of rising, interest rates fell to a point at which the trading range of the U.S. ten-year treasury note fell by over 50 basis points from its level at the end of 2013. Quantitative easing had proven so disruptive of market pricing mechanisms that even the normally staid and sensible bond market didn't know which end was up.

I have spoken and written recently about 2014 being the year of economic "cyclicalists"—those believing that the Great Recession and its aftermath have just been the result of a very severe decline in the business cycle—versus the "secularists"—who believe that what we continue to experience is the outcome of profound shifts in the way the domestic and global economy is working, relative to its behavior in the past, as is argued in *The Age of Oversupply*. Secularists, myself included, believe that cyclical upswings—while still of course present—are now both muted in amplitude and of very short duration. I expect this will continue to be the case for some time, until the global secular issues of oversupply of labor, productive capacity, and capital are either addressed directly as recommended in this book, or until the imbalances discussed herein—gradually and likely painfully—resolve themselves over a protracted period of time.

The failure of monetary policy alone to revive robust growth in the United States and the European Union (which admittedly has limited monetary tools available to it because of the Euro regime) has become evident to their central bankers. The euphoria that greeted the Bank of Japan's massive QE program—part of its government's forceful effort to reverse deflationary pressures, known colloquially as "Abenomics"—has subsided as endogenous inflation has come almost entirely from the currency market's devaluation of the yen and the resulting rise in import prices (almost entirely energy related), as opposed to wages or prices for domestically produced goods. Such a condition is unsustainable, and, as I predicted in chapter 7, Abenomics will ultimately join previous Japanese reflationary efforts in failing to reverse the disinflationary trend that, since the Great Recession, has seen the rest of the developed world join Japan's fate.

In early 2014, the U.S. economy saw a continuation of weak wage growth and ultra-low core inflation. Furthering limits on wage growth at the high end of wage sectors and the failure of the U.S. congress to extend long-term unemployment insurance benefits will pose ongoing challenges. I am particularly concerned that more folks coming off long-term benefits and being forced into taking jobs at whatever they can find will exert further downward pressure on U.S. wages. Of some alarm at the time of this writing has been recent data demonstrating falling unit labor costs with a contemporaneous rise in productivity. As I discussed in chapter 2, rising productivity that comes from weakness in wages and exploitation of excess capacity is a far cry from the version of productivity that comes from technological advancement at optimal levels of employment. The declining labor force participation rate in the United States—notwithstanding the decline in the headline unemployment rate—is particularly ominous in this regard (only a portion of this decline is attributable to the demographic shifts that are often named as the culprit). Indeed, in April 2014, the then newly minted chair of the Federal Reserve Board observed that despite the decline in the headline unemployment rate to 6.7 percent since the Great Recession, many other indicia indicated considerable ongoing labor slack.

I wrote *The Age of Oversupply* in order to offer those perplexed and frustrated by present circumstances in advanced nations a comprehensive explanation of why the credit bubble, the Great Recession, and the ensuing lack of full recovery evidence a situation that is truly apart from past economic tribulations. Shortly after the September 2013 hardcover release of this book, the often-controversial economist Larry Summers—the former Secretary of the Treasury,[11] Director of the National Economic Council,[12] and President of Harvard University—gave a speech at an International Monetary Fund[13] conference on a subject he referred to as "Secular Stagnation."[14] Summers, with whom I have had many disagreements during his terms in government, but who I credit in chapter 13 with having seen the light after his departure from the Obama administration at the end of 2010, pretty much hit the nail on the head in that speech. Summers noted that even before the global financial crisis, something was clearly amiss:

> If you go back and study the economy prior to the crisis, there is something a little bit odd. Many people believe that monetary policy was too easy. Everybody agrees that there was a vast amount of imprudent lending going on. Almost everybody agrees that wealth, as it was experienced by households, was in

excess of its reality. Too easy money, too much borrowing, too much wealth. Was there a great boom? Capacity utilization wasn't under any great pressure; unemployment wasn't under any remarkably low level; inflation was entirely quiescent, so somehow even a great bubble wasn't enough to produce any excess in aggregate demand.[15]

This book will tell you why I think Summers's insights into the present state of affairs are correct, even though I do not believe his IMF remarks presented a complete case for causality. This time in global macroeconomics truly *is* different and requires thinking outside the boxes imposed on us by the ideological limitations of the past several decades. Those differences and limitations are also responsible for the failure of policy since the Great Recession to produce a resurgence of growth, as Summers concluded in his IMF address:

> . . . It does seem to me that four years after the successful combating of the crisis, there is really no evidence of growth that is restoring equilibrium. One has to be concerned about a policy agenda that is doing less with monetary policy than has been done before, doing less with fiscal policy than has been done before, and taking steps whose basic purpose is to cause there to be less lending, borrowing, and inflated asset prices than there was before.

Speaking of ideological limitations, I must offer a small apology with this republication of *The Age of Oversupply*. The book I hope you are about to read does not deal generously with the predominant economic ideology of the Republican Party or the version of macroeconomics espoused by of the so-called "freshwater school." In fact, I am—admittedly—sometimes contemptuous of what I have seen to be self-serving ignorance from the party's increasingly more doctrinaire elements and the academic supporters thereof. The fact is that several of my more candid observations in this book have been taken by a minority as being excessively partisan and therefore dismissed by said individuals as pushing a political agenda. To the extent that that interpretation has caused people who might benefit most from an apolitical consideration of the content of this book, I wish I had not been quite as candid in assessing blame. As I noted in chapter 15, in failing to understand the underpinnings and manifestations of our unprecedented age of oversupply "no one, and nearly everyone, was wrong." With that mea culpa I urge those among you who count yourself among the most persuaded of those on the far right and your supply-side mentors to keep an open mind when forging ahead into this book. In truth, it was written for you.

THE ENDLESS SLUMP

The past twenty years have seen a transformation of the global economy unlike any ever witnessed.

In the time it takes to raise a child and pack her off to college, the world order that existed in the early 1990s has disappeared. Some three billion people who once lived in sleepy or sclerotic statist economies are now part of the global economy. Many compete directly with workers in the United States, Europe, and Japan in a world bound together by lightning-fast communications. Countries that were once poor now find themselves with huge surpluses of wealth. And the rich countries of the world, while still rich, struggle with monumental levels of debt—both private and public—and unsettling questions about whether they can compete globally.

This shift is hardly news. Starting a dozen or so years ago, we began to hear all about globalization and the economic threat that the new, "flat" world poses to developed countries. Yet since 2008, that talk has been overshadowed by the financial crisis and its aftermath—a crisis that eviscerated trillions of dollars in household wealth, created near-record levels of unemployment, and left the United States and Europe in adverse economic straits that persist to the present day (joining Japan, which has been hobbled for two decades). The causes of the crisis, it was said, lay in too much risk taking by the lords of finance, along with too big an appetite for debt among ordinary people. And so for the past five years, we've heard less about China and India and more about how to fix the financial systems and economies of the developed countries.

When people think about today's economic challenges, many of them put the problems facing the United States and Europe in separate baskets: one basket for such thorny issues as how to jump-start growth, reduce unemployment, and control the national debt; and a second basket for how to deal with trade deficits, currency issues, and competitiveness writ large.

This book argues that all these challenges belong in *one* basket. You can't understand the housing bubble and the financial crisis without appreciating how the rise of the emerging nations distorted the economies of rich countries. And you can't chart a course to more growth and stability in the developed world without recognizing that many of these distorting forces are still at work.

In the pages ahead, I argue that the central challenge facing the global economy is an *oversupply of labor, productive capacity, and capital relative to the demand for all three.*

Beginning in the late 1990s, a tidal wave of cheap money began flooding the global economy, much of it coming from Asia as China and other countries began to run huge trade surpluses and their burgeoning middle classes and thriving corporations socked away savings. Easy credit set the stage for the real estate bubble and the financial crisis. And cheap money also allowed Americans to sustain a high standard of living with low-cost borrowing and to ignore their declining competitiveness amid a growing surplus of global labor. Of course, the party couldn't last forever.

Yet five years after the financial crisis, many leaders and commentators in the United States and Europe still don't get what happened. Nor do they seem to realize that the age of oversupply is here to stay and that oversupply is a central obstacle to restarting growth. Many of the standard tools for fueling growth simply don't work. As I show in the pages ahead, cheaper credit through monetary easing doesn't yield much in an era when cheap capital already exists in abundance. And policies that seek to stimulate growth run up against the fact that there is a huge oversupply of global labor and productive capacity. Meanwhile, major risks linger in the banking sectors of the United States and Europe, where reforms have not gone nearly far enough. Today, despite the painful lessons of recent years, the global financial system is anything but stable.

Finally, the United States and Europe face a huge overhang of unresolved private debt, a legacy of the credit bubble—debt on a scale no nation has ever before confronted. These debts hold back growth, but asset holders—mostly the banks—have been loath to write these debts off and take the hit they have to take. Few political leaders are ready to force a painful resolution of these debts. And across both the political and financial worlds, hopes abound that growth will resume, inflating the value of "underwater" assets and devaluing outstanding debt.

That is simply unlikely to happen anytime soon. Economic growth won't rebound in a sustained way until the developed countries confront deep systemic problems in their own economies and the new and profound distortions in the global economy. Even though three billion people and trillions of dollars in wealth have emerged on the world scene, most policy makers are still stuck in denial about the earthshattering nature of this shift.

Can the United States and Europe get out of this mess? (And what about Japan, which has seemingly been unable to do so for decades?) I believe they can, and this book offers a road map for avoiding a future of economic stagnation and new crises.

We must begin by acknowledging how much everything has changed. Economic troubleshooters—from presidents to central bankers to lawmakers to economists—need a fresh playbook in the age of oversupply. In particular, monetary policy—historically a critical tool for fighting economic downturns—simply doesn't have, in a world of easy money, the bite it once had. And while fiscal stimulus can help restart growth, I argue that developed nations need to try this approach on a much larger scale than ever before if we are to put the advanced nations' huge surplus of workers back to work. I suggest major new investments that deal strategically with infrastructure and I detail how such investment would not only help restart growth but also lay the foundation for future prosperity.

At the same time, I propose an aggressive effort to clear away the crushing burden of unresolved debt that is a legacy of the credit bubble. This is a daunting political challenge, because it means taking on creditors who hold trillions in bad debt. But until our advanced economies can emerge from under debt overhang, strong growth will be impossible. The United States, the world's largest economy, must also confront two major obstacles to its global competitiveness: runaway costs for higher education and health care—and I suggest ways to confront these costs.

My other recommendations include further reforms to the banking sector to reduce risky behaviors and foster more stability. These efforts need to involve leaders and institutions from across the developed world if they are to succeed, given the interconnected nature of today's global financial system. Likewise, new multilateral cooperation is needed to create a global currency system that will ensure stability and a level economic playing field.

I come to these seminal challenges not as an economist or a policy expert, but as an old-school investment banker. For three decades, I have worked with a range of companies to help them find the capital they need to grow and succeed, and to provide solutions to their problems. At times, I have restructured failed enterprises and those beset by unforeseen challenges.

During my career, I've had many dealings in Japan, experiences that strongly color my views and the arguments in this book.

By now it's become a cliché to say that the United States risks turning into Japan, a country that has experienced two decades in the economic doldrums since the collapse in 1989 of a huge asset bubble of its own. Yet long before the global financial credit bubble imploded, I could see that the United States was on a path similar to Japan's and that we might someday face comparable stagnation. As it turned out, far more countries than just the United States were to be drawn into crisis.

I vividly recall sitting in a conference room with other bankers and attorneys one sunny, warm day in Tokyo in the summer of 2005. I was involved in the acquisition of a long-defaulted mortgage loan collateralized only by land, a leftover from the late 1980s Japanese bubble era, with an outstanding balance of about $800 million in today's U.S. dollars. We were in the process of closing the purchase of the loan for the shockingly low price of $50 million. But I was not particularly as-tounded. My firm had opened our office in Japan in 2000, and by 2005 I guess I was already an old Japan hand. Nothing surprised me. Al-though I mostly commuted to Asia monthly and did not reside there for long periods of time, I had spent nearly half of my recent years in Japan. This was the country in which the grounds of the Imperial Pal-ace in Tokyo—1.3 square miles of land—were once estimated to have the same value as all of the real estate in California.

I was in that conference room that day as an undertaker of sorts: a small pile of the remaining ashes of the greatest real estate bubble in history were being laid to rest.

It was all very ominous because in 2005, of course, the United States was in the midst of its own property bubble—one already quite appar-ent to the small number of us who followed the relationship among markets, lending, and global macroeconomic trends—an unusual combination of disciplines. Prices of homes and commercial properties in the United States had already become unmoored from reasonable investment returns, the ability of incomes or rents to support prices paid, and—most ominously in the U.S. residential sector—the ability of most buyers to secure ownership of a home with a conventional mortgage product. The connection between what was occurring in the United States and what I was doing that day in Tokyo did not escape me. Even as Japan's leaders struggled with the debt overhang of a decades-old real estate bubble, America's and Western Europe's leaders were turning a blind eye as an even bigger bubble (in nominal terms) inflated in the United States and Europe.

After a break, I returned to the conference table and listened to the conversation for a while. During a lull, one of the Japanese lawyers turned to me and said:

"Alpert-san, you must think we Japanese were very foolish to lend so much money against just land. You would never do such a thing in the U.S."

The Japanese, particularly the men, have a customary and somewhat endearing way of sucking wind through their teeth and screwing up their faces during moments of consternation, intense consideration, or confrontation.

I thought for a moment, smiled, and said, "Unfortunately, I think the U.S. is next up in terms of this type of foolishness."

"What do you mean?" came the reply, accompanied by much sucking of wind and quizzical facial expressions. "In the U.S., businesspeople could never do something like this!"

"I think you might be very surprised," I said—to even more sucking of wind through teeth.

Today, seven years after home prices in the United States hit peak bubble values in the summer of 2006 and five years after the financial system of the entire developed world nearly ground to a halt, the economies of the United States, Western Europe—and yes, still Japan—remain mired in severe economic dislocation.

The demand for goods and services in the developed world remains muted, relative to potential. Amid this flat demand, even the most profitable companies see little reason to invest in new equipment or hire new workers. And never has there been such bitter disagreement and deep confusion, among politicians and economists alike, about what ails the economies of the developed world and how to fix them.

To combat the ongoing slump, for half a decade despairing policy makers have employed almost every conventional, and many far more heterodox, economic countermeasures—measures that arose from a century of modern economic scholarship and experience. As a result, they have succeeded in avoiding an outright collapse of key institutions and enterprises, while kicking down the road a growing list of unresolved problems.

At this writing, an alarming percentage of the political leadership in the developed countries have flirted with or have outright implemented fiscal austerity policies. Nothing could be more damaging to the interests of the 800 million or so people of the advanced nations. Commenting in March 2013 on the dominance of austerity policies in Europe, Gideon Rachman of the *Financial Times* of London wrote, "There are many who argue that this prescription is dangerous. But the anti-austerians have failed to come up with a set of alternative policies that is coherent enough to turn the intellectual tide."[1]

The Age of Oversupply is intended to answer precisely that type of criticism: to provide a coherent intellectual rationale for why we are where we are, to deliver policy initiatives that focus on the ongoing challenges to the global economy, and, particularly, to chart a way forward toward the renewal of developed-world growth and prosperity.

CHAPTER 1

THE RISE OF OVERSUPPLY

How the Emerging Nations Remade
the Global Economy

ate December 1978 is not typically remembered as a watershed
moment for the U.S. economy. Another year of sluggish growth
was drawing to a close, with unemployment hitting 6 percent.
OPEC had announced a big hike in oil prices on December 18, a move
that would further hurt growth, but that was nothing unusual.

Many Americans weren't thinking about the economy at all as Christ-
mas approached; they were fixated on what was happening in Chicago,
where police had just arrested the serial killer John Wayne Gacy and
were hauling one body after another out of a crawl space in his home in
a Chicago suburb.

Yet 6,600 miles away, in the inner sanctum of government power in
Beijing, China, America's economic future was being set by a group of
Communist Party leaders. A historic five-day meeting took place from
December 18 to December 22, 1978—the Third Plenum of the Elev-
enth Central Party Committee—and, on the last day of that meeting,
the party issued a communiqué that committed the party to far-
reaching economic reforms. In time, these reforms would change

8

everything. This was the moment when China started down the path to becoming the fastest-growing capitalist economy in the world.

China's transformation would not only radically increase the global supply of cheap labor but also—and nearly as important—decades later create a flood of cheap money as China built up record piles of cash, thanks to its export juggernaut and the growing savings of its newly affluent population and enterprises.

Another important event occurred in 1978, far across the Eurasian continent from China: a young and little-known Communist Party bureaucrat named Mikhail Gorbachev was appointed to the Central Committee's Secretariat for Agriculture. From there, Gorbachev would move up to the Politburo within just three years. Four years after that, he would be named general secretary and initiate a series of far-reaching economic reforms that would ultimately bring 400 million people living under communist rule in the Soviet Union and Eastern Europe into the global market economy. By the early 2000s, Russia would be the biggest energy exporter in the world, a country with a half trillion dollars in foreign reserves and nearly a hundred billionaires—yet another vast pool of money looking for returns.

Economic liberalization came more slowly to India, the second most populous country in the world. But when that process started in 1991 (and was rewarded four years later when India joined the World Trade Organization) it brought another huge army of workers into the global economy—a labor force of nearly half a billion able-bodied adults, or three times the number of workers in the United States.

Liberalization also turbocharged India's economy. In just twenty years, India's gross domestic product (GDP) would grow sevenfold, with annual economic growth hitting 9 percent by 2007. India, long considered the world's basket case, would come to have foreign reserves larger than Germany's and more than sixty billionaires—every one of them looking for places to put their spare cash.

Welcome to the age of oversupply.

What we have seen in the past few decades is an unprecedented global explosion of cheap labor and cheap money. This trend is a huge driver of the developed world's economic problems. Yet most policy makers, not to mention ordinary citizens, barely understand what has happened and, worse, many political leaders, economists, and think tanks still embrace a set of solutions to today's economic malaise that aims to create even more supply—call them supply-side zombies if you will. Meanwhile, even those who do realize the need for greater demand have yet to face up to the monumental scope of the challenges we face in this age of oversupply.

But before we say more about the policy implications of oversupply, let's further explore this breathtaking shift—what I call the Great Rejoining.

THE GREAT REJOINING

The year is 1995. After severe credit and financial crises in the late 1980s and early 1990s, the United States has stabilized its economy, restarted growth, and reduced its budget deficits. Great strides in labor-saving productivity, and enormous opportunities for investment, are emerging from the acceleration of Internet technology. The United States' top economic competitor, Japan, is no longer a "rising sun" and Japanese investors are no longer snapping up iconic U.S. landmarks such as Rockefeller Center. Instead, Japan is trapped in an endless twilight of malaise and deflation. Tokyo, a once heady city now filled with depressed underwater property owners and developers, is deeply rattled after a cult releases sarin gas in its subway system, killing thirteen people. Europe is doing better, but has its own deep economic problems broadly described under the term "Eurosclerosis." Unemployment across the Continent is above 10 percent, a record postwar high.

The economist Lester Thurow, who in 1993 had published a book titled *Head to Head*, about America's coming fierce battle with Japan and Europe for economic dominance, now seems to have been laughably wrong.[1] The United States, it is clear, will be the supreme power of the millennium's last decade.

And, indeed, in 1995 the future was looking bright for America's economy. The young president who occupied the Oval Office understood the importance of investing in education and technology. Growth was picking up. The federal budget deficit wasn't just going down, the nation was on a trajectory toward a surplus.

But lurking over the horizon were entire nations, collectively outnumbering the population of the developed world by *fivefold*, that had, only a few years before, thrown off the last vestiges of socialism—in substance, if not in name, in the case of China. For decades prior, these nations had been largely inconsequential, at least in economic terms. The largest nations in the world had been cut off from free-market capitalism.

Now, in a trend largely ignored during the first half of the 1990s by economists like Thurow—experts still focused on the world's traditional industrial centers—these nations were rejoining the global economy with a vengeance. In a remarkably short span of time, a full 50 percent of the global population had been freed, or freed itself, to challenge decades—if not centuries—of the international commercial status quo. Ironically, while the Cold War, with its ever-present specter of nuclear disaster, had deeply unnerved the West, that long standoff had also sheltered the developed world from meaningful competition with the world's most populous countries.

The Cold War's end was widely seen as a triumph for liberal free-market democracies, and even as "the end of history."[2] In fact, in a grand irony, the demise of the socialist experiment set the stage for the greatest threat yet to the supremacy of the United States and other advanced democracies.

The expansion of the global labor force—and the sheer number of new workers now ready to truly go "head to head" with Americans and Europeans—has been especially stunning. Thirty years ago, most of the poorest people in the world lived in statist societies walled off from the global economy, and many were essentially peasants, inhabiting impoverished rural landscapes much as their ancestors had.

All that has changed. Today, the world has a market labor force of roughly three billion people, many of whom are in a position to compete directly for a wide range of jobs held by workers in the developed world, thanks to the wonders of multinational corporations, the Internet, and other features of a flat world.

Of these three billion workers, nearly half live in China, India, and the former Soviet Union. Which is to say that the fall of the Bamboo and Iron curtains, along with economic liberalization, has quite literally brought the other half of the world on line, doubling the global labor supply in the free market in the past two decades.

The final stage of the fall of international communism, such as it was, can be tracked to the events of 1989, with the fall of the Berlin Wall and the rise in Chinese urbanization that followed from the Tiananmen Square incident in that year. As a practical matter, the impact of these events was negligible throughout the early 1990s. The developed world's economies were weak anyway and the post-socialist world

had not yet gotten its act together. Even after the largest emerging nations' export juggernaut had commenced, the direct impact on advanced nations was muted by the enormous productivity boost arising
from the Internet technology revolution.

Only after the collapse of the Internet bubble, and after China had
joined the WTO in 2001 and become fully integrated into the global
economy, was the developed world fully exposed to the onslaught of
several billion new people who, by that point, were fully prepared to be
directly competitive.

Rapid population growth in several developing countries, coupled
with the ongoing spread of liberalization, has swelled the global labor force even more since those bright, hopeful years of the mid-
1990s. Just six countries that were all heavily statist when Bill Clinton
was president—Indonesia, Brazil, Bangladesh, Pakistan, Mexico, and
Vietnam—account for another 450 million workers.

Tallying up trends of recent decades, a 2012 study by the McKinsey
Global Institute estimated that 1.7 billion new workers joined the
global labor force between 1980 and 2010, with most of this increase
taking place in developing economies undergoing a "farm-to-factory"
shift.[3] The better pay of these jobs enabled some 620 million people to
escape poverty.

Keep this sea of cheap labor in mind the next time you pass an
empty factory and wonder why America's 150 million workers are having a hard time. Another thing to keep in mind is that this vast expansion of workers hasn't just created an oversupply of labor but has also
contributed to the oversupply of capital as hundreds of millions of
people have emerged from peasant societies to work for wages and stash
at least some of their earnings in savings accounts.

In fact, because many of these workers live in countries with insufficient social safety nets or pensions (or in nations such as China, which
is only slowly expanding its social protections),[4] they tend to put away
far more earnings than workers in developed countries. Business enterprises in those countries sock away even more (especially in China).
What that means is that the arrival of nearly two billion new workers
on the scene hasn't generated anything near the demand you might
think, in terms of these people buying goods. Instead of a balanced rise
of both supply and demand, we've seen a totally skewed situation of
ever-growing supply, particularly with regard to capital.

11

12

I'll say more about the flood of cheap money in a moment. But let me add one more piece to the labor picture—the explosion of more educated workers. In China alone, the number of students graduating annually from college has risen eightfold in the past fifteen years, from 830,000 in 1998 to 6.8 million in 2012.[5] A similar trend holds for India. In 2000, there were seats for just 390,000 young Indians in universities. Now there are spots for 1.5 million.[6] Granted, a college degree from a Chinese or Indian university is not the same as one from a U.S. or European university . . . yet. But with at least some portion of this new educated class able to undertake tasks such as accounting and computer programming, we have seen a quickly expanding global pool of white-collar workers who are earning higher salaries, saving more, and competing more for jobs previously held by workers in the advanced nations.

A SEA OF CHEAP MONEY

After so many decades of subordinating their prosperity to a failed ideology, the world's formerly socialist (or socialist-leaning) countries played a remarkable game of catch-up.

During the fifteen years from 1993 through 2007, the GDP of the emerging nations grew at an average rate of between 4 and 8 percent, with some countries, like China, famously firing much hotter than that.[7] And between 1990 and 2010, the emerging nations doubled their share of global GDP—from under 20 percent to 38 percent.[8] (In 2013, for the first time, emerging nations will account for more than half the world's GDP.)

As trade in manufactured goods and its associated jobs migrated inexorably to lower-cost labor markets, despite the productivity increases in the advanced economies the emerging nations began to develop substantial current account and trade balance surpluses.

In other words, wealth—lots of it—began to pile up in those countries.

The obvious place to start this part of the story is China, which has the biggest pile of cash of all.

Part of that pile, of course, is due to its exports. In an effort to "sterilize" its currency from trade flows that typically cause a nation's currency to appreciate and thus curtail its competitiveness, China blocked free conversion and began to accumulate vast foreign-currency reserves—to the point where, at year-end 2012, it held over $3.31 trillion in the form of dollars, mostly, but also euros, yen, and other currencies.[9] Following the Asian currency crisis of 1997, which set off fears of global recession, emerging nations became wary of borrowing in foreign currencies and floating the value of their currencies against others without maintaining sizable hard-currency reserves. China was a different story—it not only sought to protect the yuan against speculation, but also strove to control its appreciation so as to optimize competitiveness and build its employment base as swiftly as possible.

China's reserves of hard currency and related assets—chiefly U.S. dollars—totaled less than $250 billion in 2000. They grew to $2 trillion by 2008 and to over $3 trillion as of this writing, as set forth above. This vast pot of money is managed by the State Administration of Foreign Exchange (aptly abbreviated SAFE in English) and the People's Bank of China.

Talk about an outfit that has seen good times and bad: the original Bank of China was founded in 1912, when China's power was near a historic low. It is now the fifth-largest central bank in the world and among the largest lenders to the U.S. government, with quite a lot of China's reserves invested in U.S. Treasury and government agency bonds.

At the same time that China's currency reserves soared, Chinese workers and businesses were saving monumental amounts of cash. Anyone who thinks that the Japanese are good savers clearly hasn't been to China. Data from the World Bank shows that the Chinese national savings rate grew from 37 percent in 1988 to 48 percent in 2005 to 53 percent of GDP in 2011. By comparison, thrifty Japan's savings rate is now under 25 percent. The U.S. rate is at about 12 percent.[10] (Keep in mind that a nation's gross savings rate isn't just a reflection of what individual earners are socking away. It's an overall reflection of the difference between the wealth a country produces and what it consumes.)

Either way, even as China's GDP was growing by leaps and bounds, the slice of that wealth being saved also grew. In 1988, China had a GDP of just $390 billion—and $144 million in gross savings. Ten years later, it had a GDP of $1 trillion—and $390 billion in savings. By 2011, China had a GDP of $7.3 trillion and an estimated $3.8 trillion in gross savings.[11]

In a flash—at least in terms of its own long history—China went from being a poor country to one sitting on trillions in excess cash.

14

This money piled up not just because the Chinese are such religious savers, but also because China initially didn't move aggressively enough to expand public investments in the things that countries typically spend money on when they become rich: schools, libraries, parks, a social safety net, and so on.

As James Fallows observed in 2008:

> Some Chinese people are rich, but China as a whole is unbelievably short on many of the things that qualify countries as fully developed. Shanghai has about the same climate as Washington, D.C.—and its public schools have no heating. (Go to a classroom when it's cold, and you'll see 40 children, all in their winter jackets, their breath forming clouds in the air.) Beijing is more like Boston. On winter nights, thousands of people mass along the curbsides of major thoroughfares, enduring long waits and fighting their way onto hopelessly overcrowded public buses that then spend hours stuck on jammed roads. . . . Better schools, more-abundant parks, better health care, cleaner air and water, better sewers in the cities—you name it, and if it isn't in some way connected to the factory-export economy, China hasn't got it, or not enough.[12]

Maybe most notably, China's spending on health care has barely risen in fifteen years. China spent 4 percent of its GDP on health care in 1998; it spends a bit over 5 percent today.[13]

Between 1998 and 2011, tax revenue as a percentage of China's GDP nearly doubled, and China then dramatically stepped up its investments in infrastructure, energy, and education. But this spending barely made a dent in the rising mountain of money. So, instead, all those dollars needed to be invested somewhere outside of China.

And it wasn't just China that started piling up huge amounts of excess wealth starting in the 1990s. Other emerging countries did, too. Brazil's total reserves soared from $33 billion in 2000 to $352 billion in 2011. Tiny Singapore had $71 billion in reserves in 2000—and $244 billion in 2011. Indonesia's reserves grew fivefold. Russia's grew by eighteen times thanks to its natural-gas exports. Rising energy prices boosted Saudi Arabia's reserves from $21 billion to $595 billion, a twenty-eight-fold increase. (As if there weren't already enough rich Saudis looking for good places to put their money.)[14]

All told, the total foreign-currency reserves of emerging nations rose from around $700 billion in 2000 to nearly $7 trillion in 2012.

Meanwhile, several export powerhouses in the developed world also piled up more cash. Japan's reserves tripled during the first decade of the twenty-first century, to over $1 trillion. Germany's reserves also almost tripled, as did South Korea's.

What's more, many of those nations getting richer fast were just as bad as China at consuming their new wealth. Indonesia's savings rate, for example, increased to 37 percent, up from 29 percent, during the early 2000s even as GDP grew sixfold.[15]

Never before in history had so much money piled up so fast. The assets of banks and other financial entities in the world's top jurisdictions grew from roughly $110 trillion in 2002 to $240 trillion in 2008—a staggering rise in wealth, just sitting around.[16]

Of course, such money can't just sit around. As a practical necessity, most of this money went looking for decent returns at relatively low risk of loss in—guess where?—the United States and certain nations of Western Europe, with a seemingly limitless appetite for incurring debt of every kind—public, private, and corporate (Japan has tons of debt, too, but it is mostly self-funding).

With a torrent of global savings flowing back to deficit countries (mostly the United States, but also the weaker countries of Europe), their governments did not need to borrow as much domestic private capital, and interest rates plummeted. Even Japan, which had seen minor challenges to its post-bubble ultra-low interest rate environment, saw its borrowing costs plummet to new lows despite its huge debt load and poor fiscal metrics.

The enormous pool of private capital in the developed world was left to search for returns on investment anywhere they could be found—and the financial institutions of Wall Street and the City of London were happy to oblige. Borrowers were sought everywhere—in governments, corporations, real estate, and households.

But there was a problem: Over the past two decades, and especially in the early 2000s, the rising pool of capital far outstripped the rise in demand and real economic growth. Which is to say that even as rivers of cash looked for returns, there was not nearly enough productive activity to sop up all the money. As a November 2012 study by Bain & Company observed: "The rate of growth of world output of goods and services has seen an extended slowdown over recent decades, while the volume of global financial assets has expanded at a rapid pace."[17]

That was—and still is—a recipe for trouble.

CAPITAL ON STEROIDS

It's no big secret where all the new easy money ended up, at least on the U.S. side of the Atlantic. Just about every sector in the United States gorged on cheap debt, with everyone from unemployed home flippers to the U.S. Treasury to local mayors to CEOs getting in on the feast.

For starters, consider the truly gargantuan amount of money that Americans borrowed to buy and build homes and commercial real estate. In 1990, total household and commercial mortgage debt outstanding in the United States was $3.7 trillion. By 2000, it had all but doubled, rising to $6.7 trillion. Then, in just six years, it doubled once more, to over $13 trillion, and kept rising to a historic peak of $14.6 trillion in 2008.[18]

All this money had to come from somewhere, and much of it came from China, either directly or, more often, by "crowding out" domestic capital from government bond markets. In fact, as the housing bubble inflated, China became the single largest holder of government guaranteed mortgage bonds issued by Freddie Mae and Fannie Mac—with an estimated $376 billion tied up in these securities as of June 2007. Japan, with its own big reserves to invest, had also gone big into the U.S. mortgage market and found itself holding $228 billion in Freddie and Fannie securities when the crisis came.[19] Still more money poured into U.S. capital markets from domestic investors who had been effectively displaced by foreign investors willing to take low returns on government (and government-guaranteed) debt, and so set off to find borrowers who would pay more to use their money—like, say, via subprime lending.

The story of binge indebting by governments is even better known. Thanks to George W. Bush's ill-advised fiscal plan of cutting taxes while waging two wars and expanding Medicare, the federal government developed massive borrowing needs during the same period in which China and other emerging countries were piling up record amounts of cash. Total federal debt doubled to $10 trillion during the Bush presidency, with foreign governments coming to own almost half of this debt.

In January 2001, the month Bush took office, China owned a mere $61 billion in U.S. government securities. Four years later, when Bush was sworn in for his second term, that figure was up to $223 billion. And by the time the Obamas walked the Bushes to Marine One during the 2009 inaugural, China owned $739 billion in U.S. securities. As of this writing, the total stands at over $1 trillion.[20]

But while America's borrowing from China has gotten all the attention, many other foreign countries rolling in reserves also loaded up on Treasuries. Brazil's holdings soared from $12 billion in 2002 to over $226 billion a decade later. And when Russia started finding itself with piles of excess wealth, it too started bankrolling America's deficit spending to the tune of billions of dollars a year, buying over $150 billion in U.S. securities by 2010. Japan kept buying Treasuries, too, as it had for years—tripling its holdings to over $1 trillion over the past decade.[21]

American state and local governments took advantage of cheap money as well, borrowing more than $1 trillion between 2000 and 2008.[22] State and local government leaders thus avoided unpopular tax increases while providing public services at an often expanding rate. Recent municipal bankruptcies in cities such as Stockton and San Bernardino, California, are the aftermath of such practices.

Cheap money also had another effect: it put the financial sector on steroids, and helped to greatly grow and supercharge the so-called shadow banking system. Most people know this part of the story, so I'll skip all the details about how hedge funds, money market funds, private equity groups, and insurance companies turned into 900-pound gorillas, thanks to the magic of cheap borrowing and heavy leverage. In this remade financial sector, a little-known American International Group (AIG) executive named Joseph Cassano could make hundreds of millions of dollars for himself, and billions for his firm, by selling derivative products such as credit default swaps.[23]

It is truly remarkable just how quickly a growing pile of money— whether owned by sovereign funds, Indian billionaires, union pensions, Saudi sheiks, or Chinese banks holding middle-class people's savings— hooked up with legions of creative MBAs in places like New York and London. According to estimates by the Financial Stability Board, total worldwide assets in the shadow banking system grew from $26 trillion in 2002 to $62 trillion in 2007 (when one considers all non-bank financial intermediation). The United States, as the world's largest economy, developed by far the largest shadow banking system in the world, accounting for a third or more of all assets in this system.[24]

The age of oversupply created a lot of easy money for people to play with, too often with very little oversight. Bad things inevitably happened. The reckless overleveraging of a top Wall Street firm like Lehman Brothers, which collapsed with startling speed in the financial crisis, would not have been possible in a world where money was less plentiful and more costly.

It would be nice to think that such bad behavior will never happen again. In fact, though, all signs point to a future in which capital will remain cheap and regulators will struggle to impose oversight in the face of constant attack by the financial industry and its powerful political allies.

OVERSUPPLY IS HERE TO STAY

The Great Credit Bubble may have burst, but the age of oversupply hasn't ended—and won't anytime soon. Abundant labor, excess capital, and cheap money are here to stay.

For all the modernization and urbanization in India and China, vast swaths of the population of both these societies are still rural peasants, and these people will continue to make their way to cities to join the global economy. Fifteen years ago, just a third of all Chinese lived in urban areas. Today 51 percent do, which means that while urbanization is growing at a rapid pace, with literally millions of Chinese moving to cities every year in one of the greatest mass migrations in history, nearly half of China's vast population still live in the countryside. So even though China's population is aging, thanks to its one-child policy, that country hasn't yet touched the bottom of its labor barrel. A study by the Asian Development Bank estimated that the growth of China's labor force wouldn't flatten out until after 2020.[25]

India has an even bigger pool of untapped labor, given that 69 percent of its fast-growing population—over 800,000,000 people—still live in rural areas and that half of all Indians are under the age of 25. It's been estimated that 275 million new workers will enter India's labor force between 2000 and 2030. That army of new, able bodies is nearly as big as the entire U.S. population.

A similar story can be told about other developing countries. Indonesia's labor force is now growing by 2 million new workers a year; the Philippines is adding a million every year. And 20 million new workers have come on line in Vietnam since 1990, with more still to come. In Central America, a third of the population is under the age of fifteen.[26]

Overall, while the growth rate of the global labor market will slow substantially over the next two decades, it will still get vastly bigger in absolute terms. The McKinsey Global Institute estimates that a total of 600 million workers will enter the labor force between now and 2030.[27]

Millions of residents of poorer countries will also get better educated—to the extent that by 2020 41 percent of all young adults with a college degree in leading countries worldwide will be either Indian or Chinese (up from 29 percent in 2010). The number of Chinese and Indians with more-advanced degrees—and thus capable of earning higher salaries and saving more money—will also soar.[28]

The expanding savings accounts of an exploding middle class is only one reason, among others, that cheap money is going to keep flowing. Exports are another, as in the past. In fact, in the five years since the financial crisis, the foreign-currency reserve holdings of emerging countries have more than doubled, according to the IMF.[29] China alone has piled up over $1 trillion in new reserves since 2008. Brazil's reserves have nearly doubled during the same period. A study by Bain & Company, aptly titled "A World Awash in Money," notes: "Capital superabundance will continue to exert a dominant influence on investment patterns for years to come. Bain projects that the volume of total financial assets will rise by some 50%, from $600 trillion in 2010 to $900 trillion by 2020, even as the world economy increases by $27 trillion over the same period."

That's a lot of new money. However, the Bain study also notes that many of these assets don't have real, tangible value underlying them and that the gap between actual assets and financial assets will only grow: "As it has for more than the past two decades, the large volume of global financial assets will continue to sit on a small base of global GDP. . . . Total capital will remain 10 times larger than the total global output of goods and services—just as it is today—and three times bigger than the base of nonfinancial assets that help to generate that expanded world GDP."[30]

Even with all of the easy "play money" floating around in recent years, it may be that we haven't seen anything yet.

Capital superabundance helps explain why monetary easing by the Fed and other central banks, together with today's record low interest rates, hasn't done much for the economy. In "normal" times, easy money would incentivize lending and investment that would jump-start economic expansion. Monetary easing does this in two ways: not only does it make money cheap to borrow, but it makes the low returns on the safest investments so unattractive that those with capital should be willing to take greater risk. In extreme cases, it induces a condition known as "financial repression" in which the nominal rate of return (interest rate) earned on government bonds and other high-credit-quality investments falls below the rate of inflation so that merely holding those instruments becomes an exercise in losing money on a real (inflation adjusted) basis.

Ultimately, the mechanisms of capital formation—banks, non-bank financial institutions, and the capital markets at large—should normally transmit the surplus of cash resulting from extraordinary easing into longer-term, less-liquid investment in physical assets—plants, infrastructure, major equipment—and other new capacity that spurs additional production, job creation, and thereby new demand, in a virtuous circle. Also normally, the additional demand for labor and goods and services would spur wage, price, and asset inflation.

Too bad these aren't normal times.

The transmitters of easy money to the rest of the developed economies are blocked. Via extraordinary monetary-easing measures, the developed world's central banks have turned trillions of dollars of financial investments into so much cash that it is metaphorically bulging out of the pockets of banks and other investors. Yet it is not getting lent and it is not getting invested in new capacity. Why?

In a nutshell, the reason that the enormous ocean of liquidity is not being deployed is that there is so much global supply and excess capacity of labor, plants, equipment, and goods and services relative to present demand that there is little reason for private-sector investment in the development of additional capacity to produce additional supply.

What we have on our hands is a supply-side nightmare scenario.

CHAPTER 2

OUT OF BALANCE

Debts, Surpluses, and the Broken
Global Economy

The study of economics is pretty much the study of choices. The fundamentals begin with choices—the choice to produce and the choice to consume, yielding supply and demand. Economists study incentives, behaviors, physical inputs, and productivity. But what matters most is the basic will to produce and the desire to consume. That's pretty much the beginning and end of all economic activity.

And when economies are working normally, it usually isn't all that hard for political leaders and central bankers to influence supply and demand. Yet in recent years, as I've said, things haven't been working normally. In the new age of oversupply, all the rules are changing.

In normal times, managing an economy is like managing a busy urban intersection. Veteran policy makers and central bankers are like traffic cops. They've been around long enough to know what's happening and how to get motorists to behave in certain ways: speed up, slow down, turn left or right.

What's happened in the past fifteen years or so is that the familiar intersections of economic life have been transformed. New superhighways carrying vast quantities of capital and labor are now feeding into the intersections of commerce. But the intersections haven't been reconstructed to handle this influx and the traffic cops don't agree on how to handle the relatively sudden swell of economic traffic. And who can blame them? Western economic policy makers have never before seen a few billion new workers, and trillions of dollars in new capital, pour into the global economy.

To make matters worse, economists who lead policy debates don't all have the same theories of how "drivers" in the global economy behave individually. And, more and more often, they disagree about such basics as how to get economic players to speed up, slow down, or turn. In fact, they even disagree about what the role of economic traffic cops should be.

No wonder the past few years have been among the most confusing in world economic history.

A Closer Look at Global Imbalances

The huge new global imbalances that arose in the 1990s are not exactly a secret. Less obvious, though, is just how fundamentally the rise of the emerging nations has remade the global economy—and the ways this shift fueled the Great Credit Bubble—and how all of that explains why the advanced nations can't get out from under the present slump.

Sure, we've all heard a million times that globalization has changed everything. But what most people don't realize is that these changes go far beyond call centers in India or factories in China. The most profound change of all has been capital flows from surplus to debtor nations—flows that have proved devastating for developed economies over the past fifteen years. Yet even now, how exactly this imbalance arose is not well understood. That's a problem, because many of the drivers of imbalances are still in place.

So let's walk carefully through why this situation arose—and why we ended up with chaos at the global macroeconomic intersection.

Step one is identifying the three major players in the story. I classify them as follows:

- The traditional advanced economies of the northern hemisphere, excluding Japan: the United States, Canada, and the nations of the European Union;

- Japan itself; and

- Emerging/LOw-Wage current Account Surplus Economies and
Energy-exporting Nations, for which I have created a somewhat
cumbersome acronym—ELOWASEENS ("eh-lo-wah-seens"). The
ELOWASEENS, by 2006, included China, Russia, Saudi Arabia,
Singapore, Kuwait, South Korea, Malaysia, Thailand, Indonesia, Qatar,
Nigeria, Venezuela, and Libya. I have left aside India and Brazil
(otherwise considered powerhouse emerging markets) because in 2006
they were still only on the cusp of being able to sustain current account
surpluses. They are nevertheless very large nations with huge populations
that are likely to further destabilize the global macroeconomic
intersection—and are all but ELOWASEENS. But in 2006, at the
climax of the credit bubble in the developed world, they were not quite
yet a force in the overall equation.

Now you may ask, what is a nation's "current account" to begin with?
Good question: the current account balance (surplus or deficit) of a
country, together with gross domestic product and trade balances, is
among the key statistics in measuring the relative size and trading position of countries. Somewhat more simply put, if a nation takes in more
goods in trade than it sells to other nations (measured in payments),
after adjusting that equation for the net of earnings on foreign investments minus payments made to foreign investors, and general cash
transfers, that country (or region) is running a current account *deficit*. If
the inverse is true, the country is said to be in current account *surplus*.

Currently, and for many years now, the world's biggest current account surplus is earned by China, and the biggest deficit is incurred by
the United States. So it is basically economists' calculation of what nations are "in the red" (consuming more than they produce) versus "in
the black" (producing more than they consume). Pretty simple when
you think about it that way, right?

Okay, back to what happened.

In order to explain how the prevailing global imbalances have
changed everything, we need to look at the world economy before and
after these imbalances emerged. In the following pages, I do this by
examining the relationships among and within each of the world's
three main economic players for two different points in time.

First, I look at "before"—1995. While most Americans spent that year obsessed with the trial of O. J. Simpson, I think of 1995 as the year right before the world economy was turned upside down. The Internet and other information technologies were about to dramatically boost productivity in the advanced nations, but that hadn't happened yet. AOL's dial-up service—"you've got mail!"—was still the main way people accessed the Web. Meanwhile, the big economic boom outside the rich countries, in the ELOWASEENS, was just getting under way. These nations were coming into their era of great expansion and were just starting to pile up their huge account surpluses.

Second, I look at 2006 as my "after" point, when the global imbalances had fully emerged. The big focus of media attention in 2006 was the disastrous war in Iraq, but actually a bigger catastrophe was in the making as the developed world's credit and asset bubble reached an apex.

Comparing these two points in time, 1995 and 2006, is startling. The macroeconomic "traffic" flowing through the world economy not only grew substantially during this period, but the direction of the flows changed considerably—with traditionally poorer nations becoming huge creditor countries.

This revolutionary change happened without any makeover of the global monetary system or implementation of other global reforms that might have updated the macroeconomic intersection. The fall of the Iron and Bamboo curtains was, in many ways, as significant as the end of World War II. Yet there was nothing like a United Nations or a Bretton Woods Conference to create a new global financial system. No new institutions were created, like the IMF or World Bank were after the war. While everything in the global economy changed, the infrastructure to manage it remained untouched.

Perhaps this should not be viewed as all that surprising, because in 1995—six years following the fall of the Berlin Wall and the Tiananmen Square incident—the principal source of trade pressures on rich nations was still *within* the developed world. The main challenge to the economic dominance of North America and Europe—initially, in light manufacturing and, later, heavy manufacturing and advanced product design employment—came from *Japan*.

By 1995, Japan's economy was in the doldrums and America's hysteria about that country's rise had long since abated. Books like Michael

Crichton's *Rising Sun* were no longer flying off the shelves as Americans fretted about a takeover by Tokyo. But Japan was still seen as America's main economic rival. The United States and the Western European nations were still collectively running big current account deficits in 1995 with Japan (and also, to a lesser extent, the energy-exporting nations).

Increasingly, though, Japan was a manageable rival. The competition with Japan—which had pursued an export-based trading model since the 1960s and was joined by the four "Asian Tiger" nations during the 1990s—was no big deal as advanced nations emerged from their recession of the early 1990s. That's because the United States and the rest of the developed world were embarking upon a productivity explosion as the Internet and other technological breakthroughs emerged.

At the same time, the ELOWASEENS were only beginning to stir. China, long a sleeping giant, was still having its morning coffee in 1995. These countries were not yet piling up the account surpluses that are so familiar today. Indeed, they actually had a slight account deficit with the developed world in 1995, and an aggregate GDP of only $2.8 trillion (in 2005 dollars).

In 1995, then, the global macroeconomic intersection of the three groups of nations we are examining in this chapter looked like the drawing in figure 1 on the following page:

At this stage, the accelerated growth of information technology—chiefly, the Internet and its many applications—initially forestalled the rise of huge global imbalances. This new technology was not just the basis of new businesses in developed countries—from Amazon to wireless firms—but made any number of existing companies more efficient and profitable. The late 1990s shaped up as something of an economic golden age, especially in the United States, which enjoyed the longest peacetime expansion in its history. Political scientists talked of the dangers of American hegemony in a "unipolar" world, while dot-com gurus forecast an endless array of riches. The number of American millionaires grew by leaps and bounds. Even the federal budget deficit, to everyone's surprise, began to disappear. The swiftly burgeoning economic China and other nations were barely discussed.

Yet already, evidence was everywhere that the twenty-first century would not be another American century. Among other things, it wasn't long before America's golden advantage, the Internet, was to put work by poorer countries and became a driver of their growth—and new

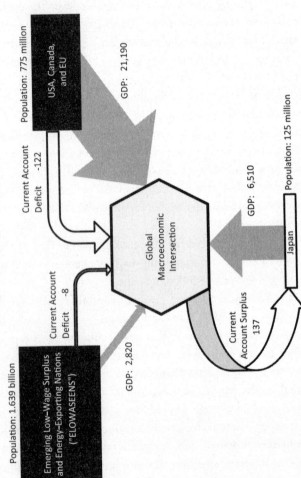

FIGURE 1: The Global Macroeconomic Intersection
Gross Domestic Product and Current Account Surplus
1995

(billions of chained 2005 U.S. dollars, except population)

Population: 775 million

USA, Canada, and EU

GDP: 21,190

Current Account Deficit -122

Global Macroeconomic Intersection

GDP: 6,510

Japan

Population: 125 million

Current Account Surplus 137

Population: 1.639 billion

Emerging Low-Wage Surplus and Energy-Exporting Nations ("ELOWASEENS")

Current Account Deficit -8

GDP: 2,820

Notes:
1) ELOWASEENS include China, Russia, Saudi Arabia, Singapore, Kuwait, South Korea, Malaysia, Thailand, Qatar, Nigeria, Venezuela, and Libya.
2) Country group boxes sized to relative population.
3) GDP and Current Account arrows show relative size.

global imbalances. After all, the Internet added immeasurably to the ability of emerging market exporters and processors to expand rapidly in the late 1990s and into the early 2000s. Ironically, the Internet (developed by the United States) made it easier than ever to move production overseas and, in time, to move services as well—even legal services.

For a time, though, during the late 1990s and first few years of the new millennium, the impact of information technology in the West—chiefly the United States—gave the countries of North America and Western Europe a huge boost in productivity and capacity. But in no small sense, the Internet bubble was not dissimilar to the gold rush, one of the great misallocation of capital resources of all time (and coincidentally, I suppose, both were centered in San Francisco and its environs).

The less attractive attributes of the bubble were excused by many with reference to theories of "creative destruction," a term originating with Karl Marx but promulgated in the context of the benefits of potentially wasteful investment theorized by the Austrian American economist Joseph Schumpeter (a story for another book). But notwithstanding the huge productivity boost that resulted from the IT revolution, it reduced pressure on the advanced nations to focus on labor-intensive productivity enhancement—such as heavy infrastructure redevelopment and expansion—even as they faced the challenge from a huge pool of cheap labor abroad. In fact, it should be noted that technology actually reduced the need for workers.

The magnitude of this increased productivity in the United States is illustrated in figure 2, which shows the dramatic rate of change in productivity growth during the boom compared to the periods immediately before and after. The steep growth reflected in the trend line marked "Productivity Burst" was akin to productivity growth at the advent of other major technological leaps in telecommunications and transportation. The years just before the turn of the new millennium were remarkably similar, as many commentators noted, to the era a century earlier when innovations like electricity and the assembly line were coming into widespread use.

Thanks to this burst, the advanced nations had an enormous head start on emerging nations that were just throwing off the burden of socialism. Arguably, the rich countries had plenty of time to plan for the tsunami of competitive labor and resources that were about to challenge their standard of living. After all, the emerging market "usurpers" didn't step forward overnight. They had to transform their industrial,

FIGURE 2

communications, transportation, financial, and political sectors in order to be competitive.

China, for example, had to build all sorts of things during the 1990s
to connect its vast labor force to the rest of the world (things that those of
us in the advanced nations often take for granted): a new national highway system, modern airports, and the urban water and electrical systems
needed to accommodate tens of millions of peasants pouring into rapidly
expanding industrial cities. The percentage of Chinese living in cities
increased from 17 percent in 1978 to 46 percent in 2009 to just over 50
percent by year-end 2012, with much of that migration—the largest in
human history—occurring during the 1990s.[1] Amid its growing pains,
China didn't look anything like the economic superpower we see today.

Also, some of the emerging countries—especially the Asian Tigers—
initially overborrowed in hard-currency denominated loans; not a

smart move. And the resulting Asian financial crisis beginning in the summer of 1997 tempered the accelerating pace of expansion in the ELOWASEENS for a brief period, giving the advanced nations further breathing room.

So what did the developed world do during the 1990s to plan for the enormous changes in the global economy that winning the Cold War had set in motion?

Pretty much nothing, as I discuss in more detail in the next chapter.

And among the ominous trends that emerged in the late 1990s was the way that developing nations handled all their surplus money. The lesson that emerging nations drew from the 1997 Asian financial crisis was that they should abjure borrowing in other currencies and boost their savings rates. Instead of *issuing debt* in the currencies of their trading partners, they began to accumulate foreign reserves in the currencies of their trading partners and invest those reserves in the debt securities of hard-currency nations—particularly in U.S. Treasury securities, with China's share alone growing from less than $60 billion at the end of the 1990s to over $1.1 trillion by the end of 2011.[2]

Two other phenomena can be traced to 1997. By the end of that year, U.S. real household median income began to stall. Such inflation-adjusted income would reach an all-time peak in 1999 that would never again be repeated to the present day.[3] Yet even as incomes stalled in the late 1990s, inflation-adjusted housing prices in the United States began bubbling relentlessly upward.

The five-year period from 1997 through 2002 was highly transitional, encompassing rapid productivity growth in the advanced nations, the demise of the Internet bubble, the introduction of the euro, the global terrorist events of 2001 and the military aftermath, together with the ongoing acceleration of growth in the ELOWASEENS and their inexorable accumulation of excess savings.

Oh, and let's not forget China's entry into the WTO in 2001, along with its gaining permanent "most favored nation" status from the United States that same year.

The global economy turned upside down with remarkable speed. In 1997, the aggregate current account deficits of the United States, Canada, and the European Union was just $94 billion. By 2002, that figure had ballooned to $467 billion—a stunning shift.[4] The rise of the ELOWASEENS remade the global economy in just five years.

These shifts contributed to subdued inflation in the United States, which hovered generally between 1.5 percent and 3 percent during this period, except in 2000, when inflation spiked slightly higher. That's because lower-cost imports, particularly from low wage countries, tempered any overall rise in prices. Prices for things like microwave ovens and cell phones fell sharply, offsetting rising prices for other things, such as health care and college tuition. Walmart was opening an average of two discount stores every week between 1997 and 2002 and pressuring its key suppliers to move to China in order to lower costs.

As a result, central banks could reduce short-term interest rates after 2001 without incurring much in the way of an inflation penalty. This, of course, fueled demand from private-sector borrowers even further. Suddenly, cheap money was everywhere.

Thus, the stage was set for the period we normally associate with the credit bubble—but, in truth, the period 1997 through 2002 was its first act.

PILEUP AT THE GLOBAL MACROECONOMIC INTERSECTION

Let's return now to the global macroeconomic intersection. By 2002, the emerging nations of the world, growing by leaps and bounds, were firmly tied to the broader global economy. The vast populations of the ELOWASEENS were now linked to the free markets by the economic and trade equivalents of modern highway interchanges—interchanges that had been under construction for a dozen years prior—in communication, shipping, capital access, and financial services. Nowhere were these linkages more visible than in China, where massive port and shipping facilities were built or expanded, particularly in Guangdong Province and to the north in Tianjin, to handle the goods from factories that, in some cases, operated around the clock.

And just down the road, albeit linked to the global economy more by an access road than by a highway interchange, were the additional 1.2 billion people of India, which was still marginally in deficit but growing rapidly. Japan, meanwhile, remained an export powerhouse with big trade surpluses throughout this period, even as its economy otherwise stagnated.

FIGURE 3: The Global Macroeconomic Intersection
Gross Domestic Product and Current Account Surplus
2006

(billions of chained 2005 U.S. dollars, except population)

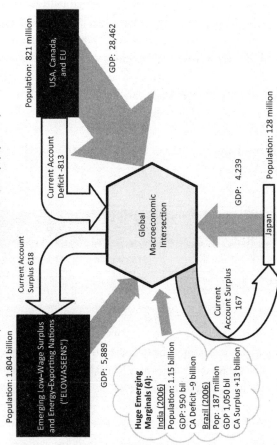

Notes:

1) ELOWASEENS include China, Russia, Saudi Arabia, Singapore, Kuwait, South Korea, Malaysia, Thailand, Qatar, Nigeria, Venezuela, and Libya.

2) Country group boxes sized to relative population.

3) GDP and Current Account arrows show relative size.

4) Indian and Brazilian current account deficits have since widened, to (current dollars) -$52 billion (2010) and -$53 billion (2011), respectively.

The GDP of India and Brazil have since skyrocketed, however, to 2011 levels of $1.85 trillion and $2.45 trillion, respectively (current dollars).

By 2006, the last full year of the credit bubble, our complex global economic intersection was therefore dramatically altered from its state in 1995. The GDP of the ELOWASEENS had more than doubled in size to $5.9 trillion, while the combined GDP of the United States, Canada, the European Union, and Japan rose by a scant 18 percent during the same period.[5]

Of far more importance, the current account deficit (and remember, these figures are all in "constant"—i.e., inflation-adjusted—dollars) for the United States, Canada, and the European Union had ballooned by 566 percent, to $813 billion from $122 billion, while the account surpluses of the ELOWASEENS had exploded to $618 billion from what had been an $8 billion deficit eleven years earlier.[6] Figure 3, on the previous page, shows what the global macroeconomic intersection looked like in 2006.

And the above was hardly the end of the story. In 2011 the GDP and current account balances of the various parties looked like this in 2005 U.S. dollars:

	GDP	Current Account Balance	% of GDP
ELOWASEENS	$7.1 trillion	+$753.4 billion	10.60%
U.S./Canada/E.U.	$34.3 trillion	-$629.3 billion	-1.84%
Japan	$5.7 trillion	+$135.0 billion	2.35%

Because of the Great Recession, the deficit of the Western advanced nations had narrowed somewhat, but the ELOWASEEN surplus grew ever larger.[7]

All flavors of Keynesian macroeconomists rightly point out that the global economy is suffering from a demand shortage. This is correct, of course, but begs the question of *why*. Unless we recognize that the dramatic changes to the global macroeconomic intersection are historically unique in both context and scope, we will never have a prayer of addressing today's economic challenges.

An insufficiency of demand is the flip side of an excess of supply. But the analytics bearing on the two versions of the same problem are different. A demand shortage can be caused by a sudden falloff in economic activity resulting from a natural shock, a war, or a debt overhang of the type discussed previously. In any case, it represents a falloff in aggregate demand relative to a static or steadily growing supply of goods and services.

But what if a historical event rather suddenly created a huge boost in supply? What if global aggregate demand was more or less steady, or even growing, but supply was growing much faster and growing independently of demand? What if the existence of inexpensive labor and capital created its own form of supply stimulus, much as lower tax rates or other policies that foster capital formation would do (in theory) in an otherwise supply-constrained economy?

If all that happened, the advanced nations would find themselves living in a changed world. And, if these nations were smart, they would change, too. Right?

Wrong. As it turned out, the developed world handled the rise of oversupply in about the worst possible way. Too much supply didn't have to become a nightmare. But it did, thanks to missteps of historic dimensions.

CHAPTER 3

MAKING THE WORST OF IT

Bad Policy, Denial, and Decline

I t is not often that two billion new workers and trillions of dollars of excess cash appear on the world stage. In fact, nothing like this has ever happened before. So you can kind of understand it if policy makers in places like Washington, London, Frankfurt, and Tokyo don't exactly know how to handle the situation.

Still, what's remarkable is the degree to which these policy makers made all the wrong choices, starting with the United States, where regressive ideologies and bad public policy ensured that the global explosion of labor and capital would snowball into a disaster that decimated America's industrial base, deeply indebted the country, fueled a record rise in inequality, and led to the financial crisis. This disaster is far from over.

So exactly how did the United States screw up?

The short answer is that America's leaders gave up on managed capitalism at exactly the moment when we needed it most.

A longer answer is about the overreach of laissez-faire ideas, the perversion of conservative ideology, the ongoing embrace of supply-side economics, and the compounding damage that occurred when centrist Democrats fatefully misread the global economy.

36   I know that's a long list of culprits. So let's unpack the failed U.S. economic and policy response to oversupply in more detail.

THE GREAT REACTION

The rise of the emerging nations in the 1990s came at a fateful moment. By 1997, the United States had been engaged for over fifteen years in a "great reaction"—an economic experiment that rejected decades of post-1932 managed capitalism in favor of unrestrained liberty, laissez-faire government, and a previously rather eccentric backwater economic notion called supply-side theory.

Emphasizing consumption and easy credit as the principal means of achieving growth, this economic philosophy proved attractive to a population that had grown tired of activist government. For a baby boom generation that had seen opportunities diminish amid the hyperinflation and deindustrialization of the 1970s, what could be more seductive than a rejection of the scrimping, saving, and collective sacrifice of its "greatest generation" forebears in favor of more spending, more stuff, and, well, "me"?

Most stunningly, winner-take-all capitalism—rejected by the public for decades following the excesses of the Gilded Age—was rehabilitated in the 1980s and sold to an aspirational middle class as a virtuous paradigm that promised everyone not merely a good job, a home for their family, and education for their children but also a shot at *Lifestyles of the Rich and Famous.* Tellingly, *The Waltons,* Hollywood's paean to grit and community during the Great Depression, went off the air just after Reagan took power, and *Dynasty,* a TV drama about a wealthy oil family, began an eight-year run days before he took the oath of office.

So-called conservatives led the laissez-faire revolution, from Reaganomics to the Contract with America. But the economic and political strategies they embraced were decidedly not conservative in the prudential sense of the word. Not even close. Broad claims were made about the virtues of small government and low taxes, and about how efficient markets and rational consumers could solve any number of societal problems—claims that any number of Republicans embraced.

Essentially, though, there was no historical proof for many of these claims, including the basic logic chain of supply-side economics, namely, that lower taxation would spur greater investment and consumption, create a greater supply of goods and services, produce a larger economy, and yield larger tax revenue overall. Whereas American conservatives had once preached caution and incrementalism in the economic realm, they suddenly turned into radical gamblers, swinging for the fences with untested ideas and putting the nation's fiscal health at risk in the process.

Supply-side theory had, before the late 1970s, been a fantasy of a small minority of economists who remained on the far fringes of the mainstream during the early postwar era. Many of them found academic homes at the University of Chicago and other midwestern universities in the Great Lakes region (hence the terms "Chicago school" and "freshwater school" to describe these economists). Over the years, they blended a cocktail of ideas into a plausible vision of economics. They argued that more freedom—freedom from taxation and regulation— would produce a greater supply of goods, services, jobs and, of course, wealth.

Freshwater economic ideas arrived at a propitious moment. They fit perfectly with a distrust of government and a new embrace of individualism in American society. Also, the essential optimism, even utopianism, of these ideas seemed quintessentially American, like the heartland from which they sprang. The bright future they offered felt like the perfect antidote to the nightmare of the Vietnam conflict, the economic shocks of the 1970s, and the malaise of the Carter years. The planets were aligned to turn consumption and lifestyle aspirations loose, financed with tax cuts and borrowing rather than toil.

So, by the early 1980s, the pattern of the next quarter century would be set. The great engine of industrial American capitalism began to recede into memory, replaced by a new "service" economy that specialized in instant gratification. (More on that below.) Also, thanks to the rise of shareholder capitalism and other trends, quarterly profits became all-important, shifting the focus of corporations away from long-term innovation and toward whatever steps it took to make a buck by the next quarterly filing.

Consumption as a percentage of GDP steadily increased from the average 62 percent to 63 percent range (where it had hovered during the period from the end of World War II through the early 1980s) to 70 percent of GDP by the 1990s. Most of this additional consumption would be financed not by greater productivity but by credit. And overall outstanding debt in the United States would explode from the 150 percent of GDP of the postwar years to over 350 percent by the peak of the Great Credit Bubble in 2009.[1]

Meanwhile, America's political leadership, particularly Republicans, learned an alarming (as it turned out) lesson during the 1980s: that "deficits don't matter," as Vice President Dick Cheney would later say. Politicians could win office by pandering to the public's desire for low taxes and lots of spending, and leave the bill to future generations. Once upon a time, Republicans were the main opponents of this free-lunch approach; in the 1980s, they became the chief proponents of something for nothing—all under the guise of championing growth and freedom. The old conservative ethos of pay-as-you-go was dead and buried by the time Reagan was reelected in a landslide in 1984. And in subsequent years, as the GOP moved even more to the right, the most positive aspects of conservatism—fiscal prudence and a reflex toward balanced restraint—all but disappeared, leaving the right to morph into the most economically reckless ideological movement in American history. What many Republicans sought to put across was not really *conservatism*—although they wore the moniker with gusto—but that magic combination of prosperity and populism that assures political success.

When Ronald Reagan came to power in 1981, he and other advocates of economic liberalization made some good arguments. Yes, there was too much regulation in some parts of the economy. And yes, the top tax bracket of 70 percent was, in fact, way too high. Certainly there was a strong case to be made that more free-market dynamism was needed to foster faster growth.

As Daniel Yergin and Joseph Stanislaw wrote in their book, *The Commanding Heights*, the Reagan Revolution was part of a larger global pushback against too much government intervention in the economy.[2] Ultimately this drive for liberalization would fundamentally remake societies around the world, with capitalist practices eventually pushing aside a heavy-handed statism, particularly in the Soviet Union, India, and China, as we have already discussed.

Ironically, though, the very same movement that gave rise to new competitors in the developing world—and ushered in the age of oversupply—would end up going too far in the United States. While China and other competitors never abandoned a strategic role for government in choreographed economic growth, such thinking became anathema in a Republican Party that controlled much of the U.S. government from 1981 to 2009, an all-important period of change.

By rejecting managed capitalism as major competitors gained power, the United States economically disarmed itself just as the age of globalization began. The hard realities of geoeconomic power were ignored by a Republican Party that embraced the beliefs of earlier times: that economic liberty and less government involvement in commerce would inevitably result in long-term, steady prosperity. Their economic message—balanced and smaller government budgets, lower taxes, less national debt, reliance on the common sense of individuals to save and invest, and the reduction or elimination of socioeconomic engineering and entitlements—sounded very attractive and, in fact, it is attractive. In some parallel universe there may be an America that lives plainly, that consumes only what it can profitably produce, that requires fewer services and less support from government, and that lives within its means and sacrifices for the common wealth of family and nation.

That nation, however, is not the America of the past three decades. It may or may not be an America that ever actually existed. But it is not the consumerist, overly leveraged country of the present day.

The evasions and denials of this fact by those of a broad range of political stripes helps account for several problems I discuss later on, particularly regarding massive deficit spending. Yet the bigger problem with the new so-called conservative economic vision is that the right embraced supply-side thinking just as the world was entering the age of oversupply.

SUPPLY-SIDE DREAMS

Starting in the early 1980s, a focus on tax cuts stood at the core of supply-side arguments embraced by a generation of Republican leaders. Supply-siders argue that economic growth and prosperity is driven by increasing the supply of goods and services by making an investment in the increase of such supply economically attractive to those with capital and other resources.

Supply-side adherents hold that consumption (demand) merely derives from an increase in supply. By offering incentives—and limiting disincentives, such as taxes—to those capable of increasing the supply of goods and services, the benefits will trickle down to all participants in an economy. If goods and services are being produced at a lower cost, people will be able to buy more of them—increasing demand, spurring more hiring, and growing the economy. All of which, the logic goes, will result in more tax revenues, even though rates are lower—an alluring outcome also known as tax revenue optimization.

Now, as it turns out, tax revenue optimization theory was developed by none other than John Maynard Keynes, though without all the supply-side trappings. Keynes postulated that there was a point of the curve of potential taxation rates at which government revenues would be maximized by virtue of the relative incentives and/or disincentives caused by tax rates. The supply-side economist Arthur Laffer, as political mythology has it, drew this curve on a napkin for none other than future Reagan advisers Dick Cheney and Donald Rumsfeld, along with the writer Jude Wanniski, in the cocktail lounge of the Washington Hotel in 1974 to illustrate the need to avoid tax increases proposed during the Ford administration.

The "Laffer curve" (so christened by Wanniski) would dominate conservative economic thinking for thirty years. It rested on the notion that tax revenues could actually be made to increase if only tax rates were lowered. This was a slight bastardization of the curve's original postulation by Keynes, and even of the reason Laffer drew it on the famous napkin, which was to prove that increasing tax rates did not necessarily increase government revenues but could decrease them. The inverse, some economists and many Republican politicians believed, had to be true as well—didn't it?

Actually, it was all a bit of wishful thinking fueled by strong populist appeal. Nearly every element of the supply-side worldview was popular with a good chunk of the American electorate: lower tax rates for all, with substantial cuts for those at the top tier to trickle down to those below; smaller government with fewer restrictions on individual liberties; higher consumption based on the simple premise of there being more things to consume; and, best of all, the promise of unlimited economic growth.

Who wouldn't sign up for that plan? And sign up America did—in fact, swallowed it hook, line, and sinker.

41

One problem with the above formula, though, is that if overall tax revenues didn't rise sufficiently amid a new golden era of growth ushered in by lower tax rates, as the Laffer curve predicted, a fiscal disaster could ensue—unless there were big cuts in government spending. A second problem is that this scenario required the maintenance of respectable levels of net savings versus investment by rational consumers.

Those were two big "ifs." And there were no historical reasons, or other forms of proof, to show that these conditions would ever be met. And indeed, both hopes turned out to be pipe dreams. During none of the periods in which supply-side theory dominated economic policy making in the United States did things ever go as the theory imagined. Most notably, lower tax rates never sparked enough growth to generate more revenues overall—not by a long shot. And during the two decades that Republicans held the White House, between 1981 and 2009, there was basically no political will to bring government spending into line with the reduced government revenues orchestrated by Reagan and George W. Bush. The Republican Party, once the guardian of fiscal responsibility, became something else altogether as its adherents learned that they could get elected by cutting taxes, or promising to cut taxes, and then leaving spending cuts for another day.

When the budget was actually in surplus during a few of the Clinton years, it was accomplished mostly through higher government revenues together with a truly booming economy driven by huge technology-induced productivity increases. The Laffer curve never really worked, at least fiscally.

Nor did supply-side economics work for ordinary Americans, many of whom saw their earnings stagnate as the lion's share of winnings went to the top 10 percent of Americans. But flat earnings didn't stop the cost of living from going up, which explains why personal savings went into a nosedive. The personal savings rate, which hovered between 8 percent and 10 percent in the United States in the decades prior to 1980, has declined steadily since the supply-siders began to weave their fabric of hyper-investment and consumption, falling to near zero by the mid-2000s.[3]

Meanwhile, personal debt rose. With wages lagging behind living costs amid record levels of inequality, consumers turned to credit cards, home equity lines, and other forms of credit to make up the difference. And thanks to deregulation of the banking industry, along with growing supplies of cheap money, it became easier and easier for Americans to borrow as much as they wanted. So even as supply-side economics was failing, new ways to keep the public pacified and living standards high emerged.

This model, of course, would not be sustainable in the long run.

Deregulation was also an important part of this picture. Laissez-faire theorists touted less government oversight of the economy as an essential step (along with tax cuts) to achieve limitless growth. And like tax cuts, this wasn't a very tough sell to Americans, with their historic distrust of government and the post-sixties ethos that elevated individual choice over the authority of institutions. In any case, it wasn't the public that needed to be sold on deregulation; it was elected leaders and policy makers in Washington. And many gladly went along with deregulation, including deregulation of finance, both because they believed it was good for the economy and because major campaign donors made sure it was good for their careers. For example, between the early 1980s and the financial crisis, Wall Street spent literally billions of dollars on lobbying and campaign donations to shape the regulatory rules that governed their behavior.[4]

As a practical matter, fewer rules on Wall Street and the banking industry made it easier for ordinary Americans to tap into the world's growing sea of cheap money—and thus remain insulated from the consequences of stagnant wages and rising inequality.[5] Sure, America's economic system had stopped working for the bottom half of the income ladder by the 1980s, but deregulation of the credit card industry meant that just about anyone could get a wallet full of plastic that let them buy nearly anything they wanted. And deregulation of the mortgage industry made it easier to buy a house and then turn around and borrow against it. The opiate of cheap credit worked in tandem with low costs for consumer products to persuade the masses that everything was more or less fine.

Yet deregulation would come to have major costs, as we now know. Banks and the shadow banking industry were unleashed, and they took huge risks with other people's money—money that was suddenly more abundant than ever before.

In retrospect, it's hard to imagine a more ill-timed confluence of historic trends. Washington, enthralled with laissez-faire ideas, removed key checks on the financial industry at the same time that cheap money flooded the world as never before; and also as strapped Americans increasingly looked to credit to maintain their standard of living.

This was a recipe for a train wreck, and that's exactly what ensued.

Emerging nations—starting with Japan in the 1960s, then the Asian Tiger states, and later China and others—were both the enablers and beneficiaries of this self-destructive behavior. They sold American consumers freighter after freighter of low-priced goods to satiate our endless consumption aspirations, papering over stagnant incomes and rising inequality, and then loaned us their export surpluses so we could continue living beyond our means, oblivious to what was really happening.

But the story gets worse because, along the way, the United States gave up key parts of its ability to generate its own national wealth.

THE GREAT INDUSTRIAL DEVOLUTION

The fall of America's mighty industrial sector over the past thirty years is often described as an unavoidable natural evolution. But the truth is that U.S. industry didn't have to fall so far or so hard. What really happened is that America's leaders—either entranced by laissez-faire ideologues or cowed by them—ensured the worst possible outcomes at precisely the moment that hundreds of millions of new workers joined the global economy.

We have all heard the standard explanation for the decline of U.S. manufacturing: Rust Belt industries simply couldn't compete against low-wage nations. In a classic example of Schumpeterian evolutionary economics, the story goes, weaker companies were destroyed and new ones arose.

In fact, the actual history is more complicated. Yes, the inability to compete against low-wage nations has been an important driver of deindustrialization. But it's also true that U.S. leaders failed to take coordinated steps that could have bolstered America's manufacturing sector, steps such as rejuvenating industrial technology, improving and better-utilizing the nation's human capital via retraining, and nurturing better business practices overall.

Were such ideas floating around a few decades ago, when U.S. competitiveness first began to decline? You bet. Proposals for an American "industrial policy" started emerging in the 1970s and some were officially embraced by President Jimmy Carter. The Reagan administration rejected such initiatives, but a growing circle of economists and politicians championed industrial policy through the early 1980s. Among them was the senator and presidential candidate Gary Hart.

Yet Hart was dismissed as a charlatan when he talked up "new ideas" to make America more competitive, and early advocates of industrial policy such as Robert Reich and Lester Thurow were painted as quasi-socialists.[6] Many in Washington rejected on ideological and political grounds the concept of developing a broadly defined national economic policy or, more properly described, a national competitiveness policy.

For generations, such policy was unnecessary, given the United States' strength and resources. It was something that developing countries needed to do in order to compete with the developed world. Yet even as the situation changed, and industrial powers like Japan and Germany showed how effective a strong national economic policy could be in fostering growth, many U.S. leaders resisted such policy on the grounds that, ultimately, only markets could allocate wealth and resources efficiently. It was deeply unfortunate timing that the so-called conservative movement arose at precisely the moment when the United States needed to use government more proactively to compete in the global economy.

Of course, the United States has for decades had a de facto national economic policy in the hodgepodge of subsidies and tax credits offered to various industries either directly or through low-cost government insurance or guarantees. The United States has long heavily subsidized the housing sector through the mortgage interest deduction, the health-care sector through the employee insurance deduction, Wall Street through the 401(k) pension deduction, and a few other sectors, such as energy and agriculture. So it's nonsense to imagine that Washington has been dominated by some purist opposition to a government role in the economy.

The problem is that there has been nothing strategic about these subsidies, at least from a geoeconomic perspective. This potpourri of perks has mainly aimed to satisfy political constituencies, not to bolster the country's comparative advantage relative to its competitors. For decades, we have annually wasted hundreds of billions of dollars in tax expenditures that have had nothing to do with the arguably most important challenge facing the United States—retaining its ability to create wealth and compete globally. Conservatives pooh-poohed industrial policy as the wrongheaded picking of "winners and losers" even as they largely accepted a tax structure that did exactly that—only not in ways that were actually useful.

We have seen entire industries vanish from our shores that could have been retained with tax credits, modifications to business practices, the targeted bolstering of human capital via retraining, and investment in state-of-the-art technology and systems. Businesses lost to competitors go beyond old-school manufacturing, and encompass the most modern and labor-intensive industries—including ones such as animation and computer graphics, which Canada, India, and China have sought to emphasize.

If you're an advanced nation, the right response to rising global competition is to start making products that offer a higher added value—and consequently higher gross profit margins—from specialized and/or sophisticated manufacturing processes. Japanese advanced electronic components and German machine tools and manufacturing equipment offer excellent examples of this phenomenon, as do parts of the U.S. economy, to a somewhat lesser extent.

This path isn't without challenges, of course. Demand in the so-called high-value-added market is more limited than that for general manufactures—so if everyone is pursuing that portion of the market, margins become squeezed. Also, what was high-value-added at one point in time (computer chips, for example) has a tendency to become commoditized over time. Finally, this approach doesn't necessarily produce a lot of jobs. The highest margins of all are obtained by "industrial" companies that design and distribute but outsource all manufacturing to lower-cost labor outside of their principal high-wage markets. A "U.S." consumer product company named Apple comes to mind in this regard: massively profitable as a margin of sales because it doesn't actually make any products.

A second notion that is often floated among freshwater economists—one that was well exposed to skepticism by my grammar school buddy,

Timothy Noah, in his book on income and wealth inequality in the United States, *The Great Divergence*—is the Ricardian notion (after early-nineteenth-century economist David Ricardo) that trade among nations, even between low-wage and high-wage nations, was a benefit to both sides.[7] The argument states that the availability of low-priced goods to workers in higher-wage countries would serve to increase their purchasing power, thus more than offsetting any pressure on nominal wages. As Noah so correctly points out, that aspect of Ricardo's contribution to classical economics was put out of its misery by Wolfgang Stolper and the inimitable Paul Samuelson in a 1941 paper that proved the opposite to be true—that with significant enough wage imbalances, the loss of jobs and consequent downward pressure on wages in high-wage countries would overwhelm any benefit of cheaper goods. The only problem is that *until* the Great Rejoining, developed-world commerce did not involve such substantial wage imbalances on a high volume of trade, so no one had an opportunity to really study Stolper and Samuelson's proposition in the real world. Again, the Great Rejoining was truly a unique global event.

Ironically, the Great Industrial Devolution was actually exacerbated by one of the greatest technological leaps in the history of mankind, known generally as the information revolution. The Internet had profound and salutary effects on domestic productivity, yet it also came with three highly problematic consequences: (i) it enabled the emerging markets to have nearly perfect communication with, and access to, consumers in the developed world; (ii) it likewise made it easier for companies in North America, Europe, and Japan to employ the abundant and inexpensive new labor pools in emerging economies; and (iii) it produced enormous efficiencies in the developed world that arguably cost more domestic jobs than the technology created.

Of course, many of the Internet's most profitable applications were those that greased the wheels of consumption—something that went hand in glove with the still-powerful pull of the supply-side zeitgeist.

Nevertheless, productivity in the developed world accelerated at a rate unparalleled in postwar economic history. In an era of advanced creative destruction, during which businesses and markets sorted through the possible applications of the technology (also known as the tech bubble), productivity masked the advances in emerging markets that were on the cusp of radically destabilizing the balance of global trade.

Productivity is, after all, similar to cholesterol—there is good productivity and bad productivity when it comes to measures of unit labor cost (the cost to produce a unit of goods or services, measured in money value). Technological advances—at least in a theoretical closed universe of national labor—produce generally good productivity. A country can produce for itself more efficiently, with corresponding benefits to living standards, as workers need to work less to meet domestic demand and—again, theoretically—earn higher incomes by devoting the saved time to catering to exogenous demand. This is what we know by a more popular name: progress.

Bad productivity is when workers are paid less (in real terms—they have less purchasing power) for producing a unit of goods or a service. It shows up in statistics as "increased productivity"—but it is the national accounts version of plaque in the arteries.

The Great Industrial Devolution didn't have to happen the way it did. The United States and other developed nations could have held on to more of their industrial base (and its ability to generate wealth) by making and selling stuff. Instead, the veritable embracing of offshoring by free market supply-siders ensured the worst possible outcome amid the rise of the emerging nations starting in the 1970s and 1980s.

As the Reagan era ended, the United States turned a fateful corner and began moving toward a hollowed-out, financialized economy characterized by easy money, soaring debt, false prosperity, and outsized risk taking by bankers and traders. That's not a good mix.

One would have thought that the near-collapse of several entire sectors of the economy after the excesses of the 1980s would have tempered appetites for risky economic theories and imprudent financial adventurism. But the desire for a renewal of abundant prosperity—more accurately, the return of the satisfying feeling of nearly unrestrained consumption—overwhelmed mere prudence. And so the mistakes of the 1980s under Reagan were merely a prelude to the greater excesses of the early 2000s. But all the trends would become more magnified over time as the global supply of labor and capital expanded, deregulation went further under Bush, and the housing bubble ushered in the biggest credit binge in U.S. history.

CHAPTER 4

LET THEM EAT DEBT

Stagnating Incomes, Credit Bubbles, and the Road to Crisis

The rise of emerging nations, along with the collapse of key parts of the U.S. economy, has been devastating for a great many ordinary Americans. Even as the wealthy got spectacularly more wealthy, starting in the 1980s and accelerating far more rapidly after 1997, middle Americans saw their incomes stagnate and the working class experienced sharp declines in wages.

Competing against nearly two billion new workers from poor countries is no easy thing. Especially if your government rejects smart industrial policies and otherwise makes the worst possible choices amid the fall of the Bamboo and Iron curtains.

The rise of inequality and the decline of the American dream is old news by now. But there is one puzzle in this story that deserves more scrutiny: Why haven't the majority of Americans who were clobbered by the economic trends of the past few decades demanded stronger solutions? Why haven't stagnant or falling incomes for the bottom 60 percent or so of households resulted in more pressure on the political system? Why wasn't Washington pushed by the voters to take more dramatic action as the emerging nations ate America's lunch? And with the recent impoverishment of the periphery nations of the Eurozone, why aren't the people in the affected countries screaming bloody murder?

In the United States, liberal answers to this puzzle tend to focus on the false consciousness of the white working class, as described in Thomas Frank's book *What's the Matter with Kansas* or the dominant role of money in politics.[1] Many conservatives, meanwhile, argue that most Americans have done better than it might seem and that, in particular, falling prices for consumer goods have allowed people to buy whatever they want.

But let me offer a better—and more obvious—explanation for why Americans didn't demand a stronger response to declining incomes: the public was showered with easy credit that allowed them to make up for lost income and maintain living standards—at least for a while.

THE LOGIC OF EASY CREDIT

Marie Antoinette famously said of the poor, "Let them eat cake." America's contemporary economic elites, whether consciously or not, decided that offering easy credit to Americans was better than addressing the causes of declining incomes. In effect: "Let them eat debt."

The past few decades have famously seen the "democratization of debt" whereby more Americans have found it easier to borrow more money in more ways. As Alan Greenspan said in 2005, "Unquestionably, innovation and deregulation have vastly expanded credit availability to virtually all income classes."[2]

Before explaining this shift in more detail, consider the elegant ways that the winners of the new economic order benefited from pacifying millions of Americans with easy credit, starting in the 1980s and reaching an apex in the early 2000s.

Japan, and later China, benefited in several ways. First, as I have described, export powerhouses needed to do something with their surpluses, and America's insatiable appetite for both public and private debt proved the perfect solution. Second, providing America with cheap money enabled American consumers to keep buying more and more imported goods even as real incomes for most Americans stagnated or declined. So not only did our competitors find a safe place to park all their extra cash, they also found a way to pump up demand for their exports. In a self-reinforcing dynamic, the more imports Americans bought, the more cheap money that countries like Japan and China had to lend back to American consumers to buy yet more things and generate yet more cheap money. Meanwhile, as I noted earlier, the ongoing offshoring of production for more and more lines of goods allowed prices on many consumer items to fall, so that inflation remained low even as money grew cheaper, and this allowed the Fed to keep interest rates low—thus allowing more borrowing and more consumption.

But there was a third way that our competitors benefited from keeping Americans fat and happy with cheap money: they helped put off the day when the United States would have to focus on global competitiveness in order to address falling incomes. Cheap money was like an opiate that kept the United States in a glassy-eyed economic malaise, unable or unwilling to do ambitious things like reconfiguring its industrial base, rebuilding its infrastructure, or investing more heavily in scientific research and education. As long as Americans had their Visa cards and home equity lines, they didn't push Washington too hard to respond to the rise of global competitors. And that was good news for the emerging nations.

A pacified public was also good news for America's wealthy, and it's not hard to count the ways they benefited from the false mass prosperity enabled by easy credit.

For starters, the financial industry benefited in a big way by doling out credit to just about anyone with a heartbeat. More indebted Americans meant more interest payments and fees on credit cards, consumer loans, and home mortgages. In turn, those payments meant bigger profits for banks and other lenders—and, ultimately, bigger payouts to their executives and shareholders. Through much of the 1980s, the financial industry's profits totaled under 20 percent of all U.S. corporate profits. That figure jumped to 45 percent at the height of the booming—or rather, bingeing—2000s.

Peddling mortgage debt, in particular, was extremely lucrative. Executives at Wall Street firms that gorged on mortgage-backed securities, like Merrill Lynch's Stanley O'Neal, scored historic paydays before "the music stopped" (to paraphrase another winner on Wall Street, former Citigroup chairman and CEO Charles Prince). Mortgage kingpins like

Angelo Mozilo of Countrywide made even more money. But issuing credit cards was also very profitable, thanks to deregulation of the credit card industry in the late 1970s that let banks charge whatever interest rates they wanted.[3]

A second benefit to the upper class from deluging Americans with a river of easy credit was that it distracted people's attention from rising inequality and the winner-take-all economy. As long as ordinary people could buy flat-panel TVs and granite countertops, nobody looked too hard at how the economy was mainly benefiting those at the top. Easy credit helped create the illusion that a rising tide was lifting all boats, when in fact only the yachts were truly moving up while everyone else was temporarily bobbing higher in a sea of red ink.

In earlier eras, America's upper class felt compelled to share the wealth created by capitalism because, in part, they worried that social instability would result if they didn't. As Henry Ford is often credited with noting, America's workers are also America's consumers, and well-compensated employees mean more sales. In the past, as well, government did more to stem inequality as strapped voters demanded policies that better spread around the fruits of prosperity. Yet thanks to easy credit, the new era of inequality that began in the 1980s was accompanied neither by social instability nor public pressures on politicians to do something. The parking lots at Target and Walmart were full, and all seemed fine.

Easy credit didn't just prevent Americans from seeing inequality. It also helped obscure the fundamental ways in which a good swath of the public lost out under globalization even as America's highly educated classes prospered in a flat world.

Under normal circumstances, the pain and dislocations caused by globalization would have triggered a massive backlash against the free-trade regime largely embraced by both political parties starting in the early 1990s. Yet easy credit helped salve the wounds of downwardly mobile Americans and silence dissent. Sure, the plant may be closed and the jobs shipped to China. But with adjustable rate mortgages at rock-bottom rates and Home Depot offering no payments for a year on new kitchens, the good times could go on.

To progressive economists, it's been obvious for many years that America's postindustrial economy doesn't work for most of its citizens.

Unfortunately, it only recently became apparent to the citizens themselves when the bills for the borrowing binge truly came due.

And, of course, the biggest problem with all the cheap money and easy credit is that it created a profoundly dangerous credit bubble that brought down the U.S. economy. Actually, it created two credit bubbles—the first in the 1980s and the far, far bigger one that began to deflate in 2007.

The story of these two credit bubbles needs to be told before we move on.

STAGNANT INCOMES, RISING DEBT

America's great borrowing binge began in the early 1980s with the onset of what we might call the Lesser Credit Bubble of 1982–87. This bubble coincided with the emergence of Japan as a major economic challenge to the United States and the rapid erosion of the American industrial base—a process that began in the 1970s but accelerated with the recession of 1980 and 1981–82, and with Japan's rise.

The 1980s was a period during which the United States should have started to grapple seriously with its competitiveness problems and the fact that real incomes for many Americans, especially the working class, were stalling or falling. Yet although the sun was setting on American economic dominance during this decade, perhaps the most memorable phrase of the 1980s was that it was "morning again" in America—a slogan of Ronald Reagan's reelection campaign.

A large expansion of the credit markets helped create the illusion that the sun was rising in America, not setting. The federal government started borrowing like crazy, with the Japanese buying record quantities of Treasuries, allowing Americans to have their cake and eat it, too: low taxes and lots of public spending to provide services and fuel growth. But an equally big story was all the borrowing by ordinary Americans. Between 1982 and 1987, credit markets as a share of GDP rose from just over 150 percent to nearly 250 percent, and the amount of debt held by American households grew by leaps and bounds.

At the beginning of 1982, Americans held just $63 billion in revolving consumer debt—credit card debt. By October 1984, when the famed "morning again" ad was blanketing U.S. airwaves, that figure had risen to $95 billion—a 50 percent increase in just two years. And by the time Reagan left office, it would be up to $189 billion—more than a 200 percent increase since 1982.[4] Because the deregulation of credit card interest rates made it more profitable for banks to issue such cards, they showered consumers with credit offers as never before. And every year, a greater percentage of Americans got credit cards, allowing them to buy now and regret later. In 1980, 56 percent of adults had at least one credit card; by 2001, 76 percent had at least one card.[5]

Nonrevolving consumer debt—auto loans and the like—grew at a slower rate but still almost doubled during the Reagan years.[6] Exotic mortgage loans also first started to appear during the 1980s, thanks also in part to deregulation. The Garn–St. Germain Depository Institutions Act of 1982 allowed banks to offer adjustable-rate mortgage loans for the first time, providing borrowers with yet another way to increase living standards now and worry about the full consequences later.[7]

The expansion of credit markets in the 1980s was not just the result of a general economic expansion. Yes, the economy grew and credit use did, too. But what we also saw during the 1980s was many Americans starting to spend more than they earned and borrowing on credit cards or home equity credit lines to make up the difference.

A few figures tell this story clearly. The ratio of household debt to disposable income rose from under 70 percent in 1980 to nearly 80 percent by the late 1980s, the start of a steady upward climb that would continue into George W. Bush's second term. Household debt as a percentage of GDP also rose in the 1980s, by about 20 percent.[8] Finally, as already noted, the personal savings rate dropped substantially during the 1980s—from about 10 percent to 7 percent. This trend, too, would accelerate in coming years.

Now, one could look at these figures as evidence of a rampant new consumerism and live-for-today mentality. And, to be sure, American society did become more materialistic during the 1980s. With millions of people watching shows like *Dallas* every week, and with huge new malls cropping up across the country, it's no wonder that splurging rose in the Reagan years.

But the more accurate story behind expanded borrowing beginning in the 1980s is that large numbers of households turned to credit to make up for stagnant or falling wages. Yes, some Americans borrowed to live it up. But many more borrowed to make ends meet. As Elizabeth Warren and Amelia Warren Tyagi detailed in their book on the rise of personal bankruptcy, *The Two-Income Trap*, it is simply a myth that overconsumption is the main driver of debt and bankruptcy among Americans.[9]

According to the Congressional Budget Office, median household income in the United States increased only modestly in the 1980s, a decade typically remembered as a boom era.[10] And the incomes of the bottom fifth of Americans actually fell during this decade, mainly because the labor market collapsed for workers with only high school degrees as factories shut down amid the rise of Japan and other competitors.

Stagnant or falling incomes for most Americans during the 1980s was a big problem because the cost of living kept rising—for housing, health care, transportation, and so on. Borrowing was one way to close the gap.

Meanwhile, even as most Americans just treaded water in the 1980s, signs of affluence were everywhere as the wealthy began doing better than ever—and taking an ever larger share of the overall pie. The best data on income trends at the top comes from the French-born economists Emmanuel Saez and Thomas Piketty, who have analyzed income gains by different groups across many nations since the early twentieth century. Their data shows that between 1980 and 1988, the share of all income going to the top 10 percent of American households went from 34.6 percent to 40.6 percent. The share of income going to those at the tippity-top, households in the top 0.1 percent, doubled during the same period, reaching 6.8 percent by 1988.[11]

So basically what happened in the 1980s is this: the rich got richer, the poor got poorer, and the middle class barely held on. And again, all this took place amid—and was partly driven by—a meltdown in U.S. competitiveness. Up until 1970, the United States enjoyed decades of trade surpluses. Those surpluses turned to deficits during the 1970s, but the worst was yet to come. In 1980, the United States had a $19 billion trade deficit. By the mid-1980s, the United States was routinely running trade deficits of over $100 billion a year—or more than a five-fold increase (although the deficit declined somewhat during the period surrounding the recession of 1990–91).[12] As much as half of this trade deficit was with Japan.

In a prelude of bigger things to come in the early 2000s, Japan turned around and pumped much of its new wealth right back into the U.S. economy. As *The New York Times* reported in 1985, the influx of money pouring into the global economy from Japan—between $50 billion to $100 billion annually—rivaled the flood of petrodollars during the 1970s, and roughly half of this money was going to the United States as the Japanese invested in Treasury securities to finance Reagan's deficit spending. "It's potentially the biggest single flow of capital in world history," said Brian Fernandez, chief investment officer of the New York branch of Nomura Securities, the Japanese investment firm. "The funds represent the nest eggs of frugal Japanese consumers, who save more than 20 percent of their wages, and the profits of Japanese industry's conquest of world markets with automobiles, video recorders, cameras, and computers."[13]

With the rise of the BRICs—the emerging economies of Brazil, Russia, India, and China—fifteen years later, all this Japanese money of the 1980s would turn out to be a drop in the bucket.

The 1980s, to sum up, was a surreal decade. It was a period when the United States finally lost its industrial dominance to countries it had defeated in a war just a few decades earlier, and became indebted to those nations as well. It was a time when America's blue-collar workers, the heroes of the early postwar industrial era, saw their world shattered as plants were shuttered. It was a time when the great American middle class stopped expanding and began to fight for survival. It was a time when wealth inequality not seen since the Gilded Age became the norm, turning the oldest democracy in the world into the least egalitarian of all the advanced nations.

And yet there was almost no pushback to all of this. Borrowing, and then more borrowing—by consumers, government, corporations—distracted Americans from the sharp decline in the nation's collective economic fortunes.

Even when the Lesser Credit Bubble burst in the late 1980s, with the savings and loan disaster and the collapse of the real estate market, there was no great uprising against the nation's economic policies. Instead, just a decade later, the United States would do the same thing all over again—only on a much larger scale and with more disastrous results. And this time, having spread the gospel of greed across the Atlantic, it helped drag Europe into its own debt trap as well.

BIGGER AND BADDER: THE GREAT CREDIT BUBBLE

In the first decade of the twenty-first century, a confluence of trends created one of the largest and most destructive credit bubbles in world economic history. These trends included a rising sea of money pouring into the global economy from China and other emerging nations, stagnant wages in the United States, and massive borrowing by ordinary Americans and their government that perpetuated the illusion that all was well—until the inevitable crash came.

We had seen this movie before, in the 1980s. But the sequel turned out to be bigger and badder in every way. If debt had been the opiate of the masses in the 1980s, it became more like crack cocaine in the 2000s—faster acting, more addictive, and deadlier.

Let's take a look at what happened to explain why the credit bubble of the early 2000s got so completely out of hand. And why, even today, many of the basic conditions that fueled that credit bubble are actually still in place.

A good place to start, again, is with the incomes of American workers. During the boom of the late 1990s, incomes increased for nearly all groups for the first time in years. The wealthy got spectacularly more rich, but those in the middle and the bottom also saw steady income gains. These good times ended with the 2001 recession, and even when the economy rebounded, it failed to deliver either good jobs or significant income gains to the majority of American households. An analysis by the Pew Research Center found that "the recession in 2001 triggered a significant decline in household income through 2004. As the recovery strengthened, the median household income in 2007—$54,489— nevertheless stood at a level that was approximately the same as in 1999."[14]

In other words, as the new millennium began, most Americans spent a full decade pretty much running in place. Shortly before the second President Bush left office, *The Washington Post* ran an assessment of his economic record and concluded:

President Bush has presided over the weakest eight-year span for the U.S. economy in decades, according to an analysis of key data, and economists across the ideological spectrum increasingly view his two terms as a time of little progress on the nation's thorniest fiscal challenges. . . . The number of jobs in the nation increased by about 2 percent during Bush's tenure, the most tepid growth over any eight-year span since data collection began seven decades ago. Gross domestic product, a broad measure of economic output, grew at the slowest pace for a period of that length since the Truman administration. And Americans' incomes grew more slowly than in any presidency since the 1960s, other than that of Bush's father.[15]

One reason for the stall in median income growth was the declining quality of jobs. Middle-class jobs—those that brought in over $50,000 a year—shrank as a percentage of all jobs through the 1990s and the Bush years. At the same time, low-wage jobs proliferated, with places like Walmart and McDonalds hiring like crazy. A 2012 study by the National Employment Law Project found that "since the first quarter of 2001, employment has grown by 8.7 percent in lower-wage occupations. . . . By contrast, employment in mid-wage occupations has declined by 7.3 percent since the first quarter of 2001."[16]

And it's not just that the low-wage jobs proliferated as mid-wage jobs declined. In fact, wages for both kinds of jobs declined.

The usual story is that middle-class jobs disappeared thanks to the shuttering of factories. But what also happened is that many "good" jobs were turned into "bad" jobs as corporations focused ever more aggressively on pumping up profits and squeezing workers. The decline of unions, hastened by an attack on labor regulations, reduced the ability of labor to bargain with capital for its fair share of the pie.

In other words, income polarization didn't just "happen." It was accelerated by gains to the upper class. Ultimately, the incomes of the top 1 percent would grow by 275 percent between 1979 and 2007, according to the Congressional Budget Office.[17]

What was particularly tough for ordinary Americans is that the tepid income gains of the early 2000s came amid unprecedented spikes in the cost of key life necessities. Housing prices shot up dramatically during this period, of course, but so did out-of-pocket health-care costs and college tuition. Middle-class families found themselves far more strapped in the Bush years than they had during the stagflationary years of the late 1970s and early 1980s.

There were other bad trends during these years, too. China's economic rise accelerated rapidly after it was granted permanent normal trade relations in 2000, leading to huge job losses in the United States—nearly 3 million by 2010, according to one analysis.[18] Another study, published by the National Bureau of Economic Research (NBER), estimated that increased trade with China caused U.S. manufacturing employment to decline by almost a third.[19]

Nearly every state felt some of this pain as a new flood of imports swamped a variety of American businesses, including many that had felt very little competition from the earlier industrial competitors of Germany and Japan. A study by the Economic Policy Institute detailed how thousands of jobs were lost even in states that you wouldn't think would be hit hard by China's rise, such as Colorado, Florida, and Maryland.[20]

Up until the mid 1990s, the United States ran relatively modest trade deficits with China. That changed in a big way during the 2000s. The U.S. trade deficit with China rose from $83 billion in 2001 to $162 billion in 2004 to $258 billion in 2007—a stunning increase that helps explain why the Chinese ended up with more cash than they knew what to do with.[21]

Yet even as Chinese imports to the United States eclipsed those from Japan, it should be noted that the huge trade deficit with Japan kept growing as well: from $63 billion in 2001 to $84 billion in 2007, a solid 30 percent increase. America's trade deficit with countries such as India, Bangladesh, and Vietnam also soared. All told, deficits with the rest of the world nearly doubled during the Bush years, from $361 billion in 2001 to $698 billion in 2008.[22]

Given this track record, you'd think that Americans would have been in open revolt against the economic order of the early 2000s. They weren't. According to many polls, Americans were a pretty complacent lot during the 2000s when it came to the economy. And a big reason, to be sure, was that U.S. households were borrowing more money than ever, and at lower interest rates than ever, to achieve living standards that otherwise would not have been possible given weak income growth and the fact that U.S. manufacturers were getting squashed by an ascendant China. Ironically, all that debt that the United States was taking on—much of it from our competitors lending their winnings back to us—allowed Americans to keep living well and keep deluding themselves into thinking that everything was okay.

Between 2000 and 2008, the amount of revolving debt held by consumers increased by nearly 50 percent—from $675 billion to $976 billion, with most of this in the form of credit card balances.[23] All told, well over a billion credit cards were in the wallets of Americans during this period.[24] In 2006, credit card issuers mailed out over 8 billion solicitation offers— or about 73 for every U.S. household.[25] In some cases, even toddlers and pets received—and even post-credit bubble still receive—these offers!

Research on how Americans were using their credit cards revealed that such cards were increasingly functioning as a "plastic safety net" to help people make ends meet, particularly when they were unemployed, ill, or just not earning enough money.[26] One 2006 survey found that "29 percent of low- and middle-income households with credit card debt reported that medical expenses contributed to their current level of credit card debt."[27]

Student debt also exploded during the early 2000s as college tuition rose sharply, in part because of cutbacks to state aid for public universities (where the vast majority of college students are enrolled). Even relatively affluent households had no choice but to turn to loans as tuition increased by leaps and bounds, nearly doubling between 2000 and 2009. Outstanding student loans rose from about $200 billion in 2000 to over $800 billion by 2010, a stunning fourfold increase.[28]

Of course, the biggest way that Americans made ends meet was by borrowing against their homes. Many other people simply bought homes they could not afford, trying to achieve a standard of living that was beyond their means. More than anything else, as we now all know, it was the huge borrowing in the housing sector that largely inflated the mother of all credit bubbles.

How much borrowing are we talking about? Well, consider that way back in 1990, all outstanding home mortgage debt in the United States totaled $2.4 trillion. By 2000, after home prices had begun their historic run-up in the late 1990s, that sum had doubled—to $4.8 trillion. And that was just a taste of what was to come.

By 2004, outstanding mortgage debt had spiked way up, to $7.8 trillion. Two years later, it was up to $9.8 trillion. And in 2007, home mortgage debt hit its historic high point of $10.5 trillion. Never in history had individuals—in any country or at any time—borrowed so much money so quickly.[29]

And never in U.S. history had Americans raided their home equity—once revered as a slow-building piggy bank—with such abandon. Back in the comparatively innocent year of 1995, before the housing boom got going, Americans pulled out just $21.7 billion in equity from their homes (either in the form of cash-out refinancing or home equity lines of credit, or HELOCs). That figure would increase more than threefold by 1999 as the housing party got under way—to $71.1 billion. And within two years, that amount almost doubled, as home owners pulled out $135.5 billion in equity. In 2003, Americans pulled out a stunning $260.6 billion in equity—more than ten times the amount they borrowed just eight years earlier.[30]

And the borrowing kept rising. In the three craziest years of the housing boom—2005 through 2007—Americans pulled out a total of $916 billion in equity from their homes.

Back in the late 1990s, mortgage equity withdrawals equaled less than 4 percent on average of disposable personal income. During the boom years, they were over 8 percent on average.[31]

So what did all this money get spent on? The question is not so easy to answer, although the Fed analyzed the issue during the boom years and various economists have tackled the topic.[32] Surveys have also examined how such money is used.

It appears that some of the money was used for excessive consumption, which is consistent with the tales of the era—people going wild with their home equity lines to buy powerboats or SUVs, or to go on holiday. But much of the equity cashed out was used for a more pedestrian purpose: paying off older credit card debts connected not only with overconsumption but with just making ends meet. Parents of teenagers also leaned more on home equity lines of credit as college tuition soared.

As a result of all the borrowing by Americans—through credit cards, student loans, and mortgages—household debt as a percent of GDP soared to heights never before seen in the United States.

A word of context: For two decades, during the 1960s and 1970s, the ratio of household debt to GDP changed at only a gradual pace. Then, during the Lesser Credit Bubble of the 1980s, household debt as a percentage of GDP spiked from 47 percent in 1982 to 57 percent in 1988—almost a 25 percent increase in just 6 years. But this was merely a warm-up for bigger things to come. Between 2000 and 2008, debt to GDP rose from 67 percent to 97 percent—a nearly 50 percent increase.[33]

The Great Credit Bubble also saw a phenomenal rise in America's external debt. After all, the money Americans were borrowing hand over fist at relatively low interest rates had to come, either directly or indirectly, from somewhere, and much of it came from overseas—and specifically from China and other competitors looking to do something with their winnings. Never before had any country in the world sucked in so much money from other countries so quickly. And this was possible, of course, because never before had so much money existed in the world.

As we know all know, the Great Credit Bubble ended badly—to put it mildly. By early 2011, an estimated 28 percent of all home owners with mortgages found themselves underwater.[34] Which is to say that a huge amount of today's outstanding $10.5 trillion in household mortgage debt was not properly secured, and much still is not properly secured. Meanwhile there is $2.6 trillion in unsecured consumer debt outstanding, which, by definition, is unsecured. About a trillion dollars of this is in the form of student loans.

During those heady bubble years, those of us who knew the party couldn't last often discussed whether the housing market would face a hard landing or a soft landing when the end came.

The answer to that question has been more brutal than almost any of us imagined. Today, six years after the bubble peaked, the economy remains stricken.

CONFUSING SIGNALS AFTER THE BUBBLE BURST: "STAG-IN-DE-FLATION"

My good friend, a commodities trader in Chicago named Lincoln Ellis, was perplexed in 2010. At that time it seemed certain that the commodities markets would inflate enormously—what with the massive increase in the U.S. monetary base, which doubled from late 2007 through early 2010 and created unprecedented access to cheap money.

After all, far smaller examples of monetary easing over decades had inevitably resulted in inflation. If people can borrow lots of cheap cash, they will all try to buy anything of value at the same time, pushing up prices. So it was that Ellis, along with many others, believed that the unparalleled levels of monetary easing during and following the Great Recession, combined with the $831 billion in U.S. fiscal stimulus, would ultimately result in sustained inflation or even hyperinflation. Basic laws of economics almost dictated as much.

But it didn't work out that way on a sustainable basis. Not in the commodities market or elsewhere. During the Federal Reserve Bank's first round of quantitative monetary easing (QE1), from late 2008 through March 2010, commodities at first rose steadily into the third quarter of 2010, by about 60 percent, and then remained in a relatively narrow trading range before stalling out just after the end of QE1 of 2010, falling about 15 percent.

With the end of QE1 coinciding with a renewed U.S. economic slowdown in the summer of 2010, the announcement of the Fed's QE2 in August 2010 (after an altogether brief respite) sent commodity prices off on a tear once more, with the S&P GSC Index rising just over 50 percent to its peak and leveling off up 38 percent at the end of QE2 in June 2011. Commodity prices then adjusted downward once more, falling 22 percent from their 2011 high through their low in the third quarter of that year. Finally, with the by-then-perennial summer slowdown triggering expectations of an additional tsunami of liquidity, commodities began to rise again in the fourth quarter of 2011 until investors were rewarded with the advent of the European Central Bank's (ECB) LTRO—long-term refinancing operation (albeit credit easing rather than traditional quantitative easing) in December 2011. Commodities bounced up smartly again by 21 percent, only to backtrack by 22 percent after the final round of LTRO in February 2012. The commencement of the Fed's ongoing QE3 effort in the second half of 2012 barely registered at first, but then sent equity markets to all-time highs in the first half of 2013.

My friend was perplexed even back in 2010. He coined the term "stag-in-de-flation" as a play on the term "stagflation," which had emerged to describe the combination of economic stagnation and high inflation that dominated the late 1970s. He was right, to a great extent; the commodity markets did appear to be exhibiting a yo-yo type of behavior within an otherwise stagnant economic climate, inflating, then deflating, in turn. But this was not a single cyclical phenomenon—it was occurring almost annually. The advanced economies, however, were very much stagnating.

As time passed, the relationship between repeated periods of expectation of additional monetary easing, the easing itself, and the end of each cycle of liquidity pumping could be overlaid with price movements in tradable commodities became clear. It became apparent that the desired inflation brought about by easing was transitory, emerging in anticipation of, and ending shortly after, the easing itself. Stag-in-de-flation was not a new economic phenomenon, it was a spectacle brought about by the inflationary desire being almost wholly unrequited. While the excess money itself had to go somewhere, it simply bounced around, looking for returns in secondary markets.

For the changed flow of traffic heading toward the Global Economic Intersection used as an analogy earlier, all had something in common—one could call it "blown transmissions."

I may be taking the auto/traffic analogy a bit far, but that's pretty much what has happened: the normal economic transmission mechanisms that would translate all the monetary easing into a mass of "welcome" reflation (growth in nominal GDP), did not function—for the reasons covered in earlier chapters—as they would in normal times.

Because the historical reason for unprecedented levels of monetary intervention is nearly always, with the exception of extreme natural disasters and wars, the need to recover from a severe recession or a depression linked to an earlier credit bubble (excessive supply creation), the resulting inflation is the most expeditious way of reducing the debt overhang holding back the economy in the first instances. And, as flooding the globe with one's currency is generally a good way to ensure that the value of your currency relative to others will decline, loose monetary policy is a handy way of increasing exports to countries with currencies that thereby have greater purchasing power in the country that is the subject of this description.

Truly, all of this should operate—in any normal environment—relatively predictably, albeit with the risk that if monetary authorities aren't particularly careful in the use of their blunt monetary instrument (monetary policy is not a surgical exercise, it is more on the order of general chemotherapy) to reverse the process at the earliest possible moment of sustained recovery, hyperinflation can result. Even if it takes some time to build up sufficient deferred and unsatisfied demand and/ or to see population and household growth add incrementally to the need for housing and durable goods, the last century has taught us that a long and deep enough slowdown in supply generation during a severe recession should, with the help of sustained monetary easing and early fiscal stimulus, generate a cyclical recovery.

History, however, is proving of little value in the present case other than as a paradigm against which current economic behavior can be compared; this should enable us to identify what is really "different this time" and explore policy options that address unprecedented scenarios.

As noted earlier, the transmitters of easy money to the rest of the economy are blocked today because there is so much global supply and excess capacity of labor and goods and services relative to present demand that there is no reason for the private sector to produce additional supply.

But here are three points that should be considered as we think about that last statement:

▪ While there will always be demand for money (both risk capital/ equity and loans), and while innovation is critical to the long-term growth of economies and societies, capital allocation to unproven innovators and their ideas is generally done in a hit-or-miss fashion. By deploying small amounts of capital across a reasonably broad spectrum of opportunities to see if a few of those opportunities "hit," venture capital is a vital business, but a relatively small user of capital. It furthers economic competitiveness, and therefore the growth of demand, over the long term. But it is neither unique to any country nor is it a producer of net demand in the shorter term, despite what the "American exceptionalism" school of thought would imply (the Romneyesque argument that the United States has a lock on innovation). Sadly, the innovations we most associate with success, such as consumer technology, often do not result in a substantial net increase in domestic employment. The availability of the freedom—and the capital—to innovate should therefore not be conflated with a functioning transmission mechanism for excess money. In other words, the argument that using monetary policy to encourage risky ventures is perhaps more persuasive in theory than in practice.

■ The investment most closely associated with growth of employment and overall economic demand is investment in physical plant infrastructure and equipment—factories and commercial buildings, of course, but also housing and related long-term durable goods (heating and air conditioning equipment, for example). The expansion of these are by far the biggest users of capital and the biggest employers of domestic labor— albeit, with today's sophisticated manufacturing processes, increasingly skilled labor. But amid the prevailing supply glut, the private sector sees little incentive to invest in new plants and equipment—evidence the nearly $1.7 trillion in excess cash on large corporate balance sheets. The household sector is underemployed and, when you throw in the debt overhang, most individuals are unable to consider capital investments such as the purchase, expansion, or renovation of homes.

■ Some say that banks won't lend in the current climate because they fear reregulation or are overly burdened by legacy losses embedded in their assets but as yet not fully recognized. While there is some merit to the latter point of view, excess reserves of U.S. banks that are on deposit in cash and cash equivalents with the Federal Reserve Banks were, in January 2013, $1.5 trillion over what banks are required to keep in reserve. To put that in context, prior to the Great Recession, excess reserves hovered consistently between $20 billion and $60 billion from the 1980s (far less before that) through 2008. Even at the end of the Great Recession, excess bank reserves had risen to "only" $800 billion. They have almost doubled that since. In fact, excess cash reserves held by the U.S. banking system currently well exceed the regulatory common equity of all of the banks in the United States, combined. This doesn't mean a thing in terms of bank solvency; losses in other assets could erode equity. But it is an unprecedented phenomenon and implies far more than banks' mere "unwillingness" to lend that can somehow be overcome with ever-cheaper money.

Are banks behaving this way solely out of fear? Commercial banks are chiefly in the business of lending their money and getting it back with a premium we call interest. From the late 1990s until the Great

Recession, banks got more heavily into trading and equity investing—to no good end. But the principal mission of banks is capital formation through (hopefully) disciplined lending. The current problem, however, can best be characterized by the fact that banks are not making enough of a nominal return on loans—at least in the present environment—to warrant much risk of not getting their money back. In normal times, banks assess the creditworthiness of borrowers to determine risk. That generally amounts to an assessment of the overall financial health of a borrower, as well as its future prospects, assuming a variety of economic conditions. Today, however, most obviously creditworthy borrowers have little incentive to increase net debt—as they themselves are not expanding—and less creditworthy borrowers are overly vulnerable to shifts in macroeconomic outcomes, even if they would consider rolling the dice. So much of whatever small-loan demand exists is simply not a reasonable risk—entirely without regard to the future of bank regulation or the quality of legacy bank assets.

The stagnation part of "stag-in-de-flation" is hard to argue with. The developed world's economies are all stagnating simultaneously. The few bouts of inflation we have seen since the advent of the Great Recession are, I have argued, merely an unsustainable aspect of extraordinary monetary easing (and central-bank credit easing) in the absence of operating transmission mechanisms to assist developed economies to turn the corner toward substantial growth. In theory, central banks could get further into direct credit easing—as the ECB already has, to some extent, and as the Bank of Japan (BOJ) seems intent on doing—identifying sectors in which it essentially pushes banks to put out money by having the central bank essentially finance those loans directly. But the notion of central banks allocating capital is fraught with unintended consequences and, even to this progressive, smacks uncomfortably of central economic planning combined with the worst aspects of cronyism.

The deflation part of "stag-in-de-flation" is also very real and, as I illustrate throughout this book, has been with us for longer than we think—evidenced by slow employment growth and low rates of inflation even in an economy overheated by massive credit creation during the boom years of the 2000s.

CHAPTER 5

NATIONS IN NEUTRAL

The Output Gap and the Vanishing of Wealth

The first place one can see the sun rise in the United States is from the summit of Cadillac Mountain in Acadia National Park in Maine. Yet within fifteen minutes of this first glimpse, the entire eastern seaboard is bathed in morning sunlight. And on any given weekday, tens of millions of people are getting up to start work, as the world's fourth-largest labor force begins a new day.

Yet for millions of Americans (and millions of Europeans), a typical weekday is one of *not* working. And not producing. And not paying taxes. And, in many cases, if part-time work is all that can be found, it means not earning and consuming at levels they would be if they were working full-time.

The worst of the economic crisis may be over, but the large economies of the advanced world—the most powerful wealth creation engines in history—are still grossly underperforming, with huge human and economic costs. Never mind the huge gains in the stock market in recent years. And never mind the near-record corporate profits we've been seeing. The hard truth is that the United States and the rest of the developed world remain mired in one of the worst economic slumps in modern history—a slump that shows little real sign of ending, whatever the tidbits of good news from Wall Street or corporate headquarters.

"Output gap" may sound like a technical term, but it's pretty simple: an output gap is the difference between the *potential* output of an economy at the so-called natural rate of unemployment that results in neither inflation nor deflation and the *actual* level of output at any point in time.

If the gap is a positive one, an economy is producing at a rate higher than its long-term potential, and wages, prices, and assets tend to inflate. If the opposite is true, as is the case today, actual output lags potential output and the condition is deflationary—or at least highly disinflationary. And that is where we are five years after the financial crisis. America is stuck in neutral, if not reverse, along with the rest of the developed world.

WASTED HUMAN CAPITAL

There are 245 million Americans of working age (and not in jail or in the military), according to the U.S. Department of Labor. In April 2013, as I write this, 155 million of these people are officially part of the labor force—63.3 percent. Of that number, 143 million have jobs.[1]

This leaves about 100 million Americans who, on any given day, are not working. Millions of these people aren't working by choice—they are students, stay-at-home parents, or retired but still able. Millions more would like to be working, but can't find a job. By the Department of Labor's count, just under 12 million of the 100 million nonworking Americans are "unemployed." Another 8 million of those who are officially counted as employed are working part-time because they can't find full-time work and 3.6 million are counted as "marginally attached to the labor force" or "discouraged workers," for a grand total of about 23 million people who should be working full-time, but aren't.

The Bureau of Labor Statistics tallies up another number to capture this picture, a number that most people have never heard about and the media rarely mentions: the U-6 unemployment rate. In a dry table on "Alternative measures of labor underutilization," the BLS offers up a more accurate unemployment rate. While the standard <u>unemployment</u>

rate in March 2013 was 7.6 percent; the U-6 rate of underemployment was 13.8 percent.[2] The often disregarded U-6 underemployment rate incorporates workers who are not included in the "civilian labor force" because they have given up looking for work even though they desire and are available to work and does not count as employed people who work part-time because they can't find a full time job. The standard unemployment rate, by contrast, counts as employed anyone who worked at least one hour in the employment survey week, even if they were part-time for reasons of not being able to find a full-time job. In fact, even the U-6 rate counts that one-hour-a-week worker as "employed" if they are working that one hour by choice rather than because of a lack of alternatives.

Of course, even this number may be way too low since it is impossible to truly calculate how many of the remaining 87 million non-working Americans, who are considered not in the labor forces but who are of working age, would rather have a job but gave up looking long ago, and the survey instruments used by the Department of Labor are incapable of divining this number. If you've been sitting home in your pajamas (so to speak) for a decade, the government probably doesn't know it.

John Williams, who writes the *Shadow Government Statistics* blog, compiles an alternate unemployment rate that estimates the number of long-term discouraged workers and adds that number to the BLS estimate of U-6 unemployment, which includes short-term discouraged workers. In March 2013, Williams's SGS unemployment rate stood at around 23 percent—nearly twice what it was in 2000 and ten points higher than in 2007, before the crash.[3] While Williams's economic data is sometimes criticized, and for some good reasons, his numbers here seem pretty on point to me.

European countries also tend to undercount the number of unemployed, counting as unemployed only those who have looked for a job in the past four weeks. But we don't need to quibble with those details because the official levels of unemployment there are plenty alarming. Across the Atlantic, even more human capital is sidelined and idle than here.

The European Union has the third-largest labor force, behind China and India—about 225 million workers. Officially, 26 million of these people are out of work—a record high. Looking just at the Eurozone, which has a population of 332 million (slightly higher than the United States), we find that 18.8 million people are officially unemployed, with overall unemployment at a record high of 11.8 percent in January 2013.[4]

Of course, these aggregate numbers don't capture the total meltdown of labor markets in southern Europe, where unemployment rates are at levels comparable to those at the height of the United States' Great Depression. As of this writing, Spain's unemployment rate stands at 26.6 percent; Greece's is 26 percent; and Portugal's is 16.3 percent. Beyond that, four other Eurozone countries have an unemployment rate of more than 14 percent.[5]

Youth unemployment in Europe has now hit previously unthinkable levels: It's at nearly 25 percent in the Eurozone and over 50 percent in both Spain and Greece.

What's particularly insidious about the unemployment crisis in the developed world is how many people have been unemployed for a year or more. In a normal economic downturn, people lose their jobs and then, when things get better, get rehired pretty quickly. That experience is like falling and being caught by a safety line just before you hit the ground. If people are rehired after a few months, they are less likely to completely exhaust their life savings, use all their allowable unemployment benefits, and come to the end of the goodwill of friends (and charity).

This downturn has been different, particularly in the United States, where the ranks of the long-term unemployed are larger than they have been since the Great Depression. According to a 2012 Pew study based on BLS data, about 29.5 percent of the nearly 13.3 million Americans who were unemployed in early 2012 had been jobless for a year or more. Many of these people lost their jobs when the financial crisis hit in late 2008 and early 2009, and never found new work.[6]

And perhaps never will.

There is much research to suggest that once you're unemployed for a year or more, employers will presume that your skills have eroded. Make that two or three years and you're really in trouble. In fact, the long-term unemployed are so looked down upon by employers that many employers would rather hire no one, leaving jobs vacant, than hire people who last worked in, say, 2009. That was the finding of a paper from the Boston Fed in late 2012.[7] A depressing *60 Minutes* segment earlier that year showed, in wrenching terms, exactly how the long-term unemployed typically can't even get a foot in the door—and that discriminating against such workers, or rather, ex-workers, is entirely legal.[8]

A survey of recruiting and hiring managers published in September 2012 found that these gatekeepers considered the long-term unemployed harder to place in jobs than those who were employed but had a criminal record.[9] Other research has documented how employers think less of job candidates who are unemployed, no matter how short a time they have been out of work.[10]

Worse, the long-term unemployed tend to turn against themselves. "There is no comparison to being unemployed for six months and being unemployed for ninety-nine weeks. Your needs change in a drastic way," said a state unemployment official quoted in the *60 Minutes* segment. "The change is the mind. That two years of unemployment erodes your self-confidence, your self-esteem. It separates you from your profession, your education, whatever you might have done previously. There's all sorts of things. It causes divorces. It causes problems with children."

Unlike in previous recessions, more of the unemployed today keep falling once they have started to fall—until they hit bottom.

Some end up like Janis Adkins, who once had a prosperous plant nursery in Moab, Utah. She lost the business when the real estate market crashed, and people were no longer buying drought-resistant shrubs for their new homes—or second homes—in southern Utah. Adkins spent a year sending out résumés and cover letters, looking for work. Nothing. Eventually she burned through her savings and lost her home.

In 2012, a reporter from *Rolling Stone* profiled Janis Adkins and described her life at the bottom—living out of her car in Santa Barbara, California. And, of course, it's even harder to climb up from the very bottom: "It's weird," Adkins told the reporter. "When people find out I'm homeless, it changes how they feel about me. I get declined for jobs. As soon as they learn I live in a van, I'm a thief."[11]

VANISHING WEALTH

So what does all this mean? What does it mean that nearly a quarter of all workers in the United States who want to have full-time jobs can't find such jobs? Or that 26 million Europeans are unemployed? In total, we're talking about between 40 and 60 million people in Europe and the United States who should be working full-time, but aren't.

Human costs aside, all these idle people—and eroding human capital—means far less wealth creation overall than would be the case if those people had jobs. In the United States, it's generally estimated that putting 1 million people to work adds roughly about 1 percent to the nation's GDP—or about $150 billion. So if all 12 million Americans officially looking for jobs had had them in 2012, the nation's GDP would have been $1.2 trillion greater. Kick in millions of other people who, ideally, would be working full-time, and we're probably talking about over $2 trillion in lost domestic production due to unemployment and underemployment in the United States.

Of course, though, not every single person who wants a job gets one—the United States has never had truly "full" employment—and so it's not realistic to muse about $2 trillion in lost wealth from unemployment. Anyway, there are more dimensions to the output gap than just those related to idle workers. The gap also reflects efficient use of technology, capital, and other resources.

Overall, for 2011, the IMF calculated the output gap in the United States at 5.1 percent of GDP. Since U.S. GDP is approximately $15 trillion per annum, the output gap would represent an annual loss of $765 billion in potential economic activity. That's a lot of money; the losses in 2012 will probably be comparable when the final data is available. Looking further back, the IMF estimated that the output gap was also 5.1 percent in 2010 and 6.9 percent in 2009.[12] Based on the GDP levels of this year, the total U.S. output gap in those three years was about $2.5 trillion.

That number is similar to the output gap estimated by the Congressional Budget Office in 2011. Taking stock of the past and future effects of the economic crisis, the CBO estimated the output gap from 2008 through 2015 at $5.1 trillion, with $2.8 trillion incurred between 2008 and mid-2011.[13]

The output gap of the Eurozone is also substantial, although the IMF estimates it as smaller than that of the United States—at least up through 2010, where IMF data ends. The output gap in the Eurozone was 3.5 percent in 2009 and 2.3 percent in 2010—figures that represent tens of billions of dollars in wealth that never was produced but would have been produced under normal conditions. The output gap has surely risen again as the Continent has sunk back into recession.

And let's not forget about Japan, with the third-largest economy in the world. Its output gap in 2011 was 4.5 percent, which translated to about $261 billion of wealth that wasn't produced.[14]

All told, the brutal fact is that the advanced countries of the world—the United States, the European Union, and Japan—have a combined output gap well north of $1 trillion a year as growth sputters or falls, and tens of millions of workers sit on the sidelines. The picture looks grimmer if we pull the lens back further to include more countries. It is estimated by various sources (The World Bank, the Bank of Canada, and the G20, among others) that the current gap between potential and actual GDP for the G20 nations—which represent almost 90 percent of global GDP—is at this writing running between $3 trillion and $4 trillion. This has been going on for years, and in Europe the situation has been getting worse, not better.

And could get worse still.

In a much-cited paper on "Hysteresis in Unemployment," the economist Laurence Ball argued that long-term unemployment has a tendency to become permanent.[15] It's not hard to see why this would be so. When able-bodied workers are sidelined from the labor force—many in the prime of their careers—and then find it impossible to again get into the labor force in a meaningful way, a society loses earners who create demand. More broadly, it loses a slice of human capital that is no longer able to generate wealth. In other words, large-scale unemployment reshapes the level of demand in a society—and in a bad way that becomes self-reinforcing.

That's the big risk today: that millions of the long-term unemployed across the developed world may never reenter the workforce. Meanwhile, older workers who have jobs are retiring later or not at all, leaving less room for younger workers.

Other factors are also at work in influencing output. Economic output doesn't just rise and fall in cyclical fashion. Productivity advances, infrastructure development, discovery of natural resources, changes in population demographics—all these act to change the potential output of nations. Changes in geopolitical circumstances—wars, for example, or the relatively sudden emergence of new capacity (the core event underpinning this book)—act to hugely change not only potential global output but also the gaps within nations.

While potential economic output has (unsurprisingly) risen consistently over the broad sweep of global history, economists have come to understand that factors at play in individual national economies can permanently reduce potential output as well. Shrinking populations (either naturally or through war or disease) in the absence of offsetting technology-led productivity gains is a good example of how an economy's potential can decline. We may be seeing such an ongoing reduction in output potential in Japan, as aging there accelerates to the highest level in the developed world. Although if any country can at least partially offset that problem with technological advances, it is Japan.

The wealth lost so far to economic stagnation and decline may be nothing compared to what is to come. Without the resumption of growth, the lost wealth from unrealized output could range from $6 trillion to $9 trillion by 2017. For the G20 nations, according to the Bank of Canada, that would be a shortfall of 12 percent to 15 percent of potential GDP by 2017. And one should note that the shortfall is decidedly skewed to the developed-nation members of the G20, because the large emerging nations, such as China, are operating close to their current capacities.

THE FISCAL SQUEEZE

An underperforming global economy is bad news, and for many reasons. But economic stagnation and a persistent or rising output gap has especially ominous implications for financing the public sector—and, among other things, affording the social-insurance programs that aging populations will depend on.

If you listen too closely to the politicians in Washington talk about budget deficits, you're apt to get an entirely wrong view of why government faces a fiscal squeeze. Republicans repeatedly say that the federal government has a "spending problem" while Democrats often blame budget shortfalls on today's historically low tax rates for most Americans (more about all that later). Some version of the same debate is heard in many European countries.

There is truth in both charges, of course—particularly in the observation that rising health-care costs are a central driver of deficits in the United States. But the biggest factor behind today's fiscal squeeze is slow growth—or, in some countries, negative growth.

Take the United States, where taxes at all levels of government have hovered between 25 percent to 29 percent of GDP over the past few decades. Most tax revenue in the United States is raised from income and payroll taxes, with such revenue rising or falling with the economy. But wealth is also taxed through taxes on estates and on the value of real property. Overall, more revenue rolls into the coffers of government when the economy is growing and asset values are rising, and less when it is not.

So let's go back to that IMF estimate that the United States lost $765 billion in potential economic activity during 2011. During that same year, taxes amounted to 25 percent as a share of GDP. Which means that the U.S. output gap for 2011 translated to nearly $200 billion in lost government revenue for 2011—not enough to close the budget deficit, but enough to make a serious dent. Or consider the bigger figure of $2.5 trillion in unrealized U.S. wealth for 2009 through 2011. Government missed out on some $625 billion in revenues as a result of those three years of reduced output.

The fiscal costs of the output gap are all the more sobering when projected into the future—a future in which thousands of baby boomers will be retiring every day (and if not retiring, at least requiring health care); and the United States will need every dime of tax revenue it can find. Yet a modest but persistent output gap over the next decade could easily diminish tax revenues by $1 trillion, which is big money.

In short, growth matters—a lot. Just as slow growth and a persistent output gap could have extremely negative fiscal implications, the opposite is also true: much faster growth could erase several trillion dollars in projected debt over the next decade.

All the same is true for Europe—a continent that also faces huge pressures on its entitlement programs and public treasuries as its populations age. In fact, because taxes make up a much bigger share of the GDP in most European nations, the fiscal effects of the output gap are greater across the Atlantic.

The fiscal squeeze on the United States and other advanced countries doesn't just affect their ability to pay for entitlement programs for the aged, the costs of which increase literally every day. The squeeze also undermines the ability to invest in the foundations of prosperity—particularly education and infrastructure. In a self-reinforcing dynamic, that underinvestment could ensure that the current output gap becomes permanent—or gets worse. At some point, in other words, the investment gap will begin to exacerbate the output gap.

With respect to infrastructure alone, the American Society of Civil Engineers in its January 2013 "Failure to Act" report calculated that "overall, if the investment gap is not addressed throughout the nation's infrastructure sectors, by 2020 the economy is expected to lose almost $1 trillion in [annual] business sales, resulting in a loss of 3.5 million jobs. Moreover, if current trends are not reversed, the cumulative cost to the U.S. economy from 2012–2020 will be more than $3.1 trillion in GDP and 1.1 trillion in total trade."[16]

This isn't a pretty picture. What we have today is no ordinary cyclical downturn. Not by a long shot. Instead, present economic conditions are far more akin, as Paul Krugman has argued, to the Great Depression.[17] That economic crisis also began with a financial crisis. And many experts believed that it was a merely cyclical phenomenon—that pent-up demand would eventually get the economy humming again. But that didn't happen, and the hard times ground on for year after year—eventually for a decade.

Things aren't nearly as bad today as they were in the 1930s (unless you live in Greece or Spain). But one obvious parallel is the widespread assumption that things will naturally turn around, given enough time.

They won't. And those who imagine a "natural" solution—or, more bizarrely, a return to growth brought on by cutting government—don't recognize that we are in a new era in which many of the rules have changed.

CHAPTER 6

THE EMPTY TOOLBOX

Why Policy Makers Can't Fix the Economy

During the most threatening days of the financial crisis and the Great Recession, on April 8, 2008, former Federal Reserve Board chairman Paul A. Volker gave a speech before the Economic Club of New York in which he observed, prematurely but correctly, "By force of circumstances, the nation's spending and consumption are being brought in line with our capacity to produce." Five years later, this has barely begun to occur.

The developed world has instead fallen back on attempts to spur the supply of goods and services with low interest rates and massive injections of monetary liquidity. Even the small amount of fiscal "stimulus" we saw way back in 2009 and 2010 was weighted far more toward tax relief and budget assistance for the states than to direct job—and hence demand—creation. (Although Japan announced in 2013 that it planned to embark on a new round of fiscal stimulus to reverse continuing deflation.)

And there is a problem with the big focus on making capital cheaper, namely, that it is akin to fighting fire with fire. We cannot continue to try to generate supply to spur demand in an environment in which there is a demonstrable excess in the supply of nearly everything linked to production. As long as there is a global glut of labor, productive capacity, and capital (relative to aggregate demand) there will be little reason to add to additional physical resources or employ additional labor. More supply is not the solution when the problem is oversupply.

At a broader level, though, most of today's policy leaders just don't get how much the rise of the emerging nations has changed everything. And on top of this denial, these leaders are more ideologically divided than ever. The result is that economic policy debates have devolved into fierce and fruitless battles over whether to implement any number of outdated, small-bore, Band-Aid approaches—none of which even comes close to grappling with the deep, systemic problems confronting the United States in a changed global economy.

Consider the responses to new U.S. employment data every month—and the *Groundhog Day* feel around arguments over the American jobs scene.

Economists are notorious for getting worked up by numbers, and these days no data dump triggers a sharper frisson of excitement than the two dozen or so tables of employment numbers released at exactly 8:30 a.m. on the first Friday of every month by the Bureau of Labor Statistics at the U.S. Department of Labor.

It's not just economists who eagerly await—or dread—the U.S. "Jobs Day," as this Friday has become known in Washington.[1] It's also politicians, stock analysts, policy wonks, and journalists. Amid the worst economic run of our lifetime—a crisis that keeps morphing and whacking us again—everyone is looking for signs of what's coming next.

If you're waiting on Wall Street for the numbers, you're wondering whether you're about to make money or lose money. But if you're sipping coffee in Washington on Jobs Day or sitting in an editorial office or the faculty lounge of a place like Harvard or the University of Chicago, you're getting ready to spin the numbers to support your beliefs about how the economy works. No matter what the numbers, you'll have something authoritative to say on Jobs Day (even I always do)—an analysis of exactly what's going on with the economy and, most of all, a set of solutions designed to ensure growth and jobs. If Jobs Day is nothing else, it's a chance to make the same points you've made before and tout the same solutions you always tout.

Yet here's the thing about all the experts and politicians with all their solutions: most of them are pulling solutions out of the same toolbox. And that toolbox is pretty much the same one that economic and policy leaders have been rummaging around in for seventy years. It's the toolbox that we've turned to again and again to deal with recessions, inflation, slow growth, and other economic repair jobs. Economists, politicians, and policy makers haven't always agreed about which combination of tools works best, but few complain about what's actually in the toolbox.

So when this latest crisis came along, starting in 2007, it wasn't surprising that America's economic elites—left, right, and center—pulled out the trusty economic toolbox and started proposing the usual ways to fix things.

The problem, though, is that this time it's different, and none of the tools have worked to really offset the loss of jobs during the Great Recession—or will work, except incrementally, barely keeping pace with the increase in civilian population of working age. Nevertheless, even four years into the crisis, everyone keeps waving the same rusty tools, saying they have the solution.

So let's recount a typical grim Jobs Day of the past year—July 6, 2012.

The news that morning was inescapably bad: Just 80,000 new jobs were created in June, according to the BLS—many fewer than widely expected. (Such disappointment with surprisingly bad jobs numbers would occur again, for example, when the March 2013 BLS report showed just 88,000 new jobs created.)

As if on cue came a torrent of opinions about what the June numbers meant and what the United States should do next. Before the day was over, various commentators had proposed all the usual solutions as ways to jump-start the economy—each as sure as the next that they could fix things if only their solution could be fully enacted.

WHY STIMULUS HASN'T WORKED

Let's start on the left, with its dreams about the miraculous effects of fiscal stimulus.

At 8:29 a.m., just a minute before the June jobs numbers went live at BLS, the Brookings Institution published an analysis that argued that states with higher government spending since 2009 saw smaller increases in unemployment. In other words, stimulus spending worked.[2] And what we needed was more of the same: "It is instructive to consider the latest evidence that active budget policies enacted today can help boost employment and speed recovery."

Brookings's call for more stimulus was not only highly muted, it was couched in part as a path to reducing the deficit: "The best prescription for improving the budget deficit over the next few years is to return the economy to health," the analysis said. Read: spending more government money to create jobs.

The Economic Policy Institute was much more direct. Less than two hours after the June numbers were posted on the BLS site, EPI pronounced the grim report "a useful moment to assess how this recovery stacks up against earlier ones, and to identify obvious policy measures that could ameliorate glaring weaknesses in the current recovery."

And nothing could be more "obvious" than additional stimulus.

As two of EPI's economists explained, one major reason the June jobs numbers were so bad was that so many state and local government workers had been laid off since the recession started in 2009. And that was still happening. If the federal government could stop these firings with more stimulus spending, things would get a lot better. "The public sector continues to shed jobs, causing job loss throughout the economy and creating an enormous drag on the recovery. To reduce these job losses and the suffering for American families they cause, Congress should provide aid to state and local governments to keep austerity in that sector from continuing to weigh down the recovery."[3]

Nine months later, when the dismal March 2013 jobs numbers came out, EPI would say something similar: "The nation's labor market remains weak, and we continue to need aggressive fiscal stimulus to create jobs."[4]

Every point we've just heard makes a fair amount of sense. States that stimulated more did do better, and firing public workers in a recession is plainly stupid and a drag on the economy. More generally, various studies—including a report by the CBO—have found that Obama's stimulus package created or saved (mostly saved) 3.3 million jobs. An even bigger stimulus, better targeted, could have had better results—and indeed, I myself proposed a new and larger stimulus in a

82

paper I coauthored with Nouriel Roubini and Robert Hockett for the New America Foundation in October 2011. (More about that proposal in a moment.)

So why am I saying that the stimulus tool, as it was used in 2009, was not up to the job at hand? One answer is that this tool was designed for an earlier era, one in which national economies were more self-contained, and not for the current era of global oversupply. The other answer is that our political system has been incapable of forging a stimulus tool that is big enough to really have impact.

Let's look first at how the stimulus tool is dated. While many mainstream economists agree that putting people back to work in the developed world is ultimately the only way to increase internal demand, few have puzzled through the global dimensions of the challenge we face and how government stimulus just doesn't fix things like it used to. The problem, of course, is that the developed world's private sector has no incentive to grow capital assets (plants and equipment) or human assets (employees) when "renting" them from emerging markets comes at so low a relative cost.

Even some modern Keynesians don't know what to do about this.

It all used to be so much simpler. The well-worn Keynesian solution to the problem of too much supply and not enough demand is to have a central agent of the public—what we call government—step into the breach to hire people for all manner of employment. And so it was that during the Great Depression the United States embarked on big public works—some necessary (the Tennessee Valley Authority, for example), others less so (grand art in public buildings). These projects were commissioned and funded by government during a time of extraordinarily low labor cost, a surplus of goods, and very low government borrowing costs. The great mystery of this period is that we will never know what its true result might have been: the Roosevelt administration curtailed spending and the Federal Reserve tightened money supply (prematurely, as it turned out), causing the recession of 1937, and the military expansion leading to World War II had an overwhelmingly positive impact on growth. A global war, it turned out, was the mother of all government stimulus programs.

Keynes viewed government spending principally as a way of restoring demand in the short term through the creation of jobs, until the private sector could take over. With government jobs halting wage declines and stemming deflation, the excess supply would be worked off and the economy would automatically start chugging along again. As with "priming the pump," once things are going, they tend to keep going, organically.

The Keynesian vision was perfectly suited to the United States of the 1930s and 1940s, when the country was very much a work in progress, with huge unmet basic needs related to infrastructure, parks, and human well-being (given the lack of electricity and plumbing in some of America's poorest regions). The private sector didn't have incentives to meet those needs, but having government do so was clearly warranted, given absent demand and excess resources.

Then, as now, the principal underutilized resource in the United States was labor. Employment fell by 8.9 million jobs from the pre-Depression high in 1929 through its low point in 1933—a full 18.5 percent of all employed people lost their jobs, a massive demobilization of American workers on a scale never seen before. Putting at least some of this idle army to work addressing basic national needs was great public policy. And by putting money in the pockets of these workers, the government created demand that otherwise wouldn't have existed for products made in U.S. factories by American workers—a virtuous cycle, just as Keynes imagined.

A much smaller—but still devastating—demobilization of workers has taken place in recent years. As noted earlier, over 20 million Americans would like to be working full-time but aren't, and the correct ballpark number of those ready and able to work is probably a lot higher than that. So for the foreseeable future there will be a huge reservoir of excess labor in America.

What's changed this time around, though, is that there is even more excess labor, at a cheaper cost, in countries like China and India. That means that even if more demand can be created, U.S. companies don't necessarily meet that demand by firing up factories filled with American workers in Ohio or North Carolina. Instead, they can often meet demand more cheaply by ramping up production in China or Mexico. And in fact, the disruption and downsizing of corporate operations in the United States, thanks to the Great Recession, turned out to be a perfect moment to accelerate the outsourcing of jobs in search of greater efficiencies and higher profits. Technology has offered another path to save labor costs. Once you've already fired an American (or a European), modern communications make it much easier to hire a Chinese worker to replace him.

Given this global picture, stimulus efforts that aim to put more cash in the pockets of consumers are not much of a solution when that cash may just result in busier Chinese workers in Shenzhen and wealthier corporate shareholders in Scarsdale while creating few new jobs in Scranton. Unfortunately, such pass-through stimulus is exactly what we've seen in recent years.

And that brings me to the limits of our political system to enact the kind of stimulus that might really make a difference.

In 2009 Congress, at President Obama's urging, passed the American Recovery and Reinvestment Act (ARRA), allegedly the largest economic stimulus effort (in nominal terms) in U.S. history, with spending that was estimated at the time at $787 billion and totaled some $840 billion at this writing. Subsequently, Congress approved hundreds of billions of additional tax cuts, in the form of a partial payroll tax holiday, and extended the Bush tax cuts and the alternative minimum tax patch for an additional two years. It also extended unemployment benefits well beyond what was normal.

All told, if we include both ARRA spending and additional tax cuts and extensions, as well as unemployment benefits, Washington approved fiscal stimulus to the tune of $1.5 trillion between 2009 and 2011. These efforts, along with monetary intervention, certainly contributed to ending the financial panic and rapid economic decline. And yet by the second half of 2012, underemployment (U-6) was still over 14 percent (for comparison, pre-recession it averaged around 8 percent and at its Great Recession peak hit 17 percent) and GDP growth was actually declining. The biggest stimulus in postwar U.S. history turned out not to be nearly commensurate with the challenge at hand.

Why?

The reason can be found in the composition of the stimulus, which was heavily weighted to putting cash in the hands of consumers as opposed to ensuring that the unemployed actually got jobs. Consider the ARRA package approved by Congress in 2009. Sure, the legislation has been called Keynesian a million times, but let's be clear: ARRA wasn't designed by Keynesian economists; it was assembled by a dysfunctional, balkanized Congress amid a frenzy of horse trading.

While $840 billion spent directly on public jobs, particularly on jobs to repair and expand the nation's infrastructure, would have had enormous impact, that's not the stimulus Congress passed, and, in the end, only a small portion of the funds was devoted to direct expenditure on employment.

Instead, the biggest chunks of ARRA were devoted to supply-side stimulus, the most substantial of which was federal tax relief—$298 billion to appease Republicans in Congress, although not a single House Republican ended up voting for the stimulus—and entitlement relief to reeling state and local governments for a total tax and social-welfare stimulus of $526 billion, or 63 percent of the ARRA package.[5]

To be sure, aid to the states saved many public-sector jobs from being cut, but that's not the same as creating new jobs. Other items in ARRA, while certainly necessary, also provided no dollars to direct new employment. The bulk of the $95 billion spent on education and jobs training, for instance, was used to plug holes in state programs that were already active but lacked funding. The remaining $219 billion in ARRA and related funding contained some funds for infrastructure and energy programs that produced net new hiring, but at best we are talking about 250,000 to 300,000 new jobs relative to the 7 million to 8 million estimated lost as the result of the Great Recession. Compared to the jobs created during the New Deal, through direct hiring programs like the Works Progress Administration, the United States didn't even give itself a chance to stimulate a strong recovery through increased employment.

What's striking is that the U.S. political system was unable to even seriously debate a stimulus that was up to the challenge at hand. The tool of stimulus—an invention of the left—had to be reforged in ways acceptable to the right. Most notably, direct government job creation was largely off the table—dismissed as un-American in favor of indirect strategies to generate consumer demand that, ironically, did just as much to help Chinese workers as American ones.

So what would a real stimulus have looked like?

In October 2011, I tried to offer an answer to that question, writing with Nouriel Roubini, the New York University economist and economic consultant who foretold the global financial crisis well before anyone else thought it possible, and Robert Hockett, an economist and professor of law at Cornell University Law School. Together, we developed a proposal for a major jobs program focused exclusively on infrastructure repair and replacement in the energy, transportation, education, research and technology development, and water treatment sectors.[6] The paper we wrote on behalf of the New America Foundation, "The Way Forward: Moving from the Post-Bubble, Post-Bust Economy to Renewed Growth and Competitiveness," noted the following:

> U.S. public infrastructure is in shambles and is rapidly deteriorating. The American Society of Civil Engineers estimates that the United States must spend $2.2 trillion on infrastructure over the next five years to meet America's most basic infrastructure needs but that less than half that is currently budgeted, leaving an approximately $1.2 trillion shortfall. A multi-year program designed to close that infrastructure deficit would not only help fill the demand hole but make the economy more productive and efficient in the long term. Indeed, long-term investment in public infrastructure is the best way simultaneously to create jobs, crowd in private investment, make the economy more productive, and generate a multiplier of growth in other sectors of the economy.

We proposed $1.2 trillion of additional public and private investment aimed at creating more than 5.52 million jobs in each year of the program—both directly, through the projects themselves, and indirectly, through the multiplier effect on other sectors of the economy.

Most important, the program would have "an emphasis on high-return strategic investments in energy, transportation, and communications to eliminate economic bottlenecks and restore productivity, complemented by labor-intensive investments in energy efficiency (retrofitting homes, offices, and public buildings) to maximize job creation."

In retrospect, even that large-scale proposal was modest compared to the challenges the United States faces, with over 20 million workers on the sidelines. I'll come back later, in the final chapters, to lay out an updated stimulus plan that would directly address that challenge.

THE LIMITS OF THE FED

Monetary stimulus is another hallowed tool in the economic toolbox—
a key way in which a strong national government that prints its own
currency can step in forcefully to tame capitalism for the greater good.

And so it was that the poor jobs numbers that came out on July 6,
2012, led to calls for the Fed to do more to spark economic growth.
These pleas were nothing new, and would also be heard after subsequent weak jobs reports going into 2013. For years now, progressive
economists have been complaining that a timid Fed has been doing far
too little in the face of the worst economy since the 1930s.

In April 2012, for instance, Paul Krugman penned a screed in the
New York Times Magazine (unflatteringly titled "Earth to Ben Bernanke") that expanded on columns in which he criticized Bernanke for
doing too little to stimulate growth.[7] Krugman theorized that Bernanke was either politically intimidated by the right, fearful of uncontrolled inflation, or just too weak and shy to push his colleagues on the
Federal Open Market Committee to wage a full-fledged war on economic stagnation.

If only things were that simple.

Here's the less pleasant truth: monetary intervention is simply not
the power tool that it once was. Actually, the Fed has done a great deal,
more than ever before, only to run up against the same problem: in a
world awash in cheap money, churning out even more cheap money
can't fuel an economic recovery. Ben Bernanke is neither overly "shy"
nor out of touch with the world, as Professor Krugman would have us
believe. To the contrary, he had—for the most part—correctly assessed
the limitations of extraordinary monetary intervention and, for the
time being, stopped pressing buttons that weren't working. Although
Bernanke tried again with a third program of quantitative easing that
was announced in September 2012 and continues through this writing
the result has been an even greater rally in financial and real assets,
including—finally—housing, with the most prominent form of transmission of the additional easing to the real economy occurring through
the "wealth effect," which I will explain a few pages later.

Monetary policy is complicated and can be deadly boring, so let's see
if we can walk through this story at a brisk pace.

During the depths of the financial crisis in the dark winter of 2008–2009, the developed economies confronted a dire choice: allow the mechanisms of market capitalism to run their course and risk a Herbert Hoover–style descent into depression, or have government conduct monetary and fiscal intervention in free-market functions on a massive scale in an attempt to stabilize the situation. I am not alone in expressing gratitude that our leaders chose the latter course over the former.

Yet while the scope of the monetary intervention was larger and more globally coordinated than anything ever before implemented in such a short time frame, it has had little sustained effect on the real economy beyond the markets and market makers.

Translation: Easy money has been great for Wall Street but has barely registered on Main Street.

Opening the floodgates at the Fed is always a sure way to fire up markets. Excess liquidity fosters market confidence and, when channeled into the banking system, ends the prospect of credit runs on banks. But you can also have too much liquidity. When money is cheap but doesn't flow into the real economy to foster new investment in plants, equipment, homes, and other durables (because tapped-out consumers aren't spending), bad things can happen.

Excess cash that lies idle in the hands of banks and other investors tends to find something to do with itself, especially in an environment in which interest rates are so low as to make just having money hang about in savings instruments or government bonds particularly unattractive. The principal advantage to holding cash is the infinite flexibility that doing so represents, at no risk other than that of inflation acting to diminish its purchasing power (or devaluation relative to other currencies, if one's thinking extends beyond borders). Vast amounts of uninvested cash lying idle within economies has historically tended to result in inflation—there's too much money chasing too few goods. So the temptation among holders of cash is to seek to maintain as much liquidity as possible while simultaneously hedging inflation risk. Cash-rich folks love all their cash, but don't want it to decline in value.

And so, cash dashes off to find "money substitutes." And what are these things? Commodities, for one, especially energy and foodstuffs. Stocks in heavily capitalized public companies are another. And last, but not least, precious metals and other items that are both liquid and especially reactive to inflation—with gold at the top of the list. But let's dismiss gold for the time being. The "barbarous relic" may be an excellent inflation hedge, but its relevance to the real economy is just about zilch.

Stocks rallying on excessive liquidity can have an indirect impact on economic activity inasmuch as they result in some degree of increased confidence on the part of the owners thereof (as long as they don't read this book and appreciate that the stock market rally they are feeling good about is principally liquidity driven and therefore passing). This leads to something economists call the "wealth effect," which in theory spurs consumption. Even those owning few equities—or none at all—can be positively impacted by the sight of stock markets rising. The wealth effect—again, in theory—can be effective as a pump-primer following a more cyclical slump and has been observed to have had such an effect in the past.

But what of the present situation? The developed world has seen four postcrisis rallies in equity markets that appear to have been coincident with recoveries in consumer confidence, employment, and other fundamental economic indicia. All were associated with large-scale government stimulus (one with both fiscal and monetary intervention, and the other three with monetary stimulus only). Three of these rallies, shortly after the stimulus ended, suffered similar reversals (each time, almost mysteriously, in spring or early summer in 2010, 2011, and 2012). Developed world economic data, as if on cue, deteriorated as the calendar approached the spring equinox in 2013 and between the time of this writing and the date *The Age of Oversupply* is published, it should become pretty clear if the record-setting levels of the equity markets in early Q2 2013 were just the latest example of liquidity-fueled exuberance that ignored real economic activity.

Equity markets do tend to rally in the presence of excess liquidity. Equity markets also tend to rally in the presence of greater investor confidence—and liquidity tends to produce that confidence by creating a feedback loop rooted in the expectation that liquidity will prime the economic pump, reinflate the economy through traditional supply/demand inflationary effects, and make it cheaper to borrow by bringing interest rates below the so-called natural rate.

And yet, since the developed world's credit bubble burst, the desired impacts of extraordinary monetary easing have not been forthcoming. Many economists have correctly identified that the advanced economies all find themselves with short-term interest rates that are, as a practical matter, as close to zero as possible and are therefore in a "liquidity trap" in which additional liquidity has no further simulative effect on growth in the affected economies. In short, with money moving at slow velocity through the real economy, excess liquidity merely piles up.

The liquidity trap observation is pretty much "black letter" economics among Keynesians and, at least since the Japanese experience with a long-term zero-interest-rate environment, it is hard for most other economists to deny the phenomenon (although there are some who are still disputatious enough to do so). But many of those who understand and agree on its existence and meaning, including many dyed-in-the-wool Keynesians, still are of the opinion that despite the presence of liquidity traps in developed economies, monetary intervention can and should be used to try to reinflate economies.

This is where I get off the boat and seek my own insights. After repeated rounds of massive monetary stimulus we not only have anemic levels of start/stop growth, but we also have *no meaningful inflation.* In fact, in between rounds of monetary stimulus, we actually lapse into periods of disinflation and near-deflation! Does this signal that we haven't done enough monetary stimulus, or is it telling us something else entirely?

I believe it is the latter—that it is both unlikely and nearly impossible to reignite sustainable inflation in the United States, and to a lesser extent in other developed countries, over any sustained period of time until global wage and capital imbalances are moderated. Price inflation alone is unsustainable without wage inflation eventually joining it. And any significant wage inflation amid a global surplus of labor—relative to demand for same—is beyond the bounds of rational expectations in the near term. Moreover, price inflation without eventual corresponding inflation in nominal wages, in fairly short order, results in economic stagnation and eventually recession as unit demand is unable to keep up, and demand for labor and materials worsens further as a result. The notion of so-called cost-push inflation based on expectations, as opposed to the "demand-pull" variety based on an actual supply/demand imbalance is highly specious at best. Ultimately, expectations yield to reality in the age of oversupply, and the reality is that—at least in the tradable sectors—there is no need to pay more for labor.

Put as a mnemonic: "If wages don't track, prices fall back."

Another money substitute that attracts the excess reserves of cash piling up around the world is the U.S. dollar. As central banks seek to keep reserves in dollars, in part because of low U.S. inflation but mostly because of the relative solidity of the U.S. economy and monetary system, a dollar shortage has actually developed in the private sector—amounting to nearly $2 trillion by some estimates. This places more upward pressure on the dollar and is correspondingly deflationary (to say nothing of the adverse effect on net exports from the United States). In a supply glut, even the "exorbitant privilege"—a term coined by French president Valéry Giscard d'Estaing—of being the issuer of the world's reserve currency, and hence being able to purchase imports in one's own currency, has its downside.

And that's not all. Ineffective attempts at monetary reflation in the midst of a supply glut and a zero-interest-rate environment have had a "leakage" effect on emerging markets. The flood of hard-currency liquidity drives up prices for commodities and raw materials, creating inflation in nations where wages actually do respond to rising prices for goods and services. Not all of this is bad from the point of view of the developed world. We want prices and wages to rise in the emerging nations because it makes the advanced nations more competitive. But it also has the effect of causing the emerging markets to institute policies that slow their growth when inflation kicks up to dangerous levels. But slower growth in places like China tends to nullify a portion of the benefit that the central banks of the advanced nations hope to obtain, because it means fewer exports. The declines in Chinese and Indian growth rates in 2012 were a prime example of what happens when emerging countries put on the brakes in an environment of generalized global oversupply. And any precipitous fall in the rate of inflation in China, like that seen in early 2013, while perhaps good for Chinese consumers and the managers of its economy, is not helpful from the point of view of the advanced economies.

All in all, the resort to extraordinary levels of monetary easing is, at best, a double-edged sword. As it turns out in recent times, it has been most useful as a tool, both in the United States and Japan, to moderate deflationary pressures rather than to ignite inflation in the real economy. And perhaps that is really its best quality—offering a degree of systemic stability. But it is stability at a high cost.

AUSTERITY AND THE CONFIDENCE FAIRY

If the big ideas of the left—fiscal and unconventional monetary stimulus—don't offer real fixes to the economy, what about the ideas of the right? More specifically, what about the right's central claim that cutting government spending and controlling deficits is the key to reigniting American prosperity?

On the campaign trail on July 6, 2012, Mitt Romney called the new job report a "kick in the gut." In the weeks that followed, Romney offered new details about how he would fix the economy, touting a 59-point plan. A central pillar of Romney's plan was to restore "fiscal health"—and Romney promised that on "day one" of his presidency he would immediately cut "non-security discretionary spending by 5 percent, reducing the annual federal budget by $20 billion."[8]

Later in the summer, Romney underlined the importance he placed on fiscal austerity as an economic cure when he chose Paul Ryan, representative from Wisconsin, as his vice-presidential running mate. Ryan, more than any other politician in recent times, has pushed the idea that lowering a rising tide of red ink is crucial to creating a new "path to prosperity."

A path to poverty is more like it. Of all the supposed magic wands floating around Washington, London, and Brussels, the notion that austerity can fix the economy is the most far-fetched and wrongheaded of them all. And yet it is repeated day after day and week after week by innumerable politicians, pundits, and think tank experts. For instance, when those disappointing March 2013 payroll numbers came out, two of the Heritage Foundation's economic analysts wrote a blog post about the sluggish economy that concluded with this non sequitur: "The U.S. needs to end the government spending binge of the past five years and return the economy to the growth of the private sector."[9]

Back in the early 1990s, it was actually centrist Democrats who popularized the idea—and sold it to President Clinton—that fiscal discipline would produce economic growth. Make the bond markets happy, they promised, and good times would roll again. Today, that idea is all the rage in Europe and on the political right in the United States.

The logic of austerity holds that a nation beset by excess government debt and impaired creditworthiness, along with slow growth, can turn

94

things around by slashing government spending and demonstrating fiscal prudence. Take those tough steps, and all sorts of good will result: renewed confidence from the markets, lower rates, easier access to capital for business and consumers alike, new investments, job creation, and increased demand as reemployed workers have more money to spend.

Read that last paragraph a few times and you can come away thinking, "Yeah, that makes good sense. Who could possibly believe that fiscal prudence is not the obvious antidote to prior profligacy?"

Among those who view capitalist economies as resembling corporations and households, the notion of tightening one's belt and enduring sacrifice to enable recovery and advancement seems elementary. To those who believe that economies trade—as do financial markets—as much, or more, on confidence as they do on rigorous realities of supply and demand, taking one's medicine seems like an irresistible cure.

The problem, of course, is that the easy logic of austerity is illusory. Nations aren't like households or companies, and history shows that belt-tightening is rarely a cure to economic malaise. And why would it be? In fact, there is no empirically demonstrable "transfer mechanism" in this logic—actual proof that explains how *less* spending in a given distressed economy would result in *more* growth. Typically, the opposite is true.

Enter the "confidence fairy." That term was first advanced by Paul Krugman to illustrate how austerity advocates—or "Austerians" as he amusingly calls this crowd—paper over the flaws in their logic. In effect, in order to work, austerity depends on some alchemical reaction in the economy, and mass psychology.

Of course, that's not how national policy should be made. Math, not magic, should be the foundation of economic decisions. Austerity is more than naïve and unworkable; it's dangerous to the societies that attempt it.

I am not going to attempt to repeat in these pages the analysis of economists such as John Maynard Keynes and Irving Fisher, among many others, who have refuted the absurd arguments for austerity. But I will offer an abbreviated list—in layman's terms—of why the concept has so rarely worked.

For starters, government spending is no different than private-sector spending in terms of how it contributes to growth and GDP. If there is less public spending, there is, in the first instance, commensurately lower GDP—a simple fact. Austerity thus needs the confidence fairy to work some serious magic to create growth. Not only does she need to induce the private sector to engage in expansionary investment and employment to foster growth, but she needs to replace the money that government was spending on investment and employment. A pretty tall order, even for a fairy!

Austerians recognize, indeed encourage the notion that in the initial phases of austerity, not only should government attempt to reduce its debt at the most rapid rate possible, but so should corporations and households. Yet as Irving Fisher pointed out, that is an inherently deflationary act. The more one pays down debt, the less one spends. The less one spends, the less real economic demand there is for goods and services—which translates to less investment, employment, and production. In turn, that means less personal income and tax revenue—which creates bigger holes in government and household budgets and a greater need for additional borrowing.

And, when it comes to government, the problem is not just less tax revenue. Reducing government spending and throwing people out of work—say, 600,000 U.S. public-sector workers between 2009 and 2012—increases the demand for social safety net programs like unemployment insurance and food stamps, blowing an even bigger hole in government budgets.

With regard to households, Fisher summarized how austerity backfires in this wonderfully counterintuitive statement: "The very effort of individuals to lessen their burden of debts increases it, because of the mass effect of the stampede to liquidate . . . the more debtors pay, the more they owe. The more the economic boat tips, the more it tends to tip."[10]

Of course, the Austerians would not agree with Fisher's assessment. They would counter that, in overly indebted countries, households and governments must first curtail spending to right the boat. But there is a social and political component to that notion that begs the question: How will people live while we wait for the confidence fairy to do her magic?

The answer is, not well at all. Both public- and private-sector unemployment can be expected to *rise* as government spending and household spending is reduced. Private-sector investment will only arrive after (i) the overinvestment (excess capacity) that resulted during the period of excess debt creation is adequately absorbed and

(ii) employment (private and public) improves sufficiently to enable households to recommence spending without going further into debt. And when the private sector will not—and, as an investor I argue, *should not*—invest and employ under such circumstances, it is sheer madness to stop government from stepping into the breach. Throughout history, slashing government spending during hard times has prolonged economic slumps, worsened price declines, and created social and political instability. We're seeing all that in Europe right now.

Finally, the Austerians argue that indebted nations really have no choice but to reduce public spending. If they don't, confidence in their creditworthiness will eventually deteriorate to the point where no reasonable investor will be willing to lend them money. Various bogeymen—"bond vigilantes"—will suddenly turn on countries that are viewed as having impaired credit and swiftly push borrowing costs (and rates of inflation) to astronomical levels. After all, that's what happens to businesses and households that have overborrowed. One moment you have a nice cheap home equity line of credit. The next, after you're underwater in your home, you're borrowing from your local pawn shop at a 300 percent annual interest rate. One day, the Chinese are happily lending to the U.S. Treasury for 2 percent a year in returns; the next, they want 8 percent—or they stop buying Treasury securities altogether.

This is the most simplistic and insidious of the arguments for austerity. While such a downward spiral can happen with small nations, it is a far-fetched scenario in the case of large economies, especially those that print their own hard currency.

The risk of nonpayment by a country that prints its own money is *zero*. On any given morning, the central banks of the United States, the UK, and Japan could—mechanically, if not legally—pay off 100 percent of all government indebtedness in their respective countries simply by printing money, a process called debt monetization. In fact, through quantitative easing, the central banks of those same countries have been legally doing just that to the tune of trillions of dollars worth of their own countries' bonds: buying them out of the open market with money they conjure up with the stroke of a keyboard. Countries that issue debt in currencies that are not their own, or which peg their currencies to a hard currency (usually the U.S. dollar), clearly cannot do likewise, have far fewer alternatives, and can (and do) default on their obligations from time to time.

What does debt monetization typically result in? Well, it *should* result in inflation and lower relative value of the currency being printed. And, for sure, that could prove economically debilitating in *normal times*. But thanks to a global glut of capital, we don't live in normal times. By now, were these normal times, central-bank policies during and after the Great Recession in the United States, the UK, and Japan should have wiped out the value of the dollar, pound sterling, and the yen and hiked internal inflation to historic highs by now. Sadly, that has not occurred, since a good solid bout of currency devaluation and inflation in the developed world would be a godsend. Nor is it likely to happen anytime soon, for reasons discussed throughout this book.

Just as important, the monetization of national debt by central banks means that the central banks own the debt issued by their respective countries' treasuries. The central bank not only receives the interest paid on the debt it has acquired (and pays no interest on the "bank notes" it created to buy the debt), but were inflation to get out of hand, the central banks can swiftly siphon excess cash out of their economies by selling the bonds they bought back into the capital markets.

Yes, the central bank may suffer a loss if inflation heats up too quickly and it had bought all its bonds at high prices. But in today's situation, if the central banks of the three above mentioned economies sold their inventory of acquired domestic debt back into the market at today's prices, they'd be doing so at great profit relative to average historical acquisition costs.

In short, not only does austerity make things worse, but there is no imperative to go down this path to escape the bond vigilantes that forever stalk the nightmares of the Austerians. In the age of oversupply, there will be plenty of cheap capital around for hard-currency-printing nations, at least for the foreseeable future.

FROM REAGANOMICS TO RUBINOMICS

If austerity makes so little sense as a formula for growth, why is this dangerous meat cleaver still lying handy in the macroeconomic toolbox—and, worse yet, still being wielded by conservative parties in Europe and the United States?

The answer, I believe, starts with a well-meaning lawyer and investment banker named Robert Rubin. As an influential official in the

Clinton administration—first as director of the White House National Economic Council and then as secretary of the Treasury—Rubin fatefully misread the global macroeconomic environment of the 1990s. In advancing what came to be known as "Rubinomics," this former cochairman of Goldman Sachs turned a liberal president into a centrist and unwittingly kept the dying embers of supply-side thought from flickering out.

During Clinton's first term, Rubin famously convinced the president to reduce budget deficits in order to please the bond markets, lower interest rates, and spur growth. Then, as the economy soared in the second half of the 1990s, Rubin believed that this approach had worked. He believed that the lower interest rates of the 1990s reflected increased confidence in the fiscal probity of the United States and, equally important, the fact that government was borrowing less, leaving more capital available for private borrowers. And he believed that these lower interest rates were a key to spurring the virtuous cycle of investment and consumption that took hold in the United States in the 1990s, producing the longest peacetime expansion in the nation's history.

In fact, though, this story of how the White House appeased the bond vigilantes and sparked historic growth never held much water. The main reason for America's economic comeback in the 1990s was the leap in productivity as the information age dawned, not confidence on Wall Street and less crowding of capital markets by government borrowing. And, anyway, it's not even clear that that produced the cheaper money of the 1990s. A decrease in government borrowing is only one of several possible reasons for low interest rates. The global supply of money, as recent history has shown, is as much if not much more of a factor in establishing the cost of capital to governments. Just look at today's historic low interest rates at a time when government deficits are sky-high. And remember, the second half of the 1990s was a time when emerging nations began pumping loads of excess cash into the United States and other advanced nations.

Furthermore, low interest rates are not some great benefit to society. Again, using the events of the past ten years as a guide, such low-cost money tends to foment risky lending and investment activity as capital seeks higher/positive real returns. And it tends to push up the prices of assets, from commodities to real estate. Meanwhile, low interest rates deprive the truly prudent among us—savers—of a reasonable real return on their savings and zings retirees living off their savings. There is nothing particularly virtuous about that state of affairs.

Unsurprisingly, Rubin collaborated closely with Federal Reserve Board chairman Alan Greenspan, who in the late 1990s saw the union of his Reaganite monetarist orientation with his ideological belief in small government and unhindered/efficient markets. That he saw a Democratic Treasury secretary come over to his way of thinking must have been most gratifying to Chairman Greenspan at the time. But then something happened that cemented the bond even further.

The Asian currency crisis of 1997 was a dire event for the world economy and for a short time threatened to topple it entirely. It is too big a subject to fully treat in this book, but a short summary would go something like this:

The Asian Tigers—Hong Kong, Singapore, Taiwan, and South Korea—were well along in the process of eating into a good portion of Japan's export economy with their own more competitive exports to the developed world. They saw a combination of internal demand (much of it simply desire for more rapid growth) for capital investment funds and a willingness of "hot" foreign capital to lend—finding little demand for itself at home, and better rates of return in emerging markets—as the perfect reason to borrow copiously in U.S. dollars and other hard currencies. Many emerging countries during the 1990s had attempted to peg their domestic currencies to the U.S. dollar (in the same fashion China later adopted, though less officially) because it was good for an export economy not to allow its currency to rise in value. It also made it much more palatable for foreign lenders to lend to them in dollars and other hard currencies.

Unfortunately, the foreign currency debt-to-GDP ratios of the ASEAN (Association of Southeast Asian Nations) countries swelled mightily, to 180 percent by 1997, just as their economies started to cool and China began to emerge as the go-to destination for American companies looking to produce goods more cheaply. As inflows of U.S. dollars slowed, and GDP growth petered out, the Asian Tigers found it impossible to maintain the dollar pegs (to say nothing of paying the debt). All hell broke loose.

The IMF, along with the U.S. government and its allies, stepped into the breach and turned what might have been a meltdown of global capital markets into a manageable crisis. By the end of 1998, the world had mostly righted itself and was well on the way toward the last phase of the Internet technology-stock bubble, which Chairman Greenspan had warned about in his famous "irrational exuberance" speech in December 1996.

Rubin, Greenspan, and Rubin's deputy, former Harvard professor of economics Lawrence Summers, ended up on the cover of *Time* in February 1999 as "The Committee to Save the World."[11] And, as a result of the Asian financial crisis, a myth was set in stone: high levels of sovereign debt can lead to a failure of market confidence, skyrocketing interest rates, and the collapse of entire economies. In other words, the crisis served as further evidence to support what Rubin had argued to Clinton: that good things happen when the bond vigilantes are appeased and bad things happen when they turn against you.

The myth left little room for other factors that fueled the Asian financial crisis, such as irresponsible lending by yield-hungry foreigners wielding cheap money. Or the dependence of the Asian Tiger economies on capital investment and asset inflation for much of their overly touted "economic miracle." Or the accelerating emergence of China as a competitor to their economies. Or how a lax regulatory climate let capital markets pull the plug on an entire region overnight.

The Asian financial crisis should have stood as a warning about the toxic nexus of cheap money and lax regulation. But that's not the lesson Rubin and others took away. And today, that crisis is still cited as evidence for why austerity is so imperative.

It's often said that generals tend to fight the previous war—applying lessons from the past even when conditions have changed. Economists and policy makers do the same thing. When bad things happen economically, they fall back on solutions that worked in earlier situations. This habit explains why the developed countries cannot escape from anemic growth five years after the financial crisis. Dipping into the standard economic toolbox worked to avert a full-blown depression, but not to regain actual prosperity.

Everything has changed in the world economy over the past fifteen years, thanks to the arrival of several billion new workers and trillions in new capital. But economic thinking hasn't kept pace. We have solutions to the problems of yesterday, but not to those of today (much less those of tomorrow). Some of these solutions actually make things worse, as in the case of austerity, while others simply aren't up to the challenge at hand. In particular, the most potent tool of all—monetary easing to create cheaper money—is, in a world awash in capital, of little use at this point in the game.

To make matters worse, in recent years the United States has faced ideological gridlock that thwarts big new initiatives. Quite apart from the dysfunctionality in Washington, economists are divided as rarely before about the way to go forward. Partly these divisions are ideological; partly they reflect plain confusion about what to do. Regardless, when economists fail to speak with a cohesive voice and offer conflicting road maps to recovery, governments have a tendency to do nothing—which plays directly into the hands of ideologues who believe fervently in unregulated market economies and small government. That's ironic, to say the least, because it's precisely these laissez-faire ideas that helped the United States get into its current mess.

And it's not just the United States that is totally stuck. In fact, economic confusion reigns in the entire advanced world. Elsewhere, in fact, things are even worse than they are in the United States.

CHAPTER 7

THE DETOUR ECONOMY

How Advanced Countries Are Dodging the Real Economic Challenges

G iven the historically unprecedented events of the past fifteen years, it should be no wonder that many economic traffic cops (economists, regulators, and other policy makers) don't know how to handle the differing information coming their way. There is substantial doubt in every nation, and within economic blocs of nations, about what direction to head in, about how to get there, and about what needs to be done to repair and improve the economic roadways.

Because things are such a confusing mess, most economic policy making since the financial crisis has amounted to nothing more than creating temporary detours around the dysfunctional Global Economic Intersection described in chapter 2. And the problem with those detours—extraordinary monetary interventions, financial-sector bail-outs, sovereign and bank "bail-ins," monetization of public debts, or stimulative tax policies that increase those debts—is that none of them address the underlying causes of our troubles to begin with. Moreover, while the detours may help things for a while—and especially benefit certain savvy market participants—they are no substitute for real repairs to broken economies. Still, even now—five years after the 2008 crisis—policy makers across the developed world labor to construct even more detours and widen some of the detours (such as quantitative easing) into nearly permanent roadways.

Let's look at some of those detours before we go on. Because the problems and available detour solutions differ from region to region, I will separate this part of the discussion into three regional summaries—Japan, the Eurozone, and the UK—before bringing the discussion back to the United States.

JAPAN

No advanced country has been more economically confused (and confusing) than Japan. And none has spent more time trying to troubleshoot a deeply troubled economy. Japan, in fact, is the oldest detour builder around, and has been in the business of inventing temporary economic fixes for nearly two decades—all the while continuing to be an export powerhouse, either in current account surplus or showing small deficits.

Ever since its bubble economy burst in the early 1990s, Japan has tried everything to get back on track economically. For starters, it engaged in any number of major stimulus efforts, spending billions on all sorts of projects aimed at jump-starting growth. Unfortunately, it targeted sectors and projects for which there was no obvious source of demand—new highways and "bridges to nowhere," for example—as opposed to, say, the revitalization of urban infrastructure or the development of senior-care facilities for Japan's rapidly aging population. Eventually, Japan's leaders pretty much gave up on the idea that fiscal stimulus could fix the economy.

Flipping to the monetary side of things, Japan's interventions have been the most significant of any developed country. Interest rates in Japan have long been reduced to the lowest levels on the planet. In fact, the benchmark interest rate in Japan has not been above 2 percent since the early 1990s, and has hovered around zero percent for most of the past fifteen years.[1] Also notable is the degree of monetization of both government debt and other assets by the Bank of Japan relative to the size of the economy, which vastly outstrips that of any other country.

Then, of course, there is Japan's staggering national debt, now over 200 percent of GDP—a cause of endless and seemingly insoluble concern.

Japan's large household wealth and its trade and current account surpluses make the huge debt possible. Thanks to all the wealth the Japanese have sitting around, much of Japanese debt is held internally— by its households, corporations, pension funds, and insurance companies—with only about 5 percent of Japanese government bonds (JGBs) held overseas, in comparison to nearly 50 percent of net U.S. debt (after central bank and other government holdings) and over 50 percent of Germany's.

Japan's trade and current account surplus and its enormous debt would seemingly place Japan in a class by itself among developed countries. But caution is urged with regard to certain "cultural anomaly" assumptions often drawn as a result. Japanese investors in their country's government bonds are not, as some would have it, a bunch of flag-waving isolationists paralyzed with fear about venturing abroad with their investments. To the contrary, since deflation took hold in Japan, JGB investors have been paid handsomely—in real (inflation adjusted) terms—to hold their government's securities.

The aforementioned surpluses enjoyed by Japan are completely inter-related with the very same deflation to prices (and wages) as offset, in part, by a strong yen that was the inevitable result of its increased internal purchasing power. To complete the feedback loop and truly appreciate matters in Japan, one also has to consider the willingness of the Japanese to carry on "enduring the unendurable" of wage and price declines.[2] As discussed elsewhere in this book, the prime victims of deflation are holders of capital assets such as stocks and real estate. Japan, with its own massive post-1989 bubble debt overhang and under-capitalized financial sector, has been particularly vulnerable to the wealth destruction that deflation brings.

And, wow, has wealth been destroyed in Japan.

Taking the assets and liabilities of the entire Japanese economy into consideration, the net worth, so to speak, of the country is today (and has been for a while) as severely diminished as one can imagine for a large economy (it is still a huge amount, but I am speaking in a relative sense here). And that's assuming the government statistics showing the net worth of the private financial sector at 3 percent of assets in 2010 are accurate—which, if financial sector assets were marked to market, would not remotely be the case. Of course that's all a bit irrelevant because the primary creditors of Japan are its own citizens. But Japanese businesses and financial institutions were so highly leveraged going into their crash two decades ago, and the nominal value of their assets has fallen so greatly, that the net worth of the country exists in the spread between household wealth that has not been lent to the government and those remaining physical assets and natural resources that are not "hocked" over their market values.

Inasmuch as wealth is more evenly held in Japan than in nearly any other developed country, the pain of wealth destruction here has been relatively evenly shared. In short, the Japanese people have gotten poorer together in yen terms.

Employment, however, has been a beneficiary and Japan has one of the lowest unemployment rates in the developed world. Why? Because of the willingness of stoic Japanese workers to accept wage deflation (not that they had much choice). This, along with the nation's tolerance for the "unendurable" phenomenon of price level erosion, has maintained for Japan a global level of competitiveness. It has also ensured a strong currency that, while posing a challenge to exports even net of the internal deflation, is making foreign direct investment by Japanese corporations highly profitable.

But after decades, the unendurable eventually gets old.

Japan has reached the point at which price and wage deflation alone is no longer allowing it to maintain its competitiveness, and it is seeking both to drive its currency down in value relative to others and resume its 1990s behavior of supplementing private employment with government-funded projects and related jobs. To move that agenda forward, in 2012 its people elected one of the most nationalist Japanese governments in postwar history.

At the beginning of 2013, Japan's government and its central bank began to aggressively "jaw-bone" the yen down by adopting a formal inflation target. At this writing they have been hugely successful, with the yen losing about 25 percent of its value against the dollar. This was intended to grant some relief from the strong yen, reminiscent of the response by the government to the *en-daka* (strong-yen) crisis of the late 1980s, which set off Japan's great bubble as the Bank of Japan flooded the banking system with yen. Nevertheless, when Haruhiko Kuroda ascended to the governorship of the BOJ in April 2013, he immediately set in motion an aggressive program of quantitative easing (much larger than the Fed's QE3 in relative scale) and both JGB yields and the value of the yen responded accordingly. Ten-year JGB yields initially plummeted from the 0.75 percent range to the 0.50 percent range and the yen reached a four-year low against the U.S. dollar—joining the global currency "race to the bottom" in order to further domestic advantage. Then, as markets fretted about the possibility that the BOJ might actually be successful in igniting inflation, bond yields shot up again to where they were. This volatility clearly replayed that of U.S. Treasury bonds during the various cycles of the Federal Reserve's quantitative easing actions. But just as the Fed has been unable to ignite reflation in the United States, there is little reason to believe the BOJ will meet with any greater success.

In an age of oversupply, with Japan being on the other side of the table (as a developed country rather than an emerging one), the country and its central bank will be limited in what they can do, or ultimately will want to do, notwithstanding present resolve. A weak yen policy, in my opinion, is unlikely to stick unless the economy truly begins to reflate. And—as I have pointed out earlier in this book—without wage growth (something I don't foresee in the developed world in general) inflation is unsustainable.

The big question, yet to be answered at this writing, is whether Japanese exporters will use a weakened yen to raise prices (in yen) to push up domestic earnings or to lower prices and go after market share to raise earnings. Both are possible, but the former would be so uncharacteristic for Japanese businesses as to lack plausibility from my point of view. Moreover, with excess manufacturing capacity in Japan, why wouldn't manufacturers seek to benefit through increased volume rather than price? Either way the economy will benefit, but going the volume route will certainly set off alarms among Japan's trading partners and competitors. And if that happens, the yen's selloff will reverse rapidly.

In fact, the only way I believe the Japanese would be able to reflate their economy is if they actually engaged in inflationary fiscal spending by taxing their population's income and wealth heavily. I will be surprised if, in the alternative, they choose even more deficit spending, as I don't believe Japan will materially balloon its enormous government debt-to-GDP ratio (over 230 percent and rising in a country with a total debt-to-GDP ratio of over 500 percent). More yen printing to finance deficits will tank the yen to levels where competitor nations will be inclined to limit Japanese trade, helping no one. And if taxation is proposed to enable supplemental government spending . . . the new government may quickly find itself the former government.

Finally, as Dr. Ken Courtis, former vice chairman of Goldman Sachs Asia and easily one of the smartest Asia hands in the world today, noted to a group of my colleagues in April 2013, just after the BOJ's actions, imagine if the BOJ was actually successful and borrowing cost rose substantially in Japan.[3] In a country so used to paying little or nothing for money, even just a 2 percent rise in interest rates on Japan's debt would, over time, make the interest costs on government debt alone increase to 4 percent of current GDP and, eventually, across all Japanese debt increase to 10 percent of GDP. While much of these interest payments are retained within the Japanese economy and one would hope that GDP would grow as a result of these policies, the slightest miss could be catastrophic.

The Japanese detours constructed to address its internal debt overhang and the massive alterations to the global macroeconomic intersection (which it encountered long before the United States and Europe did) are by far the most dramatic of any developed nation to date. In addition to the foregoing, however, something of historic magnitude is lurking in Japan: Japan is shrinking. Japan's birthrate has fallen to about 1.39 children per female today, far below the 2.10 or so necessary to preserve population stability.[4]

If Japan continues to shrink, deflation actually makes sense as an econometric matter and slows the pace of collective dissaving of remaining Japanese wealth, thus buying considerably more time to either (a) figure out something more constructive than hoping monetary policy-driven expectations of reflation will offset the rest of global reality, or (b) maintain living standards at high levels until there are literally no more Japanese to worry about. The latter is, of course, merely an observation, not a prediction.

But the detour taken via Japanese policy action is a road to somewhere. And I would contend, for the foregoing reasons, that that "somewhere" is *not* the near-term sovereign insolvency some have predicted as being around the corner for Japan and its government bonds for the past fifteen years.

While default is not an economic possibility in a country that prints its own currency (although, as we have seen in the United States, theoretically a political possibility), given the still-high levels of household savings and low household debt in Japan and the massive amount of debt outstanding from the government, corporate, and financial sectors, there is really only one source of financing other than printing money. Since the crash in Japan's bubble economy in 1989, Japanese households have been funding the government by buying its bonds. And they have been richly rewarded for doing so, because (as noted earlier) despite low interest rates, Japanese deflation has resulted in fairly consistent real (inflation-adjusted) yields on government bonds and—for most of the time since the financial crisis (longer in the case of the United States)—the only positive real yields in the developed world. But the country as a whole, in the absence of growth and the racking up of debt, is dissaving and can no longer afford to keep its households' savings effectively subsidized. And with so much debt outstanding, it can't possibly allow interest rates to rise. So eventually households will be separated from their accumulated wealth via taxation or through negative real interest rates. There are a few other options, such as opening immigration, but I certainly can't see a nationalist government advancing that as a solution. If any nation needs to see the development of a new global economic architecture in order to resume its nominal growth, it is Japan. Curiously, though, while Japan's situation is not at all rosy from a nominal-growth perspective, it does have options that appear to be quite different from those of other countries in the advanced world. The third-largest economy in the world can slowly dissave and shrink itself into continuing affluence (from a standard of living perspective) for those who remain. And compared to the situation among Japan's developed brethren, maybe that's not so bad!

THE EUROZONE

By comparison to any of the other developed regions, the seventeen nations of the European Monetary Union (EMU, often known as the Eurogroup) have not merely constructed detours around the realities of the new global macroeconomic intersection, they have taken a detour to a parallel universe from which, almost certainly, they will fail to return as a union.

The EMU, as a region, suffers not only from the same macroeconomic global imbalances that the other advanced nations do, but their dozen-year monetary union without a fiscal or governmental union has brought about internal imbalances within the region that actually very much resemble the overall global picture, albeit with completely open borders and a common central bank. So not only does Europe need to find a way to deal with the bigger picture, it faces the potential collapse of its demi-union.

At the heart of the problem is the unwillingness of the electorates of the wealthier Eurozone members to tolerate a full "transfer union" in which more productive and well-off areas effectively support those that are less so, via taxation and redistribution. At the same time, at least during the bubble years of the 2000s, the EMU's common currency enabled the public and private sectors of the zone's less creditworthy countries to borrow with abandon, mostly from the more creditworthy ones.

The collapse of the global credit bubble exposed the perversity of the economic relationships among the countries of the EMU. The great sums lent by the banks of Germany, France, and the Netherlands—the so-called core members of the Eurozone—to their weaker brethren encouraged nearly every economic mal-incentive imaginable.

The Eurozone currently is divided into two very different spheres. There are a few creditor/surplus nations, greatly dominated by Germany. Then there are all the debtor nations of the zone that suffer from a combination of one or more of (i) trade deficit, (ii) current account deficit, (iii) primary fiscal deficit, and/or (iv) high levels of sovereign and/or private-sector levels of debt.

Normally, nations facing challenges like these would address their creditors with a wry smile, perhaps a nod of humility, and then proceed to devalue their currencies like mad, make their products hypercompetitive with those of their creditors, and endure inflation as measured in their own currency. In older times, nations would erect trade barriers (and raise armies to enforce them and protect themselves from creditors) to limit access to their local markets and secure internal demand. Of course, that's impossible in the Eurozone or the broader European Union.

So that leaves some combination of the following detours around the inherent problems of the Eurozone debt overhang and its internal current account and trade imbalances:

- Flood the zone with euros through quantitative easing and credit-easing operations by the European Central Bank, thus reducing interest rates and devaluing the euro relative to external currencies.

- Have the creditor countries directly subsidize the debtor countries to enable them, in return, to effectively subsidize payments owed to creditor nations' banks and other institutions (basically an indirect bailout of the creditor countries' own financial sectors).

- Have the creditor countries' institutions, the ECB, and private-sector lenders consensually reduce the debt owed by the debtor countries to levels that allow those countries to resume economic viability (i.e., avoid default) and growth.

- Or, force the debtor countries into a combination of governmental austerity (cutting public spending to eliminate primary deficits), "internal devaluation"—or deflation of wages and domestically produced goods and services, while prices of foreign-sourced goods and services, and debt payments, remain the same; and bank "bail-ins" in which depositors are ultimately forced to rescue the banks in which they have their savings (as we first saw in Cyprus in March 2013).

Each of the foregoing yields problems for one party or another in the EMU. The Germans do not wish to see inflation for a number of historical and internal economic reasons. General euro devaluation/inflation in the zone might make European exports more attractive globally, but does not in and of itself address zonal imbalances. There appears to be little willingness among the electorate in creditor countries to tolerate direct transfers to their debtor brethren, even if such transfers ultimately are applied to bail out their own financial institutions. As for those institutions, they are generally in such precarious shape that they're not going to start writing off assets in the absence of a direct bailout by their own governments or the ECB.

The resulting stalemate has yielded an ineffective and festering hodgepodge of (a) ECB credit easing to effectively lend money to marginally solvent or insolvent banks secured by collateral of debatable value; (b) limited subsidies/loans to debtor countries from creditor governments and multinational institutions; (c) limited debt reduction, but only from private-sector lenders who know that pennies on the euro is better than nothing at all; and (d) the imposition of governmental austerity measures and internal devaluation on debtor countries that can't possibly grow themselves out of their debt burden amid the deadly dual impacts of domestic contraction and the global supply glut.

This combination cannot ultimately succeed.

And that failure speaks to the larger failure of the European people and their governments to accept the need for complete fiscal and sovereign union even as they desire a monetary one. As a result, there remains an elevated possibility that the monetary union will not survive intact and one or more nations will withdraw.

The Eurozone has constructed an alphabet soup of organizations and strategies to avoid the need to address the rebuilding of the global economic intersection: the European Stability Mechanism (ESM), the European Financial Stability Facility (EFSF), and the Security Markets Programme (SMP), as well as Outright Monetary Transactions (OMT), Emergency Liquidity Assistance (ELA), and Long Term Financing Operations (LTRO)—and the list goes on. But all are half measures and based on the expectation that weakened but still sovereign nations will tear up the fabric of their societies to repay the institutions of other sovereign nations with whom they are in a marriage that can best be described as "sleeping with the enemy." There is no love in such a marriage and in the absence thereof, divorce can be postponed for only so long. This is a detour akin to hooking the autobahns of Germany to the autostrada of Italy using a rutted dirt road.

The great Eurozone experiment in authoritarian austerity is failing. To be sure, it is failing slowly and with much "can-kicking," but failing nonetheless. Eurozone unemployment rose to 12.1 percent for March 2013, an all-time high, according to Eurostat, the statistics office of the European Union. For those age twenty-five and younger, unemployment is nearly 25 percent—one in four persons—and that number is far higher in the Eurozone periphery—in Spain over 55 percent and in Greece over 60 percent.

In May 2013 Eurostat revealed that the Eurozone as a whole had contracted for a fourth straight quarter, with even France falling once more into recession, joining eight of the seventeen Eurozone nations in slump. And Eurostat said further that it expects conditions to continue for at least the balance of the year.

This book is slated to be published four days following the German federal elections of 2013, and by the time you read this, Germany will have likely reelected its chancellor, Angela Merkel. Merkel's ability to advance Germany's straight austerity regime throughout the Eurozone was undermined in late 2012 and early 2013 by its obvious failure. But, as the austerity myth is very popular in her country, until she is re-elected it is unlikely that the German government will be able to participate in the development of an alternative approach (perhaps barring the eruption of a new crisis in Europe, which is not entirely unlikely).

And a new and more realistic solution is sorely needed because the situation in the Eurozone is, as I have noted, quite different from that in the balance of the developed world. This is because of the painful coexistence of a supranational currency with independent sovereign indebtedness. In sum, then, it is also the only area featuring a real (as opposed to hypothetical) conflict between debtor nations and their creditors.

With respect to the periphery of the Eurozone, in the nations with the highest levels of total debt to GDP, the bond vigilantes arrived in 2010 and have been staging raids on the bonds of Greece, Italy, Ireland, Portugal, and Spain—often called "GIIPS"—repeatedly ever since. The GIIPS are, in fact, the only nations in the developed world that face high debt funding costs (Iceland's were still elevated at this writing but they defaulted to nearly everyone). But even with the very precarious fiscal position in which they find themselves owing enormous sums to external creditors—payable in a currency they don't print—and suffering a nearly perpetual recession, there is so much liquidity sloshing about the world that there is an active trade in the bonds of these weak nations. Perhaps not surprisingly because of the real rates of return being offered (assuming there is no default), but still notable because the markets seem to discount both the obvious risk of loss—Greece, after all, has already handed investors nearly €100 billion of losses between principal and interest rate reductions—but also the macroeconomic consequences to Eurozone debtor and creditor nations alike.

As 2013 trudged on, a battle fatigue reminiscent of the entrenched stalemates of World War I had settled across Europe. Creditor demands are essentially unchanged and economic and social conditions in the debtor nations continue to be extremely parlous. Very little to no progress has been made in the further fiscal and financial integration of Eurozone nations, and the European Central Bank has backed away somewhat from the table after repeated rounds of interest-rate cutting and extraordinary credit easing (although it finally cut its funds rate again by another 0.25 percent to 0.50 percent in early May 2013). Whatever quiet erupts from time to time in this ongoing battle merely masks the strain and pressure throughout the zone.

This cannot go on for much longer. Perhaps a year, perhaps just long enough to push past the elections in Germany. Perhaps the Eurozone has more time, perhaps less. But what is very likely is that 2013 will see a continuing deep weakness in the Eurozone. As the respected London-based macroeconomic analysis firm Capital Economics wrote in early January 2013, "We expect a 2% drop in euro-zone GDP, a much weaker out-turn than that expected by the consensus. This will both hinder the efforts of the peripheral economies to restore their public finances and maintain the opposition of core economies to further steps towards fiscal union. Against this background, there is a clear danger that the crisis re-escalates in 2013."[5] Capital Economics may have been at the bearish end of economic consensus, but it is pretty clear that growth is not in the cards.

And, as throughout the developed world, without growth the Eurozone's travails will not repair themselves. The troubles of the periphery are also spreading to the core of Europe, at this writing to France, and even self-aggrandizing Germany is taking it on the chin. The social situation in the periphery is deteriorating and governments are either falling apart or weakening.

Expecting that the GIIPS will merely take their medicine and suffer the aftertaste is folly. Reflective of the short-term thinking so typical of these times is the hope that conditions will improve merely by putting bandages over plasters. And since Europe's slump serves to further that of the global economy in the aggregate, given its size, nothing good can come of its further decline.

Many of my friends throughout the Eurozone believe that patience and support around the edges of the problem can succeed in turning things around. I can't help but think of all the ruins of great churches I have wandered through on the Continent, their facades strongly buttressed while grass and moss thrive within what used to be space protected from the elements. Other routes will inevitably be sought, and with some luck the Eurozone nations will consider some discussed in this book before the roof caves in.

THE UNITED KINGDOM

Great Britain is a far simpler story.

The United Kingdom deserves a medal for foresightedness for having rejected membership in the EMU. But the UK's earlier adoption of Thatcherism (Reaganism without the Great Communicator's spoonful of sugar to help the medicine go down) and the post–Great Recession fiscal austerity policies of the Conservative/Liberal Democratic coalition government are certainly not awardworthy.

Like the early policies of the Reagan administration, Margaret Thatcher's were a reaction to substantial efforts at social engineering during the 1960s and 1970s, a period of tumultuous change during which the Labour Party controlled the UK premiership for eleven of the fifteen years preceding Thatcher's ascension. As in the United States—and as I have discussed elsewhere in this book—there were excesses and mistakes by Labour during the '60s and '70s, to which Thatcher responded with a vengeance that was uniquely her own.

Britain, of course, is in a different category than the United States, the EMU, and Japan. It doesn't have much of a manufacturing/export sector, and hasn't for decades. Instead, it has emerged as the European global hub of the financial services industry—a trend that has shaped its economy in recent decades. And even though Britain no longer exports much of anything, save oil, it has plenty of "wealth imports" because it is generally regarded as the most stable large economy in Europe. London has an enormous commercial and residential real estate market that acts as a repository of wealth for many who have less confidence in the legal and political systems of their own countries than in the security afforded within the British realm. When things are faring well for its financial sector, and international oligarchs are feeling flush, the financial aristocracy in the UK spends and invests, and in such periods Britain has shone. And when left to its internal markets—not so much.

The lack of a highly diversified manufacturing and service economy puts the UK in a class by itself. On the one hand, it shares the ability to issue its own hard currency (like the United States and Japan but unlike the nations of the EMU). On the other hand, however, there's not much to buy domestically with sterling, other than services and financial/real assets. In fact, most of what the UK exports, other than North Sea oil, are services—many of them financial—and the place to which most of those services are bound is, not surprisingly, the Eurozone. Indeed, if one subtracted North Sea oil from the UK's GDP and trade statistics, the current account deficit of Great Britain would be larger, as a percent of GDP, than even that of the United States, similarly adjusted.

Furthermore, the UK's banking sector is a behemoth that threatens its economy in a way not shared by the United States, Japan, or the EMU. Financial sector debt in Great Britain in mid-2011 was a whopping 219 percent of its GDP, in contrast to the financial sectors of the United States (40 percent), Japan (120 percent), and the average for the four largest economies of the EMU (84 percent). The only developed country in the same neighborhood, literally and figuratively, is Ireland, which nationalized the vast majority of its banking sector with a financial services debt to GDP of 259 percent. The UK as a whole has a total debt-to-GDP ratio of 507 percent, within kissing distance of Japan's at 512 percent.[6]

The difference between Great Britain and Japan, of course, is Japan's massive industrial economy and its big account surpluses. Like the United States, both Japan and the UK have total control over their own monetary printing presses, but since the financial crisis sterling has depreciated about 20 percent against the U.S. dollar while the yen appreciated about 40 percent to its peak, before it began to decline under government jawboning in 2013. The difference is in purchasing-power differences: deflation in Japan increased the purchasing power of the yen, and continued inflation in the UK (the highest of any of the developed regions) has depressed that of sterling. But here we have a chicken-and-egg game going on: Did inflation in the UK just happen, thereby depressing the currency? Or did the currency fall in value, thereby sustaining inflation in export-dependent Great Britain?

I argue that it is the latter to a large extent, although once economic matters begin to snowball it becomes increasingly difficult to identify the original catalyst. Again, other than in connection with money flows to the UK from flight capital and for financial trading purposes, there is very little natural net bid for the pound. That is to say, if you're a national economy and you don't, net of imports, sell enough things that people want to buy (other than oil) and therefore run a huge (especially ex-oil) current account deficit relative to GDP, there is little purpose in holding your currency unless you actually live in the country in question. Your currency is therefore going to depreciate, the costs of the many things you need to import is going to rise, and internal inflation must ensue.

Then add two more factors to the UK's dismal story and we can be done with this part of the argument for the time being. First, the arrival of the Euro in 2000 made it less likely that anyone in continental Europe, in or out of the EMU, would seek to hold capital in sterling (other than for safe-haven purposes)—to say nothing of folks in other areas or the world seeking to hold currency in Europe; and second, the 507 percent debt-to-GDP ratio of the UK makes it a nearly metaphysical certainty, at least on a relative basis to the situation in other developed countries, that one day not too far down the road the UK will need to "print" more bucketfuls of sterling—again depressing its global value—when it inevitably takes over the portion of its over-levered banking sector that it doesn't already own, as was the case in neighboring Ireland.

Thus, the real exposure to the government (under the rubric of "too big to fail") is nearly threefold its 80 percent government debt ratio. That is, in my opinion, a disaster waiting to happen. And if, as predicted by most analysts at this writing, the UK enters recession in 2013, the makings of such a disaster may be close at hand. And here's the kicker: household debt in Great Britain is the highest of any of the ten largest developed economies in the world (save Australia—but let's not go there) at 98 percent of GDP! So don't go looking for help there as you might in the case of Japan.

To recap, here are the three big problems impacting Great Britain's real economy as it deals with the overall pressures of global glut and debt deflation:

- A weak currency yielding domestic inflation and eroding consumer demand in the absence of the ability to transmit inflation through to wages;
- Households in debt up to their eyeballs with no obvious way out other than to curtail consumption and hope the inflation provides a debt-reducing tailwind before households are overall insolvent; and
- To the latter two, add the "brilliant" notion of curtailing government spending to close primary fiscal deficits—which Thatcher-born, Cameron-carried austerity measures should provide the coup de grâce that kills the entire economy.

Rule Britannia! Not. The Cameron government's austerity detour threatens to send the people of Great Britain right off the white cliffs of Dover.

As 2013 dawned, it was apparent that the United Kingdom had tried and failed at the fiscal austerity game. Despite the hopes that a reduction in spending would trigger a confidence-induced expansion, the UK debt-to-GDP ratio has failed to decline and UK GDP has resumed its decline as well after recovering somewhat after the Great Recession. The latter decline, of course, makes a decline in the UK's debt-to-GDP ratio pretty much impossible under present circumstances.

Fortunately, the Bank of England (BOE) has not been willing to rely on what many of its directors and policy committee members view as unwise fiscal austerity. It has pursued much the same monetary path as its larger cousin, the U.S. Federal Reserve, and flooded its economy with liquidity. But that is all that it could do in the presence of a Tory government hell-bent on fiscal austerity. As I have discussed throughout this book, there are limits on what central banks can do—and the BOE, under its recently retired governor, Sir Mervyn King, did all that it could. No shocker, then, that the Austerian David Cameron was, at the end of the first quarter of 2013, pressing the Bank of England to do even more. Anglo-Japanese similarities are growing every day, it seems.

The UK economy is in the hands of the angels now. If it eventually slips into recession, the things that have been keeping it afloat—its low current account deficit made possible by the fact that it is a net oil exporter; its position in Europe as a repository for flight capital and investment; and its hard and respected currency—are not unlikely to be overwhelmed by a receding real economy and a vulnerable financial sector. I would rather, however, that the British government was not beholden to angels (or confidence fairies) and would step decisively back from austerity before waiting for things to come crashing down in a triple-dip recession. Either way, I am afraid, another route must be found.

THE UNITED STATES

So let's bring our account of detour building back full circle, to the United States. The United States, as already discussed, has been—with the exception of Japan, of course—the primary target of global deflationary pressures among the advanced nations. It shares with its brethren in Europe a classic post-bubble financial and household debt deflation. On the other hand, unlike Japan (and some European nations) it has a dismally low household savings rate—which could otherwise provide some element of a buffer.

The United States is heading down the same demographic path as the other developed nations—aging and with an insufficient number of younger workers to support an aging society in the future (especially in the absence of household savings). It has previously been able to offset this with immigration that has run an average of about a million per annum over the twenty years from 1990 to 2010. These immigrants, unlike the more longtime residents of the country, have tended to keep birthrates from sinking into the organic declines seen elsewhere in the developed world.

But with jobs presently scarce in the United States, there is increasing evidence that with the recession, net Mexican immigration to the United States (Mexico being the biggest source of immigrants to the States) has fallen to nearly zero, and for a period may have turned negative. This phenomenon is exacerbated by growth in the emerging world, which reduces the desire to emigrate in the first place. Positive population growth obviously yields growing demand, and is something that the United States has become accustomed to expect for centuries (barring interruptions of war and depression). And population growth is either inherently inflationary, or at the very least expansionary. Its absence or its reversal, of course, would tend in the opposite direction.

The United States, as has been more than clearly documented in these pages, is the star in overconsumption relative to its own production, and its immense negative current account balance would be unsustainable without the enormous global excess of labor, productive capacity, and capital relative to global demand. But nevertheless, the current account deficit is well sustained and can remain so for a long period of time before the underlying global imbalances are sufficiently offset by emerging market demand. And since the supply glut is going to be with us for the foreseeable future—and the earnings of the developing nations are going to continue to exceed the global real economic demand for capital for as long as it takes to absorb that glut—the cost of financing the current account and primary deficits of the United States will, as it has in Japan, remain exceedingly low.

All of the above is undeniably deflationary over the short and medium terms.

And that brings us to the final deflationary factor, the U.S. dollar. If only the futile post-crash attempts to debase the dollar had proven successful, we'd certainly have seen reflation and, after suffering some, the American worker would have seen his nominal wages rise—with perhaps a disturbing but ultimately tolerable twelve- to eighteen-month lag between nominal price and nominal wage growth.

But that was and is not to be. The dollar will not devalue as long as every nation is intent on protecting its own trade position and the source of the biggest chunk of global demand is the United States. Inflation will not occur amid existing excesses of supply and capacity. And "expectations-induced" inflation tactics—in theory inducing inflation by printing more money and making statements about long-term interest rates—has diminishing potency when after years of such tactics they fail to produce the real thing. And the United States is stuck in that mode as of this writing.

Were the United States not a diverse economy—producing products and services that people around the world want to buy if pricing, on a quality-adjusted basis, is otherwise competitive—this would not be as much of a problem as it is. But as with the Japanese yen, which is nowhere near the store of global wealth that the dollar represents, apart from its use in trade, there is always a bid for America's currency. And, as the purchasing power of the dollar remains strong or rises (as has the yen's) it actually exacerbates deflationary pressures—creating headwinds to net exports and lowering the prices of imported goods.

Nevertheless, the domestic economic meme in the United States tends to revolve around discussions of the national debt and the primary government budget deficits (and the likelihood that such deficits will remain in the absence of renewed growth, increased tax revenues and/or government spending cuts, given national demographics). This is understandable inasmuch as no one enjoys contemplating staying behind on one's bills and ruing the day it all catches up.

But governments, and especially that of the United States, are not families or businesses, and as much of the rest of this book will demonstrate, neither are national economies. The United States is in no position to survive a jump off of another "fiscal cliff" of budget cuts and tax increases in the absence of a national growth plan, and neither of the two constitutes any sort of plan at all beyond the conjuring of the confidence fairy, which, like expectations-setting in monetary policy, is merely a resort to believing in what should be, rather than being a response to a state of affairs wholly resistant to drum beating and pixie dust.

The events of late 2012 and early 2013 were complex, to say the least. On the one hand, the United States saw some economic improvement, perhaps better called stabilization. Job creation has pretty much absorbed new participants in the labor force, helped along by the fact that the labor force participation rate actually declined year over year in 2012, but it has not absorbed a material portion of those thrown out of work as a result of the financial crisis and the Great Recession. Real (inflation-adjusted) wages continued to deteriorate and nominal wage growth was less than 2 percent. (Both figures are challenged by the fact that much of the economy's reemployment is occurring at very low wage rates.) The U.S. economy, even by the end of the first quarter of 2013, had failed to replace 3.2 million of the jobs lost since its prior peak sixty months earlier, a process that would take seven additional years if the pace of reemployment remained the same. And in March 2013, the rate of job formation slowed considerably, as it had before from time to time in previous years.

American manufacturing activity, which at the beginning of 2012 was thought to be the savior of the economy, actually sputtered during much of the year before turning up somewhat and by the second quarter of 2013 again shedding jobs. The housing and consumer sectors revived a bit with more employees, a huge amount of deferred demand, and other more technical factors, but the notion that a household sector encumbered by debt equal to almost 90 percent of the nation's GDP can prove a consistent and reliable supporter of growth for the $15 trillion U.S. economy is overly hopeful.

Yet within the developed world, the U.S. economy is clearly the "winner among losers"—and has done a better job of righting itself, primarily because from the commencement of the present slump through 2012 the United States largely avoided the austerity route. Those involved in the economic debate in the States certainly talked about austerity enough, though. From the National Commission on Fiscal Responsibility and Reform (the so-called Bowles-Simpson Committee) to the Campaign to Fix the Debt and from the Ron and Rand Paul family in Congress to the Tea Party, the United States has been inundated by demands to address the fiscal imbalances in current and future budgets. Finally, with the so-called fiscal cliff and debt ceiling confrontations within the federal government in the final days of 2012 and the first part of 2013, this debate reached a crescendo.

The U.S. payroll tax holiday, enacted to spur recovery from the Great Recession, was terminated at year-end 2012. Its effect was nothing less than the wiping out (in terms of take-home pay) whatever growth in aggregate wages occurred during 2012. The effects of this were seen in the first quarter of 2013 as the economy slowed. Weekly hours and wage rates were flat or declining as the economy entered the second quarter of the year. At that rate, it is at best unclear when wage growth in the United States will be sufficient to restore to disposable income what the termination of the payroll tax holiday took away. Sure, some part-time service sector jobs were created in early 2013, but looking at the data at the time of this writing, it would appear that whatever job formation occurred was at such low wages that in April 2013, while 165,000 jobs were created in the United States (all in the services sector and, net of lost positions, all apparently part-time), the index of aggregate weekly payrolls actually declined by 0.2 percent for the month.

But by early 2013 the debate itself had already begun to shift. The reelection of President Obama in 2012 left the Democrats in Congress in no mood to compromise much on social spending, and those

Democrats who appreciate the fact that additional fiscal stimulus is still warranted have been at least emboldened, if not rendered more optimistic. Their optimism was rewarded in mid-May 2013 when the Congressional Budget Office announced new estimates of future federal budget deficits, which is now expected to fall to as little as 2.1 percent of GDP by 2015, well out of any plausible notion of a danger zone. The change in the overall policy zeitgeist in Washington does not yet include broader fiscal action to promote growth. And the lines in the sand between most Republicans and Democrats still run deep on questions of macroprudential regulation, especially with regard to the financial sector.

In my opinion, the U.S. economy is not sufficiently primed to absorb any further contraction in government spending, or any more broadly based current increase in rates of taxation, than has already been enacted. And politically I don't see much of a chance of ending the policy stalemate as long as there is any hope of even an anemic ongoing recovery. But even that modest hope may likely prove dashed by the end of 2013—the boost given to the economy by its higher-paying manufacturing sector in 2012 vanished by second quarter 2013. Also, the U.S. economy is not an island. It will be challenged by further weakness in Europe and turbocharged competitive pricing from a currency-weakening Japan which, in turn, will challenge the emerging nations and encourage wage and export stimulus there, so that the emerging nations will remain highly competitive. If I am correct in this assessment, then it would seem that such renewed decline will bring other policy options to the table.

The detours constructed to forestall disaster in the developed world, arising from the gridlock in the global macroeconomic intersection, are as complex as the problems themselves. While they differ somewhat with regard to the particular challenges experienced in the various regions, the detours—temporary measures taken to keep economic traffic flowing—all have two things in common: (i) they have been chiefly designed to rescue institutions and underpin the value of financial assets, and (ii) they assume that the phenomena that gave rise to the ongoing crisis will be repaired and that regular commercial traffic flows will be restored. Alas, none of them focuses on actually repairing the antiquated roadways of global commerce and capital flows because there is an absence of consensus in the developed world about what is at the root of our routing problems in the first place.

So what do our economists, politicians, and business leaders observe? They see inflationary and deflationary risks at the same time. They fear too little employment, too much stimulus, lower taxes, higher taxes, government deficits, and contractions in government spending hiding behind every rock down the road. They see equity markets rise in anticipation of higher nominal earnings, and they see bond markets rise and fall in reaction to tidal waves of liquidity amid expectations that nominal economic growth will be anemic, if not recessionary. And they have staring them in the face a long-term (thirty-year) downward trend in interest rates on prime government debt (for example, in the United States, the United Kingdom, Japan, and Germany) that was broken only—and only temporarily—by the biggest credit bubble the world has ever seen. And it has resumed again, impervious to any expectations-led strategies aimed at creating greater demand for global capital.

That's why my friend saw "stag-in-de-flation" a few years back. He simply couldn't identify what he was seeing—it simply made no sense.

So where does that leave the other advanced nations? Today, it leaves them barking up the wrong trees. It leaves them continuing to focus on enhancing supply and debt-induced consumption when the natural order of things dictates that domestic economic stability and growth can be recovered only by generating both endogenous demand and improved levels of household savings and financial institution capital through higher levels of employment and regulatory responsibility while continuing to endure the long wait for consumption to rise and aggregate savings to fall in the emerging nations, relative to the prevailing supply glut.

In the later chapters of this book, we will move beyond the "whys" to defend the central thesis of *The Age of Oversupply*: that there are realistically achievable, real-world solutions to the economic slump affecting the developed world . . . but they require a reorientation of recent patterns of economic thinking, especially in the United States and Europe. Not only are we caught in a slump, but the academic and political world is stuck in a rut. And one way out of a rut is to grab hold of old roots and pull oneself out.

CHAPTER 8

BAD VALUES

Why Sticky Wages and Prices
Block a Real Recovery

Markets are not working properly.

That should be clear to anyone who has read this far. The supply of global labor and capital is too great, and demand too weak, for them to resume proper functioning without powerful assistance. This imbalance has been going on for years and nobody seems to know what to do about it. Private markets haven't solved the problem, not because they are inherently dysfunctional, but because the sheer magnitude of changes in the global economy, thanks to the fall of the Bamboo and Iron curtains, has created challenges too big for private markets, acting alone, to reasonably address.

We have to face up to the realities of the supply glut. If we don't, the developed world's economies—and the global economy as a whole—will continue to fluctuate in and out of crisis. To some, the solution here is anything but more government intervention. In addition to embracing austerity, many argue that the remedy to malaise is more aggressive steps to unleash the dynamism of market actors. For instance,

Mitt Romney's 59-point plan for growth included proposals to cut business taxes, slash regulations, negotiate more free-trade agreements, roll back labor rights, and make it easier to tap domestic energy supplies.[1]

While some of Romney's ideas might well have spurred new economic activity, it is simply wrong—or quaint, really—to imagine that if government just stepped out of the way, the market would magically revive the economy. As I'll explain later, there are certainly some places where less government participation could be helpful, and I suggest exactly that. But near the core of my economic plan, laid out in coming chapters, is a lot *more* public intervention. Before getting to those details, it's important to understand exactly why private-market actors haven't gotten us out of this jam—and won't be able to without some help.

ELUSIVE EQUILIBRIUM

Most economic theories, especially mathematically expressed economic theories, tend to be grounded in the idea that markets move toward a state of equilibrium. Supply typically aligns itself with demand. Wages and prices adjust to reflect excess labor and goods—or accurately reflect the shortage thereof and encourage new entrants and offerings. In short, economic activity tends to all balance out. There is little debate, even in the notoriously fractious world of economics, that markets normally tend toward equilibrium.

Much of the earliest thought on equilibrium theory was pioneered by a less well-known but highly influential French-Swiss economist named Léon Walras (1834–1910) who, with his acolyte, Vilfredo Pareto (1848–1923), founded the so-called Lausanne School of economics.

Walras was the son of an economist, but didn't turn to economics himself until after he had floundered a bit as a young man. He first studied engineering and then worked in a bank, tried his hand at journalism, was a clerk for a railway company, and even wrote a novel. Walras laid out his groundbreaking ideas on general equilibrium in *Elements of Pure Economics*, published in the 1870s. But that treatise wouldn't be translated into English until the 1950s, which is why Walras remains little known to this day.[2]

While Walras and Pareto went on to influence some economists with whose work I do not agree, the Lausanne School gave us important concepts, such as marginal utility theory. Most important, Walras taught us how markets "clear" to achieve equilibrium and how, when capitalism functions properly, there is a natural balance between supply and demand. If there is too much supply, prices will come down. If there is high demand, prices will rise. Sounds pretty obvious now, of course, but Walras was one of the first economists to show, in well-thought-out detail, how equilibrium emerges. More broadly, Walras argued that when capitalism functions properly it tends toward an optimal allocation of its fruits that provides a sufficient level of satisfaction for a vast majority in society.

The operative clause in the foregoing paragraph is "when capitalism functions properly." And today such is clearly not the case in the developed nations. Moreover, contrary to conventional wisdom, capitalism isn't malfunctioning only (or mainly) because of screwups and greed within the advanced economies, as the left would have it, or because of a meddling and distorting statism, as the right often posits, but rather because of the unique, unprecedented rise of the developing world and the dawn of the age of oversupply.

What we have today is massive *disequilibrium*. And that state is inherently confusing to economists of all stripes.

So how is it that equilibrium theory missed the boat here? Walras and Perato may have been absolutely accurate in assuming that things would gravitate toward equilibrium within a closed system. But what equilibrium theory doesn't account for is that events could occur that create a simply massive supply/demand imbalance, and that such an imbalance could be so great that it takes a long, long time for various actors in the free market to bring things back into balance—so long that such actors simply don't have the patience or ability to engage in the activities that would bring about a rebalancing. All of which could cause an extended and self-reinforcing slump.

We have had problems of that nature before. The Great Depression was certainly one of them. But in terms of fundamentals, I believe the present situation is far more difficult to exit, both because of the magnitude of the imbalances and the obstacles to growth within otherwise wealthy countries—Exhibit A being once-booming Japan. While we have stabilized the crisis and are slowly repairing the damage it did, a cancer still infects the developed nations. At moments—when the stock market surges or a nice employment report rolls in—that cancer can seem to be in remission. Don't be fooled. The cancer isn't going away, and it threatens to turn today's large output gap into a permanent reality and chip away at prosperity for many years to come.

The only way out of this conundrum is for demand to eventually catch up with supply. And ultimately that means that the new people and wealth of the emerging nations must be fully absorbed into the global economy in a balanced, sustainable way. The good news here is that global population growth is slowing and the size of the world's labor force is expected to level off within the next two decades. Moreover, the aging of populations in countries like China and Japan should reduce today's huge piles of money as longtime savers start spending more of their incomes. Also, if middle-class people in China, India, and other emerging nations eventually demand the usual things—better schools, better mass transit, cleaner air and water, and a stronger social safety net—public investment in those nations should begin to sop up more excess wealth.

In other words, demographics and politics suggest that the age of oversupply won't go on forever. The world should be out of the woods and back in better balance in a decade or two—although nobody really knows.

Of course, that time frame is unacceptable. The United States and other developed countries need to find a Plan B that goes beyond just waiting.

What would Léon Walras say about all this? Good question. Just to be clear: when I speak of a "supply glut" relative to demand, I am not rejecting Walrasian notions that prices will respond in order to clear markets of excess. I am instead positing that the size of the global imbalances are so large that market mechanisms cannot overcome them on their own within an acceptable time frame. Walras was almost certainly right that markets invariably reach equilibrium. But that's not very reassuring if it takes decades for such equilibrium to come about. And there would appear to be a decided correlation between the *magnitude* of imbalance and the *time* needed to absorb and offset same, given the realities of both market and other human behavior.

Worse, the failure of market mechanisms to respond positively results in secondary damage in the form of a negative feedback loop that limits the degree to which growth in developed nations will resume.

While today's underlying economic problems are very serious, there are many factors—such as pent-up consumer demand and household formation—that should serve to provide a real boost. But the impact of these natural boosters has been muted due to a number of other global fundamentals. Let's explore one of the most important ones, as I see it.

THE STICKINESS DILEMMA

Free-market economics isn't just malfunctioning because of an unprecedented global supply glut. There is another big reason that the efficient operation of markets within the developed nations is stymied: *stickiness.*

Stickiness in economics refers to the way that wages, prices, rents, and assets can get stuck at artificial points instead of responding to natural forces such as supply and demand. Stickiness can result from different factors, for example, regulations that keep prices at a certain place or stubbornness as people refuse to accept the actual value of things. Whatever the factors, stickiness is another example of markets not working the way they are supposed to. And right now, stickiness is a big, big problem in the United States and other developed nations— one that greatly complicates the challenge of coping with global oversupply.

While I prefer to think of economic stickiness of as an integrated whole, and believe we face a broad stickiness dilemma, it helps to break each example of stickiness down to see how this phenomenon operates.

Sticky Wages: Given the huge surplus of labor in the world—both in the developed nations with their high unemployment rates and in developing countries with their huge populations—the logic of markets might dictate a pretty drastic fall in wages over recent years. Yet this hasn't happened.

Nominal wage rates in the United States and Europe are mainly flat or only slightly up or down. And the extent to which they are down appears attributable to lower wages accepted by returning workers rather than a wholesale repricing of labor. Which is to say that wages in the West (note that I am excluding Japan from this discussion for the moment) are sticking well above where they should be.

Why? Two reasons. First, there is still some labor force protectionism in the developed world, especially in Western Europe. Labor laws and union agreements keep wages from falling sharply for many workers in response to market conditions that might otherwise dictate such a downward shift.

But the second and perhaps more universal reason is the wage-rate rigidities that Keynes called "sticky wages" that are manifested at the most microeconomic of levels. Many bosses, faced with lower revenues, will tend to fire people rather than lower wages across the board. And many organizations will keep paying workers roughly the same wages even though they could go out and hire new people at much lower salaries. For a bunch of reasons—most notably the resistance to pay cuts and perceptions of fairness—salary levels in many organizations don't change very quickly. So, for example, a large law firm that pays its new associates $125,000 a year may keep doing so even if a slower economy means there is a much larger supply of freshly minted law grads to pick from and it would be possible to hire associates for less money. Wages are simply not always driven by macroeconomic laws, and this is one more way in which equilibrium doesn't occur as naturally as Léon Walras imagined.

Now, sticky wages have been good in many ways, the first being that they serve as a brake on deflation. "Overpaid" workers have more money in their pockets to buy stuff and keep paying high rents or leases. But clearly this is not an expression of efficient market theory with regard to labor, and the long-term consequences are troubling. Sticky wages also can keep unemployment higher than it might otherwise be if more workers were hired at lower wages. And sticky wages also have big implications for competitiveness because it's harder for the United States and Europe to compete with China or India when the former group's workers are overpaid relative to the latter group's. It should be no wonder that most of the new job creation that prevails throughout the developed world occurs predominantly in lower-wage job categories. Retail, for instance, is one of the fastest-growing sectors of the U.S. economy—with these jobs typically paying under $21,000 a year.

Japan is one place in the developed world where wages have fallen significantly in response to market conditions. Wage rates and prices have declined in Japan on a nominal basis for fifteen years. As a result, Japan has been able to maintain much of its trade competitiveness (even, until recently, against the headwinds of a super-strong currency) and enjoy a far lower unemployment rate compared to its developed-nation peers.

Uncompetitive wages can't last forever in the United States and Europe. And when wages finally do fall, so will the value of certain assets that may also be stuck at artificially high points right now.

Sticky Real Assets: The bubble may have burst, but prices for many homes and commercial properties in the United States and Europe remain well above what they are actually worth. The reason is that the current period of easy money has worked to keep asset prices high by reducing the pressure on creditors to permit the resolution of highly leveraged assets in a manner that would lead to full and final price discovery.

At moments of greatest stress since the beginning of the global financial crisis, governments have bailed out and "bailed in" banks and other major financial intermediaries, providing emergency liquidity, or forcing creditors (and, as we saw in Europe in 2013, even depositors) to relinquish claims, in order to avoid fire sales of assets and/or defaults. These actions have served to magnify the general tendency of creditors to avoid wiping out their capital by liquidating assets at substantial losses. This has been especially so, given that many creditors believe that even enormous downturns in asset values may be cyclical in nature. Just wait patiently, the logic goes, and asset values will keep inching back up—just as in the past. Waiting is especially appealing when the government is loaning money at zero interest and banks can make hefty profits—if not by adding loans, then by increasing the spread between the rates at which they loan money and the banks' own cost of funds.

So it is that, in the United States five years after residential and commercial real estate values peaked, mortgages on millions of homes are in default or foreclosure, or have yet to be liquidated or fully restructured. And hundreds of billions of dollars of commercial real estate mortgages—loans that will likely never be able to recoup their full principal—have been extended ad infinitum. Year after year, the banks have resisted facing the reality of a huge, unprecedented number of loans gone bad.

But why take a hit now when the pain can be put off till later? And the firming of the housing market during late 2012 and into 2013—even with those millions of homes with defaulted mortgages waiting to be liquidated—reinforces this view.

Creditors have kicked the can down the road—and then kicked it again—with the full knowledge of regulators who (justifiably) feared a renewed collapse of the financial system if these matters were resolved more swiftly. Officials in Washington haven't really wanted banks to deal with all their bad debt. Not now, anyway. European Union regulators are even more panicked at the thought, given the very low levels of equity capital at which banks in the European Union operate.

Sticky values for assets reflect another reality—one more pedestrian in nature—seen in the United States and a few other nations that experienced a housing bubble, which is that it's no easy thing to toss a few million people out onto the street through foreclosure and eviction, and so the wheels of resolving the housing crisis have turned slowly. Simply processing the mountain of foreclosure paperwork has proven to be a monumental task—and things got further bogged down when banks and mortgage servicers were investigated for cutting corners in that department, using "robo-signers" and other shady tactics to expedite foreclosures. Another speed bump has been the government's various—and mostly unsuccessful—efforts to aid home owners facing foreclosure. Such efforts have been well-intended, and arguably should have been far greater in scope (and still could be). But there is no question that they have slowed the resolution of bad housing debt.

What does this all mean? It translates to market distortions, such as millions of families living "rent free" for years (post-default/pre-eviction) which artificially inflates other forms of consumption. Money that would normally be spent on rent or mortgage payments is being used for groceries, gas, and gadgets. Sticky asset values also translate to distortion in supply and demand for commercial property space, as mortgages are not written down to permit rents to adjust. And that last reference brings us to a discussion of artificially high rents in general.

Sticky Rents: To start, let's go with the issue of real property rents. Rents (or what federal government statisticians call "owners' equivalent rents" in the case of those who own their homes) are not only typically the largest portion of household expenses, but are a substantial expense of businesses as well, especially small and midsize businesses. So if rents are sticking at artificially high levels, it matters a great deal for the economy as a whole.

Real "contract" rents are generally a function of the cost of money and the value of property, which itself is heavily influenced by the cost of money. When interest rates fall and money becomes cheaper, the value of real property tends to increase. Because it is cheaper to "carry" property, investors or home owners will pay more for it. So if property prices start to decline, the easiest way to prop them up is to lower the cost of money—which is exactly what the Fed and later the Obama administration, with the first-time home buyer's tax credit (the Housing Assistance Tax Act of 2008), sought to do as property values went off a cliff starting in 2007. Central bankers in other developed countries did the same thing.

As much as property values have declined in the United States and elsewhere, they would have fallen much further without cheap money acting as a buffer against a total meltdown.

This may sound like good policy, and in the shorter term it does prevent a deeper deflationary spiral. But given the huge glut of unresolved property in the United States and many parts of Europe, there are major downsides to propping up real estate prices.

First, the property sector has become heavily dependent on a zero interest rate policy, which raises the question: What will become of values if and when interest rates recover to longer-term trends? Moreover, what confidence can buyers have about the long-term value of property under such circumstances? Think about it: if you buy a house for $500,000 when interest rates are at 4 percent, what are the odds that you'd get the same price for that house if rates rise to, say, 8 percent? Maybe you would make back your money because the overall economy would improve and wages and prices would rise, but there are inherent risks to buying in a market where values are artificially inflated by the cheapest money in history. This is why experts such as Yale professor Dr. Robert Shiller (cocreator of the Case-Shiller Home Price Index) and former Reagan Office of Management and Budget director David Stockman cautioned in early 2013 that U.S. housing might be entering a minibubble reflective of artificial and unsustainable conditions.[3]

Second, over 20 percent of all single-family homes purchased in 2012, and nearly 40 percent in some markets, were purchased by investors for rental to families. This kind of buying has made good sense with interest rates low and rents high. But given that real per-capita wages are stagnant or declining, whatever inflation-beating rise we've seen in rents to date in the United States is more the result of families being unable to enter the mortgage market to buy a home than the demand for housing in the aggregate. In the absence of generalized inflation of prices and wages, rents would have to fall, and maybe sharply, when the owner-occupied housing market was finally liquidated and repriced.

In truth, had the property backlog repriced already, rents would be considerably less tight. So get ready for disruption when the four million U.S. homes facing foreclosure (to say nothing of excess housing units in the creditor regions of Europe) are finally repriced for liquidation. Sticky rents today mean problems tomorrow in the absence of substantial generalized economic growth.

The future looks even more ominous if we consider the broader subject of economic rents. Without getting too wonky here, economic rents are what owners of anything—capital, a franchise, a patent, even appointment to a rarefied job—get to keep above and beyond the fair cost of their own labor and capital. Loosely defined, it can just be called excess profits. Think of it as the economic charge for "specialness"—for the best location of a building; for the best batting average as a professional baseball player; for coming up with the "next great thing" (and having the foresight to patent it). That sort of thing. There is no inherently fair level to economic rents—they are best described as "what the market will bear."

But here's the catch: amid a condition of excess labor, productive capacity and capital, relative to demand, economic rents tend to rise—at least in the short term. If, for example, prices remain constant for some odd reason while the input costs of labor, materials and debt capital fall on a real basis, guess who gets to keep the difference? Yes: shareholders, owners, landlords, and "talent." In fact, economists have a special word for that group: rentiers. And as with "contract" or "real" rents, economic rents can actually grow in what otherwise should be a deflationary environment because of sticky prices.

Sticky Prices: As with wages, prices for goods and services are generally driven down only over extended periods. Business leaders seldom wake up in the morning and decide to drop prices unless they absolutely have to because of insufficient demand for existing inventory. Macro-competitiveness trends don't generally shape the planning agendas—notwithstanding that competition-driven pricing is very much front and center. Even productivity gains since the mid-1990s have tended not to migrate directly to nominal price reductions (or, for that matter, to be shared with labor in the form of higher wages). Instead, such gains have led to a combination of lower effective prices (giving the consumer better goods for the same price) and higher economic rents.

But one thing is for sure: an economic event like the Great Recession *should* serve to reduce prices, given the combination of too much productive capacity and too little cash in the pockets of consumers. Yet that hasn't happened. Prices did fall at first, but then quickly stabilized.

So how much should prices be down? Jared Bernstein, Vice President Joe Biden's former chief economist, calculated in August 2012 that prices should be falling by as much as 6 percent (highly improbable, but that's what his model suggests).[4] The reason is the substantial output gap in the United States, which, as we've discussed, is the difference between what the economy is producing and what it could or should be producing at so-called natural levels of unemployment and given other factors.

So why have prices continued rising slightly or remained flat? Some have attributed continued inflation to extraordinary monetary stimulus or expectations of future inflation. But clearly—especially if Bernstein is right—deflation is also being avoided by the mysterious phenomenon of sticky prices.

Interestingly too, following the Great Recession, producers have lost considerable pricing power in real terms as producer prices have tended to rise faster than consumer prices for finished goods. If there were a way to pass on the far more volatile producer prices (which bear more relation to overall monetary-stimulus-impacted global demand for commodities and other inputs than do domestic consumer prices) to consumers, producers would certainly be doing so. Recent contractions in corporate revenues and margins are beginning to reflect the limitations of price stickiness.

THE CHALLENGE OF GETTING UNSTUCK

The components of the stickiness dilemma are interrelated. Wages, asset values, rents, and prices must all, eventually, rise or fall in tandem. They can diverge for periods of time, generally due to fluke circumstances, such as excess debt creation. But any major or lengthy diversion is unsustainable, and that is the definition of a bubble.

This being the case, what is preventing the natural adjustment of all the above sticky elements to the realities of oversupply in today's global economy?

Two answers seem most relevant. The first is that the economies of the developed world are enormous and therefore able to sustain the status quo for a very long period of time through dissaving. In places like Japan, dissaving takes the form of literally spending savings. But in most of the developed nations it means going further into debt.

The second answer is quite a bit more philosophical, and boils down to this: people who have their wealth in real assets don't want to see them lose value. And there is an inherent recognition that downward wage and price adjustments inevitably threaten such value. Why? Because such adjustments translate to less ability to pay contract rents.

So, for example, if a young lawyer is paid less, she can't afford to pay as much in rent for an apartment. Which means that the apartment is worth less money. Which is unpleasant if you're the guy who owns the apartment. Assets' values fall—as do economic rents—when wages and prices fall.

Given this chain of logic, it shouldn't be a surprise if those who own most of the nation's assets favored public policies that seek to delay or prevent nominal wealth erosion, even to the point of sacrificing growth and enduring high levels of underemployment.

In a cyclical downturn this tendency makes perfect economic and social sense. Heavy and persistent erosion of wealth can result in a negative "wealth effect," discouraging both consumption and investment, and therefore impeding recovery. Stickiness can therefore be everyone's friend.

But stickiness of all types can also pose real problems. And beyond all the problems I have just described, sticky factors also tend to distort economic data. In early to mid-2012, many analysts of the housing economy (including one of the best, Bill McBride of the well-respected economics blog *Calculated Risk*) called a bottom to the U.S. housing market. Correctly interpreting housing data is important because it offers insights into the direction of the economy as a whole. But how much confidence can we really put in housing data right now, given how the real estate market has yet to be repriced in ways consistent with unstuck/sustainable wages and costs of money?

Regardless of the signs of recovery in some U.S. housing markets, at the end of the first quarter of 2013, around 20 percent of home owners with mortgages remained underwater with outstanding mortgage balances that have a poor chance of ever being collected on in full. During 2012, there were an average of 6 million home owners who were not paying their mortgages or who were more than thirty days delinquent. Yet lenders have been unwilling or unable—for legal, logistical, or economic reasons—to move against defaulted home owners on a timely basis to seize and liquidate their homes. The average post-default period through liquidation during 2012 ran over thirty months nationally and far higher in the so-called judicial foreclosure states. Accordingly, there is a "shadow inventory" of homes—many in the formerly hard-hit markets that analysts are now citing as being on the mend. And no one really knows how the liquidation of such inventory would impact prices. But it's safe to assume that the effect would be reasonably dramatic, given that the size of the shadow inventory of homes exceeds the number of all homes currently sold in the United States in a year.

All of this shows the interconnected nature of the stickiness dynamic. Consider what is distorted when price stickiness prevails in a real estate market that, in truth, is glutted by excess shadow inventory.[5]

First, the lenders who hold the defaulted loans may be carrying them at inflated values that potentially overstate the capital position of such lenders. Second, the stickiness in home prices may become reflected in rents that are higher than they would be if the excess inventory found its way into the market and resulting price declines made rents fall in tandem. Finally, and far more potentially troubling than other considerations, the families who continue to live unevicted in their defaulted homes are living, as previously discussed, rent free—they have none of the housing costs that are normally a family's largest single expense. Accordingly, nonpaying households are spending their rent-free disposable incomes on other things. And such spending may not only distort prices but may significantly distort the real health of regional, if not national, economies.

One argument advanced to counter this point has been that if a defaulted home owner loses their home, they will simply move into a nearby rental. But I challenge that. A family paying nothing for shelter (and a good portion of those remaining in default really cannot pay much of anything) may instead move in with friends, family, or worse. Even if fewer than half of the U.S. shadow inventory of defaulted residential homes ended up creating a real vacancy, it would yield a number of excess unoccupied vacant housing units far higher than it was at the peak of the housing bubble.

In short, there is a lot going on in the United States, and many mixed messages are being sent and received. Managing the world's largest economy is hard enough without the laws of supply and demand not working as they are supposed to.

Of course, the United States can take solace in the fact that it isn't Spain, the country that had the greatest housing bubble and now has the largest inventory of excess housing. Spain has over 5 million vacant housing units—20 percent of total housing stock—and has many more homes in default. Evictions—*desahucios* in Spanish—are proceeding at a pace of nearly 30,000 per quarter—over 400,000 since the crisis began, through 2012. The social impact of what is transpiring in Spain, which has a 25 percent unemployment rate, has driven up suicide rates and has led the Spanish government to ban foreclosures on the homes of poorer families. All this, and yet as of early 2012, despite a much more severe bubble, Spanish home prices had failed to reset anywhere near the degree that U.S. prices have.

A DANGEROUS WAITING GAME

Stickiness eventually becomes unstuck, but the distortions that prevail until that time can be quite severe and serve to delay remedies that might produce better outcomes. If you're lucky, though, stickiness doesn't matter all much because, by the time the accounts of the prior boom need to be finally reckoned, another expansion has begun. And if the developed world found itself mired only in a severe recession, there would be no reason to fret too much about the stickiness dilemma. I would join Keynes and others in gratitude for the way stickiness stops a free fall in wages, asset values, and prices.

But, unfortunately, that is not the case today.

We are not in a normal cyclical downturn. Given the dimensions of global imbalances, no developed nation can afford to "stick to its guns."

Imagining that cyclical forces will fix things enough to avoid far bigger adjustments is tantamount to saying that we can wait out both the absorption of hundreds of millions of more workers in developing countries who will join the global economy in coming years, and also the creation of sufficient consumption/demand in those same emerging markets to absorb the even larger excess of supply that looms on the horizon.

Waiting it out is like waiting out the biblical flood of Noah, the only allegory I can think of that compares with events currently altering the economic surface of the planet. Noah at least prepared for his flood and had faith in a higher power to restore things to normal (and, of course, his crisis lasted only forty days and forty nights). The developed world went into its present economic malaise with nary a paddle, much less an ark. And belief in a higher power—a confidence fairy, for example— just won't cut it.

Moreover, waiting carries with it the risk of being inundated by other economic forces that are already having a corrosive effect in the United States and other developed countries. Foremost among these is long-term underemployment amid an output gap. This problem is more than just demoralizing to societies, it has been demonstrated to result in labor hysteresis, which, as mentioned earlier, is a semi-permanent change in both the labor force and a nation's economic potential by virtue of loss of job skills, employer rejection of the long-term unemployed, and the disillusionment of millions of workers.

Another corrosive outcome of waiting is that it feeds a growing polarization by wealth as those with capital seek to preserve the status quo—along with their wealth—by avoiding unsticking the structure of prices, rents, and assets. While most workers have an interest in unsticking things and getting growth and employment going again, the rentier class are actually doing pretty well in the current situation. And, in a challenge to representative democracy itself, this group is very good at getting its way. For now, anyway. But big fights loom on the horizon—and indeed, some are already under way. Even in Japan, the long and painful process of repricing its economy has led to significant political instability as the pie shrinks in nominal terms.

The stickiness dilemma can't be tackled overnight. We can't just wave a magic wand and undertake a sweeping overhaul of economic relations. Rather, we are limited to the employment of multiple, incremental strategies that cumulatively can smooth the process of global readjustment while minimizing (but certainly not eliminating) the pain associated with such change.

Obviously, adjustments to wages, prices, and the value of assets can, if precipitous, be highly destabilizing. So gradualism is important. Ultimately what is needed is a change in orientation, not a pell-mell dash to economic salvation with all the unintended consequences of hasty actions.

Japan, for example, has been able to maintain a high standard of living amid enormous repricing of its wages, prices, and assets. But it has endured that which many of its fellow developed nations in the West view as anathema—and over nearly two decades. As an experiment in achieving stability amid financial disaster, the Japanese experience is, at the very least, notable. Also notable is the fact that with the change in the Japanese government at the end of 2012, the Japanese people have shown they are fed up with it.

Do the United States and Europe need to do what Japan did? Certainly not. But big changes in attitude—as well as policy—can no longer be avoided if we are to sidestep that outcome.

CHAPTER 9

BLIND SPOTS

The Failure of Economic Leadership

So what happens to a country when key industries collapse, when incomes stagnate, when ordinary people get by through borrowing, and when its top competitors become its leading creditors? Nothing good.

In the United States, the most prominent vestige of three decades of debt-financed expansion is the high level of polarization in wealth and income. As I wrote, with Hockett and Roubini in "The Way Forward," the credit bubble of the 2000s exacerbated

> a trend toward wider income disparities in the United States that already had been steadily growing since the early 1980s. . . . But the problem went beyond bifurcated wages. It also involved a major change in the shares of income received by labor and capital. Because many workers were no longer sharing the fruits of the economy's impressive productivity gains, capital was able to claim a much larger share of the returns, further widening wealth and income inequality which

by 2008 had reached levels not seen since the fateful year of 1928.[1]

During the Gilded Age of the 1890s, and again after World War I, the incomes of the top wealthiest American families grew so disproportionately large that those in the middle of the socioeconomic ladder saw their real incomes eroded despite the growth of the overall economy.

This time around, as inequality soared, starting in the 1980s, ordinary Americans were able to sustain their living standards by borrowing trillions of dollars to finance homes, consumer goods, education, and medical expenses.

This was a twenty-first-century version of the feudal lord financing the annual planting and harvesting by his marginally enfranchised serfs. In a feudal system, though, the serfs who couldn't pay their debts would remain permanently indentured—along with their offspring—until the debts were repaid. Not so in a modern free society populated by citizens who are not serfs. When the incomes of Americans proved unable to support the debt they had incurred, or when they saw their collateral for those debts fall in value below the amounts owed, they defaulted. And they continue to default on their debts as of this writing, albeit at a slower pace.

THE AGE OF CAPITAL

At the same time, large corporate profits rose after the Great Recession, eliminating the weakest of competitors and leaving the survivors to thrive. As CNNMoney commented on 2011 corporate profits: "The Fortune 500 generated a total of $824.5 billion in earnings last year, up 16.4% over 2010. That beats the previous record of $785 billion, set in 2006 during a roaring economy."[2]

Why did this happen, especially amid near zero aggregate GDP growth in the developed world? The answer is simple. Against a glut of global labor, there is no incentive or need for employers to raise the incomes of labor.

To see how dramatically workers have been losing out, consider wages as a percentage of GDP over the past sixty years. Back in the heyday of industrial capitalism, from the 1940s through the early 1970s, the share of national product going to workers every year was routinely over 50 percent of GDP. Labor unions were powerful and even top corporate leaders espoused the belief that workers should get a fair share of the prosperity they helped create, and that a modern economy worked best when labor, capital, and government worked in concert to produce steadily growing and shared prosperity. The highest-paid executive in America in 1950 was General Motors's Charlie Wilson, who made $663,000—or no more than 40 times what average line workers in the company made.

The early postwar period is often referred to as the Great Compression. The extreme inequality of the Gilded Age and the 1920s dissipated and all boats really did rise equally as productivity increased and the economy expanded. Indeed, between 1945 and 1973, the wages of U.S. workers rose in almost perfect tandem with their productivity. American workers got what they deserved, and U.S. executives and shareholders did plenty well.

All this started to change in the 1970s. Wages as a share of GDP first dipped below 50 percent around 1974, and never again would labor command half of all the country's output. If you look at a graph charting the rise of both productivity and wages since World War II, you'll see that the two lines begin to diverge in the early 1970s and the gap just keeps getting wider and wider in the following decades.[3] Workers were keeping less and less of the wealth they were producing. Owners of capital were keeping more and more.

The age of labor was over. The second age of capital had begun. By 2011, wages as a share of GDP had fallen to 43 percent. That same year, corporate profits soared to over 60 percent of GDP—the highest levels since before the Great Depression.

Labor simply is no longer a scarce or valuable resource worth "paying up" for (with limited exceptions in the high-value-added sectors). Toss in some technological developments that "saved" even more labor and you get the picture.

If you keep unit pricing static, the less paid to labor, the higher the return to capital. The greater the polarization of wealth, the fewer individuals, per capita, participating in corporate (capital) ownership and the returns thereon. And the greater the polarization of wealth and income, the greater the need to supplement income with borrowing. The virtuous circle of investment and economic growth devolved to a vicious circle of debt, disinvestment, and slump.

One would expect wealth and income polarization to be a typical attribute of emerging nations. Whether the barons of nascent, relatively free-market democracies or the oligarchs of authoritarian "banana republics," we forgive the rush to wealth and the shortsightedness present in nations just beginning to flex their economic muscle. Yet a key feature of advanced nations (until the present age, it seems) had been a widespread belief that economic strength was ensured by an economically—and, of course, politically—broadly enfranchised population. After all, an industrial economy's workers are also its consumers, as Henry Ford famously argued in the 1920s when he began paying his workers the then unheard-of wage of five dollars a day. "It is not the employer who pays the wages," Ford once said. "Employers only handle the money. It is the customer who pays the wages."

THE PLUTOCRATIC WORLDVIEW

What we are seeing today is the emergence of a global plutocracy, not only in the get-rich-quick emerging nations but in the advanced nations as well, where a Second Gilded Age has been under way.

This plutocracy's members tend to be only marginally concerned about the countries in which they actually live, seeing themselves instead (because they run corporations that operate globally) as citizens of the world. They have not merely enjoyed wealth and privilege, but have—perhaps to rationalize their station in a meritocracy in which luck also plays a significant role, or perhaps to justify it—formed an aristocracy of ideas, of self-generated and self-sustaining ideologies, and have promoted a "philanthrocapitalism" that has rendered the noblesse oblige of the original Gilded Age positively quaint by comparison.

In her 2012 book, *Plutocrats: The Rise of the New Global Super-Rich and the Fall of Everyone Else,* the journalist Chrystia Freeland writes that "the ambition of the philanthro-capitalists doesn't stop at transforming how charity works. They want to change how the state operates, too. These are men who have built their business by achieving the maximum impact with the minimum effort—either as financiers using leverage or technologists using scale. They think of their charitable dollar the same way. . . . The plutocrat-as-politician is becoming an important member of the world's governing elite . . . [and] can use his own money to bankroll his campaign directly, and also to build a network of civic support through the less explicitly political donations of his personal foundation. Some farsighted plutocrats try to use their money not merely to buy public office for themselves but to redirect the reigning ideology of a nation, a region, or even the world."[4]

In fact, the thinking advanced by some American, British, and even continental European members of this vaunted group would make the industrialists—even, perhaps, the royalty of yore—blush. And what they are saying is often mimicked by members of the political classes, especially some of those who entered politics after having made their own fortunes.

It's not easy to describe the plutocratic worldview precisely, even though I have heard it recited many times in different ways in the business and political circles I travel in. Even though politicians and the media both give this view a wide berth, here are a few key implicit points you often hear from some of today's super-wealthy (and perhaps more so from their sycophants):

- That they are smarter than other people, and especially politicians, bureaucrats, school superintendents, and old-style nonprofit leaders. Why? Because they have made their fortune reinventing whole sectors, such as technology and finance.

- That because they are so smart, and so good at solving problems and reinventing things, they deserve their fortunes, however crazily outsized these may be compared to what ordinary people earn. More than that, they deserve to be running large swaths of U.S. policy, such as education—and maybe even the executive branch, where their business smarts can be used to better manage the economy, as Romney repeatedly suggested.

- That if we want more people like them around—the people who actually create the jobs and create revolutionary new products and services—we need to incentivize risk taking and wealth creation, not squelch it. We need to stop pushing antiquated public policies that hold the "job creators" back, whether it's by taxes on capital gains, restrictions on educated immigrants, or any number of silly red-tape rules that govern the business sector, including the blizzard of regulations in the Dodd-Frank Wall Street Reform and Consumer Protection Act.

■ That the main reason Americans are holding them back—with taxes and regulation and their biases against independently wealthy candidates or billionaires dominating education policy—is because so many citizens, 47 percent according to Mitt Romney, are "takers" who benefit from keeping the wealthy down and who rely on a welfare state largely financed by the wealthy.

Sounds pretty awful laid out that way, and very self-serving, but is it that far off the mark? Of course, not all of those with substantial wealth embrace these views. Some believe they got rich because of plain good fortune and no small amount of sweat. Many are happy to pay higher taxes and believe strongly in the social safety net. And many do think that strong government watchdogs are needed to keep business honest and the financial system stable.

Still, it's hard to avoid the feeling that a good chunk of the developed world's upper class really do have a serious blind spot in these matters, and really do believe that they deserve, if anything, even more influence in society than they presently have.

BIG MONEY—AND BIGGER BLIND SPOTS

In December 2012, I had a chance to spend a moment with the technology visionary, entrepreneur, and venture capitalist Marc Andreessen. Andreessen, you may recall, created the first commercially viable Web browser, Mosaic, and went on to found Netscape and invest in and nurture many other technology companies that have become household names.

With a net worth estimated at over half a billion dollars in 2012, and a wife who is the daughter of Silicon Valley's wealthiest real estate owner, Andreessen's family is comfortably within the top 0.01 percent of U.S. households—about 11,500 families—perhaps even near the top 0.001 percent. Andreessen, who was born and raised in the Midwest and now resides in Silicon Valley, supported the presidential bid of Barack Obama in 2008 and then switched his allegiance to back Mitt Romney in 2012.

Andreessen spoke to a room of tech-fascinated young and middle-aged businesspeople, reporters, and economic policy veterans, all very interested in what he had to say—much of which was quite visionary, almost stunningly so. It was clear why Andreessen is so well regarded and has excellent timing that leads to extraordinary success—and he's a pretty nice fellow, too. He—and especially his wife—are also massively philanthropic and, apparently, socially concerned, something I truly admire and respect. But then, as he was discussing all the wonders that technology would bring—for instance, the elimination of retail stores and the potential for a crash in the value of commercial real estate (presumably retail and office), disintermediation of traditional industries, and "onshoring" of production as robotics eliminated the emerging markets' labor advantage—someone asked him what that technology would do in terms of the elimination of jobs, which are already less than plentiful.

Without jobs, the questioner asked, how is the middle class going to keep paying for all the great new products and services that get cooked up by the tech sector?

I then witnessed an interesting transformation. Here was a clearly brilliant man, not to the manor born in any respect, faced with a very relevant—and troubling—question. But what poured out of Andreessen in reply was not a visionary answer, but a fairly pointed diatribe that began with the words, "The middle class is a myth, it no longer exists."

Andreessen's view can be summarized in three points, all of which I was stunned to hear, coming from a smart futurist like him:

- The American middle class was an anomaly resulting from the World War II decimation of Europe and Japan, leaving the United States the only producing nation for the world and allowing U.S. labor an enormous advantage which, in Andreessen's view, continued over some three decades until the emergence of the Japanese forced out inefficient industries that overrewarded "high school graduate" labor.

- The U.S. labor force is unskilled and undereducated and there are thousands of jobs going unfilled for tech-savvy engineers, designers, and programmers. If only Americans understood this and were trained with the right skills.

- The federal government needs to "get out of the way" and let innovators innovate so they can provide the necessary jobs and supply plentiful and ever-cheaper goods.

It's hard to know where to start in responding to these views, which are not uncommon among America's super-wealthy. For starters, during the best years the United States ever had—from 1945 through 1975—government did anything but "get out of the way." To the contrary, government was closely involved in building the key foundations for the creation of national wealth. By building the public university systems and heavily subsidizing private universities, government helped create the largest pool of human capital the world had ever seen. By funding technological innovation, both directly through spending on science and indirectly through military projects, government laid the groundwork for innumerable innovations—including the Internet that Andreessen used to make his fortune. And by funding the Interstate Highway System and an advanced national air control system, government helped foster greater mobility for goods, services, and ideas. Tight regulation of the financial sector also ensured that the economy ran pretty smoothly, in contrast with more recent times.

As for all those unskilled or mistrained workers, they're an example of what happens when we take a laissez-faire approach to something as important as human-capital allocation. In countries like Denmark, government plays a key role in ensuring that there are enough trained workers for key growth sectors by investing enormous sums in redeploying and retraining labor as the economy changes. The United States doesn't do that, instead leaving human-capital decisions up to thousands of individual educational institutions. Sometimes it seems that the University of Phoenix—the behemoth for-profit college with 500,000 students—plays a bigger role in shaping human capital than the federal government. More about that later, too.

One could also note that in the United States and Europe, increasing the number of trained tech workers would barely make a dent in the oversupply of domestic labor, to say nothing of global excess labor. And there's a curious thing about the tech industry demanding immigration-law changes in the United States and claiming that there is an insufficient number of trained high-tech workers. As Ross Eisenbrey of the Economic Policy Institute wrote in a February 2013 *New York Times* editorial:

> If anything, we have too many high-tech workers [in the U.S.]: more than nine million people have degrees in a science, technology, engineering or math field, but only about three million have a job in one. That's largely because pay levels don't reward their skills. Salaries in computer- and math-related fields for workers with a college degree rose only 4.5 percent between 2000 and 2011. If these skills are so valuable and in such short supply, salaries should at least keep pace with the tech companies' profits, which have exploded. And while unemployment for high-tech workers may seem low— currently 3.7 percent—that's more than twice as high as it was before the recession. If there is no shortage of high-tech workers, why would companies be pushing for more? Simple: workers under the H-1B [guest worker visa] program aren't like domestic workers—because they have to be sponsored by an employer, they are more or less indentured, tied to their job and whatever wage the employer decides to give them.[5]

Finally, as one who is inundated with hardware, software, and free or nearly free apps that seem to be able to do everything except call my mother and tell her how things are going in my life, I am seeing no lack of innovation in the tech sector and certainly no evidence that big government is stifling the Marc Andreessens of the world.

But Andreessen's Q&A response was not the real story I took from that evening. After the formal presentation I took him aside for a few moments and posed a different set of questions. What, I asked, did he think would happen to wages and prices in a world already oversupplied with labor and manufacturing capacity when additional technological efficiencies eliminate even many service employees—the service sector that now provides 70 percent of all employment? From where would demand derive? Furthermore, if Andreessen was correct about the coming lack of demand for commercial real estate, for example, what would become of the wealth lodged in those assets as they deflated in value? And finally, with a decline in top line pricing power—even for tech companies with best-of-class products—as wages (the ability to pay) declined in nominal terms, what did he think would happen to the value of companies in which he was investing his and his clients' money? (Apple's fourth-quarter 2012 financial results, released at the time of this writing, brought this trend into full focus after my encounter with Andreessen—with gross margins depressed as the company's groundbreaking and superlative products are now going head to head with those just as good and cheaper.)

Needless to say, Andreessen is less of a macroeconomic visionary than a tech revolutionary. A very smart man, like many others in his field, able to see trends clearly and to tap into developments the average intellectual is generally unaware of, Andreessen had no answer—nor did I expect he would. He is an engineer, not an economist.

Clearly, this is not the time to have our best and brightest in the developed world abandon aspects of their intellect to convenient or self-serving points of view. It is time to ask if they have actually thought through what they are saying. The tech arena has always had its versions of the confidence fairy and exceptionalism described in earlier pages—it's called "the next big thing." Yet given that so many of the big things of the past fifteen years have disrupted or disintermediated more jobs-intensive alternatives in the service sector, one might ask, Who is going to buy the next big thing? And how are they going to be able to pay for it?

Might it be reasonable for tech companies, even those with enormously competitive products and services, to test their pricing assumptions—not just relative to competitors but relative to what their customers will likely be able to afford to pay in nominal terms as global wages and prices adjust? Sure, Apple sells plenty of iPhones and iPads in developing markets—and will sell more—but what exactly is going to happen if consumers in the largest consuming nations keep making less and less money as capital keeps capturing the bulk of productivity gains? Our present-day technology industrialists need to recall the admonitions of Henry Ford.

Too many business leaders simply aren't asking such big macroeconomic questions. And too many businesses are subscribing to ideologies that either ignore—or offer the wrong answers to—these questions.

I'll say more about all this shortly. But first let me discuss another consequence of today's stagnant and uneven economy that also is too often ignored by the business and political leadership of the developed world: the unraveling of the social fabric.

THE NEW INSTABILITY

In all parts of the world, developed or otherwise, economic enfranchisement is a key to maintaining stable, democratic governance. I would go so far as to assert that ultimately it is the best ensurer of private-property rights and the rule of law. An otherwise free society is asking for trouble, big trouble, if a large segment of its population can't find good-enough jobs or enjoy decent living standards. This is especially true if widespread hardship exists alongside growing affluence at the top of the economic ladder.

What kind of trouble am I talking about? Historically, three outcomes have tended to flow from mass economic disenfranchisement. First, private property, general wealth, and income may become vulnerable to appropriation via taxation, government seizure, or populist revolt. Second, the rule of law and democratic governance may be compromised or suspended, either by revolutionaries seeking "justice" or by oligarchs seeking to protect their private ownership. And three, growing crime extracts its own economic penalty in the guise of theft, corruption, or loss of physical security or life itself.

If you think none of these things could happen here in the United States, or in Europe, think again. In fact, some of this is already happening. The upsurge of populism in the United States between 2009 and 2011 stands as a major hint as to how economic instability can translate to political instability.

The Tea Party, which emerged largely in reaction to the Wall Street bailouts and the massive fiscal and monetary stimulus actions of the federal government, reshaped American politics in very short order. Among other things, the Tea Party's emergence served to further endanger all moderate Republicans—respected centrists like Richard Lugar, who suffered from a conservative backlash in 2012, were knocked out in primaries. In turn, a more extremist GOP has pushed the United States to the brink of economic disaster on several occasions—first with the budget ceiling battle of 2011 and then with the fiscal cliff standoff in late 2012. Also, it's fair to say that if another financial crisis hit today, an emergency measure like TARP (the Troubled Asset Relief Program) would not pass the Tea Party–dominated House.

The rise of the Tea Party shows how economic and political instability can interact and feed on itself. Economic disruption tends to empower fringe leaders and these leaders in turn can take steps that amplify such disruption and create further chaos.

Occupy Wall Street proved far less powerful than the Tea Party, but showcased the potential of another kind of populism—one aimed at taking down rich people. A backlash against wealth is inevitable—and given popular support in the United States for tax increases on the wealthy, is really already under way—if most people are suffering, year after year, even as those at the top see big income gains. That's been the situation in the United States for several years now, and the only wonder is that Occupy Wall Street took so long to emerge. I wouldn't be at all surprised if, given today's wealth polarization, another, perhaps stronger, anti-rich movement emerges in coming years.

Of course, social and political instability is far more widespread in Europe. Austerity has created massive pain in Spain, Ireland, Italy, Portugal, and Greece, much of it inflicted on people who had nothing to do with the reckless borrowing, both private and public, that brought these countries to their knees. Violent street protests have become common in Europe, and far-right extremist parties, such as the Golden Dawn in Greece, have emerged to command large new followings. Meanwhile, the economic pain throughout Europe has reduced birthrates and further slowed population growth, trends that pose an obvious threat to economic growth.

Some Europeans are simply giving up on life altogether. As CNBC reported in fall 2012: "A growing number of global and European health bodies are warning that the introduction and intensification of austerity measures has led to a sharp rise in mental health problems with suicide rates, alcohol abuse and requests for anti-depressants increasing as people struggle with the psychological cost of living through a European-wide recession."[6]

In the UK, the suicide rate in 2011 was 15 percent higher than in 2007, before everything fell apart.[7] Greece, which had one of the lowest suicide rates in Europe back when times were good, has been grappling with a skyrocketing suicide rate since 2010 as the country struggles with an economic calamity on par with America's Great Depression.[8] Several people have shot themselves to death in public squares in downtown Athens. Japan has a cultural history of suicide among those who have been shamed or believe themselves to have become a burden to others. Suicide in Japan has now become epidemic, with the number of deaths per capita rising by more than 35 percent from 1995 to 2009 as the "lost decades" took their toll. (The rate has slowed in just the past few years.)[9]

If you think the United States has been spared untimely deaths, you might consider that suicide rates there, among those thirty-five to sixty-four years of age, rose by 30 percent from 1999 to 2010, and among men in their 50s, by nearly 50 percent during the same period.[10] As another example of distress, consider how many disturbed people have been engaging lately in murderous rampages:

During the six painful years following the peak of the credit and asset bubble in 2006, from 2007 through 2012, the average number of people killed or injured per year in incidents of mass murder in the United States was nearly three times the average killed or injured per year in the quarter century from 1982 through 2006.[11] Bad enough, but consider this: during the happy-go-lucky bubble period, from 2000 through 2006—a period of perhaps the lowest financial stress for the broad population of the United States (despite significant geopolitical challenges)—we saw the lowest average number of people killed or injured in incidents of mass murder of any such period within the thirty-one years from 1982 through 2012, a mere 41 percent of that just over three decades' average.

The deadliest of all thirty-one of the foregoing years was the final one—2012, which alone saw deaths and injuries from such incidents at a rate over 500 percent of the rate during the entire thirty prior years, punctuated by the December murders of twenty of the youngest students in an elementary school in Newtown, Connecticut, together with six of their teachers and administrators.

Now, mass-murder statistics may not make a wholly convincing argument for present conditions rending the social fabric of the United

States, but the foregoing comparison of the bubble period to the post-crash period is at least worthy of comment.

Ultimately, economic disenfranchisement needs to be examined from multiple perspectives, and while some indicators—such as suicide—are dramatic and very visible, others—such as the erosion of the rule of law or appropriation of income and wealth—are far more gradual.

The bottom line is that extreme things happen to the social fabric of societies with bad economies and high inequality.

THE LOST GENERATION

Perhaps the biggest cost of the long downturn is the decimation of a generation of young people who have been unfortunate enough to come of age during these trying economic times. Young people were already struggling economically before the financial crisis, facing high education costs, a challenging job market, and daunting home prices. The policy analyst Tamara Draut explored these problems in her prescient 2006 book, *Strapped: Why America's 20- and 30-Somethings Can't Get Ahead.*[12]

Of course, now things are worse—a lot worse. And not just in the United States, but across the developed world.

The United States has seen a very significant drop in the labor force participation rate since it peaked at the beginning of the millennium. Beginning in 2007 that fall became a free fall, with millions of people exiting the labor force. While much of that decline was attributable to frustrated job seekers being unable to find employment, the conventional wisdom has held that the overall aging of the American population was resulting in lower participation rates. This, at first blush, seems to make sense. But when one looks under the hood of U.S. statistical employment data, a different picture emerges. As it turns out, older Americans are returning to the labor force, not leaving it, probably because of a need to keep working in the face of eroded wealth. Instead, it is younger Americans whose labor force participation rates have declined.

As my friend and fellow member of the New America Foundation's World Economic Roundtable, Steve Blitz, chief economist of ITG Investment Research, wrote in December 2012: "By some measures, the labor force participation rate of 16- to 24-year-olds has dropped from near 70% to around 55%. For those between 25 and 34, the rate is down 80% from close to 90% a decade ago. . . . The absence of so many young people from the labor force will have profound consequences for the economy. If these trends persist, future spending patterns will likely be very different than the one we have generally experienced during the past 50 years or so."

More than that, though, these figures show how in the United States, as in much of Europe, the pain of economic distress has fallen squarely on the young. In the more labor-protective markets of the European Union, not only is demand for labor slack, but there is a fear of hiring younger people as full-time employees because of the difficulty in laying them off in a downturn. As Steven Erlanger wrote in *The New York Times* in December 2012:

> Throughout the European Union, unemployment among those aged 15 to 24 is soaring—22 percent in France, 51 percent in Spain, 36 percent in Italy. But those are only percentages among those looking for work. There is another category: those who are "not in employment, education or training," or NEETs, as the Organization for Economic Cooperation and Development calls them. And according to a study by the European Union's research agency, Eurofound, there are as many as 14 million out-of-work and disengaged young Europeans, costing member states an estimated €153 billion, or about $200 billion, a year in welfare benefits and lost production—1.2 percent of the bloc's gross domestic product. . . . As dispiriting, especially for the floating generation, is that 42 percent of those young people who are working are in temporary employment, up from just over one-third a decade ago, the Eurofound study said. Some 30 percent, or 5.8 million young adults, were employed part time— an increase of nearly 9 percentage points since 2001.[13]

The economic distress being wrought upon the young is not confined only to the existing shortage of jobs, but has far more insidious and longer-term economic and social consequences.

Millions upon millions of our well-educated young are not developing the skill sets and getting the experience they need to be competitive in their domestic labor markets, much less helping their national economies compete on a global basis. As Blitz notes above, the spending patterns of the present generations of sixteen- to thirty-four-year-olds are likely to be very different than those of prior generations, with the former having little in the way of resources to consume during what are typically the peak consumption years of their thirties and forties. They are also less likely to form families and to invest in major capital items such as homes.

Of course, present pressures on our younger generation go even beyond the unemployed and underemployed. I had a conversation in mid-2012 with a woman in her late twenties—well employed and very well educated—about deflation and shopping. I asked whether she had noticed, in her own Internet-based retail behavior, that she seldom had difficulty buying goods online at marked-down prices if she merely waited for merchants to clear their inventories or by simply seeking a lower price via shopping aggregators such as Google Shopping and others. Or for that matter, whether she engaged in "store-switching" (either online or in bricks-and-mortar retail stores) in order to obtain a lower price for the same or similar goods, a practice that economists have noted contributes to hidden deflation, as it is not accurately reflected in the calculation of many consumer price indices.

What I got back was a surprising, good-natured rebuke: "What do you mean by 'shopping'? My friends and I don't shop much. After rent, food, the payments on our student loans, and an occasional drink or meal with each other, there's nothing left to shop with."

Apparently, for all my concerns about the unemployment of our young adult population, and their prospects for the future, I had missed seeing that many of those gainfully employed today entered the workforce heavily indebted and are not following older patterns of consumption.

One last thing about young people is that inherited money is unlikely, as some researchers once suggested, to bail them out down the line. Inheritance is generally a positive social trend, in spite of the conventional wisdom that the passing down of wealth serves to make the rich even richer and further increases inequality. To the contrary, the math of inheritance is that it tends to deconcentrate wealth (unless one has only a single heir and bequeaths all of one's estate to him or her). In fact, intergenerational transfer has far more of an impact on the less wealthy (as a percentage of net worth and of lifetime income) than it does on the affluent. That's why many hoped that when trillions of dollars—in some estimates, as much as $41 trillion—were passed down to younger Americans in coming decades it could serve to solve some pressing economic problems, such as the failure of many households to build much (or any) retirement wealth. Young people may be bruised by today's economy, the logic went, but they'll be okay when their parents kick off and pass down even modest estates.

Alas, though, this great avalanche of money from the old to the young is unlikely to descend, according to a 2011 study by Edward N. Wolff of New York University and Maury Gittleman of the U.S. Bureau of Labor Statistics, "Inheritances and the Distribution of Wealth, or, Whatever Happened to the Great Inheritance Boom?"[14]

Wolff and Gittleman show evidence of a decline in the frequency of bequests and suggest that this trend presages far smaller inheritances in the future than previous scholarship had suggested. The reasons are complex:

> Life spans rose over this period [from the 1980's to present]. Since elderly people were living longer, the number of bequests per year declined. . . . As people live longer, their medical expenses might rise as they age and, as a result, less money is transferred to children at time of death. [Also] the share of estates dedicated to charitable contributions might be rising over time. This trend may be particularly characteristic of the rich.

Changes in the economy are changing the social fabric of the United States and other advanced countries in profoundly troubling ways. We have lived through five years of depressed household formation rates and the phenomenon of "boomerang kids" who move back in with their parents because they are unemployed or making too little to afford lodgings, even with roommates. In our urban enclaves, we are seeing a dramatic rise in what experts now refer to as "transitional age youth"—grown, educated young adults who are literally on the street because not only are they unemployed but their families have also been hard hit and are unable to take them back in.[15] Household formation rates recovered in 2011 and 2012, but we literally lost millions of households that normally would have formed from 2007 through 2011.

Even the face of panhandling has been altered. Few of us walking around American and European cities can avoid noticing that those sitting with signs and begging for money are not the old, crusty down-and-outs of yore. They are our sons and daughters. Occasionally, I take note of what they are reading while they panhandle; they are not un-educated, either.

The trends discussed in this chapter make for an alarming mix: wealth and income polarization. Crime, social stress, and dislocation. And above all, a demographic mess as one generation that was destined to retire, now can't (and will live a long time, depleting its wealth) along with another generation that wishes to work, form families, and thrive, but for whom there is no room.

And these, of course, are the secondary symptoms of our economic times—the primary one being a lack of growth, underemployment of available labor (and, therefore, the weak position of labor relative to capital), and the global imbalances themselves. We are confronted, therefore, with the challenge of understanding how to address and remedy those primary symptoms and—in so doing—cure the second-ary impacts.

CHAPTER 10

THE STABILITY IMPERATIVE

A Responsible Approach to Economic Policy

On an unseasonably warm Monday in early November 1990, President George H. W. Bush signed a budget bill that had emerged after months of bitter negotiations in Washington.

There was no public ceremony for the signing, but a statement from the White House declared that the bill was the "centerpiece of the largest deficit reduction package in history and an important measure for ensuring America's long-term economic growth."[1] By reducing spending and raising taxes, and ensuring deficit reduction through tough reforms to the budgeting process, the bill was a textbook example of a balanced approach to fiscal policy. Both political parties gave ground and President Bush showed himself to be a flexible leader focused on the national interest by breaking his "no new taxes" pledge.

In raising taxes, Bush was following in the footsteps of his predecessor, President Reagan, who agreed to substantial rollbacks of his historic 1981 tax cut as his administration worked to tame the budget. By some counts, Reagan raised taxes eleven times.[2]

A leading architect of the 1990 budget deal was Richard Darman, Bush's budget director. A veteran of the Reagan White House and the Treasury Department, and Gerald Ford's Commerce Department before that, Darman epitomized a now bygone pragmatic conservative approach to fiscal policy and the economy. Yes, the goal was to limit the size of government, but always with a keen focus on ensuring steady economic growth and fiscal stability.

There aren't many Richard Darmans hanging around Republican circles these days.

After President Bush faced a primary challenge from Pat Buchanan and went down to defeat in 1992, Darman was widely criticized by conservatives for pushing his boss to raise taxes. The conservative magazine *National Review* called the 1990 budget bill "the most catastrophic budget deal of all time."[3] And just three years after that deal, which had passed Congress with many Republican votes, not a single Republican voted for President Bill Clinton's budget—which also featured a balanced approach to deficit reduction.

We know the rest of the story, repeated as well in earlier chapters. The GOP was taken over in the 1990s by hard-line right-wing ideologues who didn't know the first thing about managing a modern economy or balancing budgets. But they did know about winning elections by promising tax cuts now and smaller government . . . well, one of these days.

The budget ceiling standoff in 2011 showed this brand of conservatism at its most reckless extreme—with Republicans basically threatening to blow up the economy if Democrats didn't agree to spending cuts in exchange for raising the debt ceiling. Republicans did agree to modest tax hikes on the rich as part of a fiscal-cliff deal at the start of 2013—even as their intransigence ensured that the vast majority of the Bush tax cuts were made permanent, digging the fiscal hole even deeper.

Once upon a time, conservatism was about prudence. Lately it's been about zealotry. Yes, conservatives talk about growth, jobs, and balanced budgets. But these concerns routinely take a backseat to ideological principles, with GOP leaders worried stiff about how the party's extreme base and antitax interest groups will react to their every move.

To the extent that conservatives are practical, it's in the worst self-interested ways—catering to the needs of powerful industries (and big donors) without regard to the distorting effects on the economy or fiscal policy. We have seen the rise of a crony conservatism, with its leaders again and again going along with unnecessary or wasteful subsidies to industries that shouldn't be receiving a dime in taxpayer support. These actions should be just as much anathema as funding disliked government entitlement programs. The difference, of course, is that subsidized industries make campaign donations; safety-net recipients do not.

For all the conservative talk of government being "the problem," the fact remains that the federal government has grown steadily since the dawn of the Reagan years, a period during which Republicans controlled the White House for an aggregate of nearly two decades. And whether it is farm subsidies, military spending, or corporate tax breaks, the conservatives haven't shown themselves ready to scale back much of anything beyond the usual social-welfare programs. And even the significant cuts they have advocated to those programs, such as Congressman Paul Ryan's plan to downsize Medicare, have been designed to kick in years from now, so as to mitigate the political fallout. In the more recent past, under George W. Bush, Republicans actually increased the cost of Medicare through prescription drug coverage and giveaways to the health-care industry.

This weird brand of conservatism—an extreme right that embraces crony capitalism—has been so dominant for so long that it is easy to forget what *real* conservatism actually is. Or how conservative principles should translate to economic and fiscal policy.

I'm no conservative, certainly not in the "capital C" sense, as the term is used these days. But I do believe strongly in approaching today's serious economic challenges in ways that are responsible, soberminded, and prudent. And since those are terms that once were associated with conservatism, I'm going to go ahead and lay out an approach that I call *prudential conservatism.*

The gist of this approach is that after an age of excess, greed, and risk taking—and of ignoring serious economic problems festering out of sight—it is time to rein things in, take our medicine, and fix serious problems. Prudential conservatism is focused on mitigating hazards and undertaking the rebalancing needed to spur renewed global competitiveness. This approach argues that in order for the developed world economies to function effectively and regain strength, we must curb imprudent—if not downright destructive—economic and institutional behaviors.

What does all this mean in practice? The remainder of this chapter spells it all out.

STABILITY *AND* GROWTH

One of the strangest things about modern conservatives is how they have turned into cheerleaders for risk. As if by reflex, Republicans fight nearly every proposal that would force powerful economic actors to behave more prudently. Conservative leaders in Congress fight regulation of banks and other capital-markets participants at every turn. They have been against the mandating of solid capital requirements, against greater transparency around derivatives, against limits on proprietary trading—and on and on, all out of the fear that stricter rules will constrain credit creation and thus growth. Congressional Republicans, many of whom hail from the heartland and—in their defense—generally hold the coastal mega-banking establishment in rather low regard, nevertheless tend totally to buy the view that the best way to promote growth is to promote risk taking.

Of course, though, there is nothing conservative about this outlook. Nor does this thinking make much sense. If it's true that the world is now glutted with cheap money, and that there is a lack of sound opportunities for investment because of weak demand, there is no reason to believe that steps to limit risky behavior (say, by requiring banks to hold more capital) would restrain growth. The opposite may be true in conditions of capital shortage, but it is decidedly untrue today and for the foreseeable future.

The fact is that what is most important to our economies under present global circumstances is *stability*. Cheap money in the hands of profit-hungry financiers is a recipe for trouble, as we have seen. And that's exactly the situation we are in today, the legacy of the financial crash notwithstanding. Wall Street's cowboys can still engineer big and scary disasters, with J.P. Morgan's multibillion-dollar trading losses in 2012 a case in point.

Some things never change, and the way that greed can drive reckless risk taking is one of them. That's why, over the course of a century, we have created central banks, deposit insurance, and supervision regimes to moderate risk taking and ensure against panics. The unintended consequences of these stabilizers has been—ironically—the socialization of risk, which has made it easier for those in finance to play fast and loose with "other people's money." Many have tolerated this out of the belief that we need lots of risk to promote credit creation and growth. But things have changed. In the age of oversupply, the notion of taking systemic risk to spur economies no longer makes sense.

Under present circumstances, government should promote investment that is inherently less risky and involves moderate rates of return. In the private sector that may mean, for example, investment in better-capitalized banks that offer a high degree of shareholder safety in consideration of lower expected returns—returns that are still considerably above ultra-low, risk-free returns. And government itself can channel investment dollars—as I will discuss later—via infrastructure bond regimes.

The key is to keep in mind the nature of the problem today. We need jobs and the absorption of existing labor and capacity resources, but we should not advocate the development of additional unnecessary capacity in order to accomplish that aim.

With those preliminary thoughts on the table, let's move on to a more detailed discussion of the steps needed to achieve higher growth rates *and* nurture more stability in our financial system.

BITING THE BULLET ON BANKING: REAL REGULATION FOR STRENGTH AND STABILITY

Let me start with the one of the toughest—but most important—steps: fixing the broken banking system.

I am sympathetic to calls by people like former Citigroup leader Sanford Weill to break up today's megabanks into boring commercial utilities on the one hand and risk-taking investment houses on the other. I get it when Sandy Weill's former coworker at Citi, and my good friend, Sallie Krawcheck (who also ran Merrill Lynch when it was acquired by Bank of America), and others, such as Morgan Stanley's former CEO Philip Purcell, argue that large universal banks, in addition to being too big to fail, have become essentially unmanageable.

But let's be real: universal banking—i.e., banks operating in a large number of business lines, including commercial and investment banking—is here to stay. And no matter what the optimal solutions may be in terms of "breaking up the banks," the reality is that seeing these solutions achieved globally is beyond rational expectations. And because banking and trading are global activities today, the international banking system is, sadly, only as strong as its weakest links. So if one or two countries bust up their big banks, there will still be a whole lot of systemic risk as long as these banks remain deeply enmeshed with those in other nations that are less cautious.

Thus I suggest that we assume that global universal banking will endure, but that governments finally step up—on a global level—to better regulate these banks. And quickly, before another crisis. Here is what I believe must be done:

Capital and Reserves. Modern banking is often called "fractional reserve" banking. This means that a bank maintains only a small portion of its total assets in liquid reserves (either voluntarily or by law) to honor periodic demands for cash from depositors. Meanwhile, it puts the rest of its assets to work by investing to earn money, often in leveraged ways. Some conservative economists—often the same ones who decry the end of the gold standard and such—claim that fractional (or zero) reserve banking is the underpinning of weakness in our banking system. After all, if banks can merely conjure up cash—and in fact, they can and do, often merely borrowing whatever liquidity they need to maintain to meet reserve requirements—where is the discipline?

Well, the discipline in banking is not in reserves or the lack thereof, it is in equity capital requirements. Banks' principal liabilities are the relatively short-term time deposits it owes to its depositors, together with short-term borrowings. Yet because lending by banks is generally for longer terms, the solvency of banks can be protected only by an adequate buffer of equity capital that can absorb losses on assets when they occur. The problem, of course, is that equity capital costs banks a lot more than deposits and short-term debt. Accordingly, management seeks to minimize equity in order to improve earnings and, naturally, banks do everything in their power to prevent the mandating of higher capital requirements. They spend gobs of money lobbying legislators and regulators and spin out scary scenarios of how credit will contract if higher capital requirements are mandated. That is to be expected. But it should also be ignored by governments that provide the deposit insurance, access to cheap credit, lender-of-last-resort backup, and the ultimate charters under which banks operate and profit. The level of bank profitability is not a proper concern for regulators. The stability of the banking system *is*.

In continental Europe and Japan, where banking is much more closely tied to the state in terms of overall policy implementation and bilateral support, matters are even more complicated. But regardless of whether banks have a history of being nationalized (and privatized) in certain parts of the developed world, or are held more at arm's length in the Anglo-American portion, the integration of the financial system demands that a consistent and demanding set of standards apply throughout the institutions and jurisdictions that are so integrated.

Unfortunately, that's not happening right now, even after the disastrous financial crisis.

The international accords on standardization of bank supervision promulgated by the Basel Committee on Banking Supervision, organized originally by the Group of Ten central banks in 1974 and operating out of the Bank for International Settlements in Basel, Switzerland, have all been heavily negotiated political agreements, sorely lacking in the prudence they are meant to ensure. The postponement in January 2013 of the still-inadequate Basel III leverage rules for banks is a stark illustration of this. The rules were scheduled to go into effect in 2015 and the EU is concerned that many of its banks won't make the cut. And here's the clincher. The rule calls for capping bank leverage at 33 times tier 1 capital! (For wonks, that's all tier 1 capital, including nontangible equity.) That means that a *mere 3 percent shift in the value of a bank's assets wipes it out.*

This constitutes reform? I am sorry, but we need a heck of a lot more capital supporting our banks than that. Certainly our megabanks.

Now, the truth is that new Anglo-American capital requirements are higher than the Basel requirements, but they are still not high enough. A big problem here is how bank assets are valued to begin with. While the Basel III rules make some marginal improvement on the way in which banks calculate the value of their assets for the purpose of assessing capital requirements, the methods used are both questionable and lacking in transparency. One needs only to look at the levels at which

U.S. banks are trading—well below book value—to understand that the market itself doesn't believe in banks' regulatory accounting.

Without writing a complete dissertation here on how to restructure either Basel III or the regulatory systems of any particular region, I lay out below a set of basic changes I would like to see. These changes would apply only to banks in the United States, the United Kingdom, Japan, and the Eurozone initially, with wide berth given to emerging-market banks to phase in these requirements through 2025. While they are obviously much more stringent than the Basel III requirements, I'm also asking for something tougher than the U.S. Federal Reserve's Integrated Regulatory Capital Framework (IRCF) proposed in mid-2012. My changes:

- Leverage ratios of any bank clearing through the Bank for International Settlements should be no more than twenty times permanent tangible capital (that is, common equity plus perpetual capital that is not in the form of anything that can be redeemed or is intangible). Developed-world banks should achieve this threshold by 2019.

- The requirements set forth in the IRCF for banks with assets in excess of $100 billion should be tightened—with dynamic, pro-cyclical capital requirements that bar the distribution of dividends to shareholders and stock buybacks entirely until permanent capital is at least 8 percent of total assets. For banks with over $500 billion of assets, it should be 10 percent of total assets. The reliance on banks to achieve these thresholds over a time period is inconsistent with their being allowed to make distributions to shareholders in the interim or, if after achieving them, they fall out of compliance. That must change.

- In terms of valuing "whole-loan" bank assets for capital adequacy purposes, I would accept the changes suggested in the IRCF but seek more explicit safeguards to avoid future episodes wherein collateral for asset-based secured portfolio loans (loans "held for investment" by banks) declines precipitously in value without a bank recalculating the adequacy of its capital. It seems reasonable to me that if collateral value declines below 95 percent of the outstanding amount of such loans (net of any immediately realizable borrower guarantees or other deposits), banks should not be permitted to incorporate in risk-weighted asset values the shortfall between actual collateral value and the outstanding principal amount of the loan. This will require ongoing collateral revaluation. But one of the great silver linings of the mortgage crisis is the development of an entire industry dedicated to statistically reliable and relatively cost-efficient revaluation systems that is perfect for this ongoing level of regulatory oversight. We need to move beyond the "pray and delay" tactics of banks during crisis periods and institute a new meme I call "recognize and resolve." If you make a loan that goes underwater, you deal with it when it happens, because that is the prudent thing to do.

▪ As to securities and other instruments held by banks in their trading portfolios, we must be very diligent in removing the lack of transparency inherent in so-called mark-to-model (also known as "mark-to-make-believe") valuations for capital-adequacy purposes. While Basel III and the IRCF have made some strides in this connection, more needs to be done to discourage banks from taking positions in assets that are so complex or specialized that they are not traded in open markets or not readily valuable through trades in very similar assets. To the extent they take such positions they should be granted only small—or *no*—credit for such assets. If something is such a good deal that a bank is willing to position it without apparent liquidity and at value that may one day be difficult to prove, then the bank should go for it—with its equity capital.

▪ Banks in the United States continue to grossly underreport broad swaths of assets to which they are exposed, relative to the reporting requirements of their non-U.S. peers, revealing only small portions of their exposures to derivatives and keeping most mortgage-backed and other asset-backed securities off their books entirely. This makes it very difficult for investors or regulators to determine whether they are truly sufficiently capitalized. As Bloomberg's Yalman Onaran reported in an extraordinarily well-researched piece in February 2013:

> Using international standards for derivatives and consolidating mortgage securitizations, JPMorgan, Chase & Co., Bank

of America Corp. and Wells Fargo & Co. would double in assets, while Citigroup Inc. would jump 60 percent, third-quarter data show. JPMorgan would swell to $4.5 trillion from $2.3 trillion, leapfrogging London-based HSBC Holdings Plc and Deutsche Bank AG, each with about $2.7 trillion.[4]

The developed world can no longer indulge the luxury of provincial anomalies in bank reporting and regulation. In a systemically interdependent global financial world, such gaps can lead to disaster. It is time to agree to a single standard, and one which is most conservative.

While we have been wallowing in the zero (or nearly zero) interest rate policies of the advanced world's central banks, banks themselves have been quietly restructuring their liabilities. Why borrow from bondholders for long terms at high rates when you can attract nearly unlimited deposits at demand deposit and money market rates below 1 percent or (often) far less? The problem with this thinking is that depositors can withdraw their money at almost any time. But bondholders' capital stays put, even in a panic. Bank lending, however, is not run on a demand basis. Banks typically lend for fixed terms, often quite long ones. So in a panic, banks have no way of becoming liquid even as liquidity is being drained from them. And, as discussed above, if the value of their long-term loan/securities assets declines only slightly in a panic, they can be left insolvent as well as illiquid. The solution, naturally, is to mandate greater duration matching between bank assets and liabilities. This is a problem that has actually become worse since the global financial crisis, despite all the efforts at bank reregulation, and that is unfathomable.

I should note that one key difference between what I am suggesting and what is contained in the Basel III rules and the IRCF is the use of total assets, as opposed to risk-weighted assets, in the denominator of the capital requirements calculation. Why? The bottom line is that total assets is a much larger number than risk-weighted assets. Assessing capital requirements against solely risk-weighted assets is a false test, because the notion of what is safe versus what is risky continues to be highly speculative. Anat Admati of Stanford University and Martin Hellwig of the Max Planck Institute in Bonn, Germany, wrote compellingly about this in February 2013:

The idea of risk weighting is that safer assets are given less weight and therefore require less backing by equity. In practice, the system of risk weights has encouraged banks to invest in assets that are treated as safe by regulators even though they are risky, such as AAA rated mortgage-backed securities or Greek sovereign debt. The system also allows banks to manipulate their own equity requirements by using their own risk models to determine risk weights. . . . For example, the roughly €55 billion ($74 billion) in equity that Deutsche Bank AG had on its balance sheet at the end of 2011 represented more than 14 percent of the bank's risk-weighted assets—far more than required by Basel III—but only 2.5 percent of the bank's total assets.[5]

Finally, methods for modeling risk need to be standardized. Basel allows for far too much discretion at the level of each country's bank supervisors. Moreover, local regulators rely on banks' internal models for running risk weight calculations, and the banks all use different models! Imagine, for example, that food inspections by the U.S. Department of Agriculture allowed for each food-processing establishment to use its own methods of determining food safety. Well, that's pretty much what you've got in the global banking system today, and a lot of people are going to get poisoned if this keeps up.

Reorganization: In the United States, a desire to avoid nationalization of failing banks during the global financial crisis led to a huge pyramid of bailouts and other assistance granted to America's largest financial institutions—at the cost of enormous sums of taxpayer money together with the acceptance of huge moral hazard. In many cases, bank regulators said they couldn't seize the conglomerated bank holding companies that controlled troubled banks, and had their corporate credit intermingled with those institutions.

This technical problem was resolved with provisions in the 2010 Dodd-Frank Wall Street Reform and Consumer Protection Act. But we still don't have final regulations for what would be done to resolve large banks that clearly cannot be shut down. The classic U.S. method of stripping a seized bank of its bad assets and marrying the remaining "good" bank to a competitor or strategic investor in a shotgun wedding of sorts would be nearly impossible (and, if possible, wildly expensive to taxpayers) in the case of certain giant banks. Regulators call such banks systemically important financial institutions (SIFIs) and today still don't have the regulatory architecture they need to handle future melt-downs of these banks. The good news is that a clean and efficient re-structuring mechanism is readily available in the case of any large institution: expedited bankruptcy.

Expedited bankruptcy is a much better alternative way of addressing SIFI failures than bailouts, nationalizations, or the expensive process of seizing and selling a big (and broke) bank. We are fortunate that even the most troubled SIFIs tend to have large amounts of unsecured debt capital and trade payables. Through an expedited bankruptcy, creditors of SIFIs could have a healthy chunk of what they are owed converted into the restructured bank's new equity. That's it—done and delivered. No tears and no systemic pain. If creditors knew this was a possibility, banks may pay a tad more to borrow, but my guess is it won't be much, given the ongoing capital glut. "Too big to fail" should not mean too big to resolve. And making this form of resolution a requirement for large financial institutions worldwide should be a no-brainer, structur-ally, despite the political pressure from SIFIs and their foreign counter-parts who will surely try to prevent it.

Activities: This one is short and simple. As former Federal Reserve chairman Paul A. Volcker has argued, banks must be rendered relatively boring institutions once more. No more trading with regulatory capital, no more positioning real estate and other long-term assets as a principal (rather than as a lender), no more selling of risk guarantees as a principal, no theoretically off-balance-sheet entities that a bank can't afford to completely throw under a bus, and, please, no more London Whales (the risk-taking trader who lost JPMorgan Chase billions of dollars).

Banks exist with the help of government and should be accountable to government. Government subsidizes, insures, lends to, and charters banks to fulfill a public purpose. Such support of banks is inconsistent with their taking risks unconnected with their core mission of aiding and intermediating the process of capital formation (for which regu-lated banks today are not the only avenue, by the way). Such activities place the global financial system at material risk and should not be permitted in any of our major financial capitals.

Compensation: There has been no better suggestion of late on addressing bank compensation than Sallie Krawcheck's in the *Harvard Business Review* in June 2012. Krawcheck writes from experience as a former top executive at both Citibank and Bank of America. Her position is simple: while it is good to defer bonus payouts to bankers to ensure that they continue to have skin in the game, paying them with stock and stock options is counterproductive because it places further incentives on bankers to engage in risky but potentially very profitable behavior in an attempt to run up share prices. In one of the most lucid insights I've seen on the issue of compensation, Krawcheck wrote:

> Since the crisis, regulators and boards have gravitated toward increasing the amount of stock-based compensation and lengthening the mandatory holding period to induce senior banking executives to behave properly. Underlying this seems to be a belief that if a bank's CEO—let's call him Handsomely Paid—earns and holds $40 million worth of stock in his bank, rather than earning $20 million in cash and holding $20 million in stock, he will lead his institution in a more risk-sensitive manner. Don't be too sure about that.[6]

As Krawcheck explained, any number of studies over the past few years have found that financial institutions with supposedly "shareholder friendly" governance and compensation policies were more likely to have embraced extreme risk taking. Indeed, you don't need a finance scholar to make that connection; just look at the finance chiefs with some of the biggest equity stakes in their companies at the height of the bubble, in 2006. They included James Cayne of Bear Stearns, Richard Fuld of Lehman Brothers, and Stanley O'Neal of Merrill Lynch. All of these executives gambled big and lost; none of their companies would still be standing by the end of 2008.

As Krawcheck notes, equity investors tend to focus on the upside—obsessed with how to push up the value of stocks. But not fixed-income investors, who are always worried about the downsides. She writes:

> A simple but powerful way for boards to alter the risk appetite of senior bank executives would be to add fixed-income

instruments to the compensation equation. Any shift in this direction would have an impact, but the most logical end point would be a compensation mix that mirrors the bank's capital structure. Thus, as bank financial leverage (and therefore financial risk) increased, senior executives would be motivated to become more risk-averse.

An example: If Handsomely Paid's financial institution had $1 of debt for every $1 of equity, his $20 million in compensation (down from $40 million because of pressure from shareholders) would be paid as $10 million in debt and $10 million in equity, and his risk tolerance would probably remain relatively robust. If the capital structure shifted to $39 of debt for every $1 of equity—a hugely risky position—his compensation would be paid as $19.5 million in fixed-income instruments and $500,000 in equity, and the CEO's attention to risk would be heightened. He would most likely focus on enabling repayment of the debt in a timely fashion, rather than on increasing the upside for the $500,000 in equity. This structure would thus provide an automatic brake on the bank's risk taking.

To be sure, there are other details that one could put forward for further strengthening the banking system, but I view the foregoing as the core points. I don't head a SIFI (unfortunately) and my modest firm is anything but systemically critical. But I live and work in a world in which the rupturing of SIFIs means financial crisis that leaves no bread on the table for the rest of us in the industry. More important, it can lead and has led to global financial catastrophe that impacts billions of people. Downsizing SIFIs so that they resemble utilities is pretty much the only answer. These institutions will still be profitable and it is likely that their shareholders will come to appreciate their lower risk profile and increased transparency.

Amid a global capital glut, there is simply no need for overly "creative" activities on the part of our largest financial institutions. Today there are plenty of other established avenues through which capital is united with those engaged in productive economic activity.

SHUTTING DOWN THE CASINO:
REFORM TO PROMOTE STABILITY IN INVESTING

A sober and steady financial system—one that tracks with the true conservative value of prudence—would not be a friendly place for risk-addicted cowboys.

So how do we crack down on the cowboys? We must move away from what the great economist Hyman Minsky called money manager capitalism, which has been with us for many decades but grew enormously beginning around 1997 and exploded in scope after the turn of this century.[7] An ever-larger mountain of money—401(k)s, pooled pension funds, sovereign wealth funds, insurance funds, and university endowments—is now being managed by financial firms and advisers, all feeling a gun to their head to get maximum returns lest the money go somewhere else.

As my sometime colleague and co-blogger, and one of Minsky's disciples, the economist L. Randall Wray of the University of Missouri at Kansas City and the Levy Institute at Bard College has noted:

> First, there was the rise of "managed money"—pension funds (private and public), sovereign wealth funds, insurance funds, university endowments, and other savings that are placed with professional money managers seeking maximum returns. Also important was the shift to "total return" as the goal—yield plus price appreciation. Each money manager competes on the basis of total return, earning fee income and getting more clients if successful. Of course, the goal of each is to be the best—anyone returning less than the average return loses clients. But it is impossible for all to be above average—generating several kinds of behavior that are sure to increase risk. Money managers will take on riskier assets to gamble for higher returns. They will innovate new products, using marketing to attract clients. Often these are purposely complex and opaque—the better to dupe clients and to prevent imitation by competing firms. And, probably most important of all, there is a strong incentive to overstate actual earnings—by failing to recognize losses, by overvaluing assets, and through just plain fraudulent accounting.[8]

Now, don't get me wrong, I am all in favor of financial innovation, and I have been responsible for my fair share over the course of my investment banking career, creating products that disrupted and disintermediated bank lending—drawing non-bank capital-markets investors directly into primary transactions with those seeking money for growth and stability. But if the purpose of primary capital markets is to unite well-informed investors with businesses seeking to raise money, and the purpose of secondary market trading is to establish liquidity (the ready ability to buy and sell) and establish a market value (so-called price discovery), then we are well beyond the point at which we have sufficient liquidity and price discovery for the purpose of establishing a ready market. And, unfortunately, much of the financial "innovation" of late has been connected with secondary markets—especially in derivatives issuance and trading, high-frequency trading (HFT), and money management marketing.

As the following table demonstrates, the average holding period of a share of stock traded on the New York Stock Exchange has gone from eight years in 1960 to a matter of months today. There is nothing gained and much potentially lost from this activity.

Additionally, as an outgrowth of the intense competition among money managers and the fickle nature of much of today's investment capital, we are beset today by insider trading scandals, by destabilizing high-frequency trading, and by corporate and money management frauds—all of which serve to undermine the operation of the markets themselves. It's time to recognize the inherent dangers that money manager capitalism poses to the real economy and upend the status quo.

Year	NYSE Turnover	Holding Period
2009	141%	9 months
2000	88%	14 months
1990	46%	26 months
1980	36%	33 months
1970	19%	63 months
1960	12%	100 months

Source: NYSE Group Factbook. Turnover = number of shares traded as a percentage of total shares outstanding.

Reining in the Money Managers: In early 2012, a financial analyst named Simon Lack wrote a stunning exposé on one aspect of the money management industry, *The Hedge Fund Mirage: The Illusion of Big Money and Why It's Too Good to Be True.*[9] In his book, Lack very convincingly demonstrated that from 1998 through 2010, investors in hedge funds and fund of funds made almost nothing in terms of net profits. Yes, you read that right, the nearly $2 trillion hedge fund industry made its investors (net of losses and fees) an aggregate of $9 billion in 13 years—far less than such investors could have earned investing in U.S. Treasury bonds! And what did the managers of that enormous sum of money make in fees during that same period? $444 billion. The hedge fund industry took 98 percent of the profits on the money invested in it. In other words, investors put their money at risk, but their hedge fund managers kept most of the profits of that risk. Smart money? I don't think so. Smart managers? Indeed, yes. Very smart.

In all fairness, the period Lack covers in his study included the 2008–2009 crash, but only a portion of the equity markets' recovery thereafter. At this writing, the above calculus would be slightly less extreme for those managers who had the great foresight to take full advantage of that recovery. But given the modesty of most hedge fund returns, even as the markets regained pre-recession highs, very slightly less extreme, apparently.

Notwithstanding that retail investors (mom-and-pop investors, as opposed to money managers) appeared to have drifted back into the equity markets in early 2013 after a hiatus of several years, trading volumes remain near modern historic lows. High-frequency trading, in which powerful computers get a split-second edge over other investors, has, in recent years, constituted between 50 percent and 70 percent of total market volume. And money managers are increasingly trading shares not based on underlying business fundamentals but rather on how they think other people (and even others' computers) will trade on those shares. Trading and investing has become more manic, with money managers chasing each others' behavior and actions.

As a young banker, I was taught by sales and trading veterans that when push comes to shove, "bonds are bought, equities are sold." Investors generally seek safe havens for the major portion of their wealth, often turning to government, municipal, and higher-grade corporate bonds at returns that exceed inflation by a few percentage points during normal times. Equities, on the other hand, are—in theory at least—investments in businesses, with all the risk that comes with owning a share of a business one doesn't manage (especially with the misalignment of management incentives we have seen over the past decades). Generally speaking, other than in the case of professional money managers, equities used to be sold by brokers to their clients based on a number of motives: the desire to earn their clients money and protect that money from erosion due to inflation; the desire to earn commission income; and/or the internal financial rewards derived from assisting the investment banks they work for in selling securities those banks have underwritten. In any event, someone used to have to sell equities.

Today's complete dominance of money manager capitalism has changed these relationships. With the rise of the mutual fund industry during the 1980s leading to the enormous expansion of the hedge fund industry and, finally, the exchange traded fund industry, demand for equities has soared as more money management professionals wake up every morning needing to buy equities to make a living.

This doesn't make a lot of sense, at least for investors. Fundamentally, equity ownership has turned from an investment to a "trade." Money managers have become more like Las Vegas sporting-event bookies than productive actors in our all-important system of capital formation. Indeed, Maynard Keynes noted in *The General Theory of Employment, Interest and Money,* "When the capital development of a country becomes a by-product of the activities of a casino, the job is likely to be ill-done."[10]

I prefer the sporting-event bookie analogy to that of a general casino because the outcomes in equities are not predominantly based on random luck; but the great man had a point.

The twin purposes of a secondary stock market are to (i) establish liquidity for one's investments (enabling an investor to readily exit an equity investment by bringing interested buyers and sellers together) and thus (ii) establish the value of such investments. There is no further social or economic gain to be realized by making secondary stock markets into anything more than that. That's not to say that there isn't opportunity for profit in trading; there certainly is. But the argument that these activities produce liquidity for liquidity's sake pale when exposed to the reality of unacceptable levels of volatility and just how much wealth ends up in the hands of middlemen.

One more point before I discuss what I think needs be done. There is a myth that markets are not only efficient but that the players in those markets are all possessed of perfect, or at least nearly equivalent, knowledge about what it is they are buying and selling. That the players are making rational decisions based on good information is the essence of the notion that market values bear any resemblance to fully informed reality. Many market economists (among them, by the way, Milton Friedman) have defended anything that enhances liquidity and are willing to stomach the resulting volatility based on this premise alone.

Too bad this is a lot of nonsense.

Professional investors, in fact, often have dramatically different information—as insider trading scandals have demonstrated. And in the absence of complete and roughly equal information, they end up discounting the actions of other market participants rather than the possible outcomes for the businesses in which they are "investing."

Professor Lynn Stout of Cornell University Law School makes very salient points on this subject in her 2012 book, *The Shareholder Value Myth: How Putting Shareholders First Harms Investors, Corporations, and the Public.*[11] Good corporate managers, of course, have far better information than any passive investor in public shares, legal disclosure requirements notwithstanding. So almost by definition, public market valuations are not much different than odds setting and opinion-arbitrage among bettors on a football game.

It is vital, therefore, that securities markets be channeled to support their primary purpose for existing in the first place. This was far more easily done when the exchanges themselves were merely mutual cooperatives owned by the principal brokerage firms and a few wealthy investors. But today, the world's major exchanges are all public corporations seeking to make a buck regardless of the impact on the public purpose they were organized to further.

Worse, the exchanges have been engaged in "competitive deregulation," lobbying within their respective jurisdictions for the most casino-like environments they can muster in order to usher the greatest number of bettors through their portals. And because the exchanges are not playing this game with "house" money—as in a casino-sponsored poker game, they are merely taking a "rake" on all transactions conducted within their respective domains—they really care only about the volume of trades, thus insuring that the job of providing liquidity and considered price discovery is, in Keynes's words, about as "ill-done" as can possibly be imagined.

The problem with all of this is not merely that the vaunted equity securities markets of the developed world are no longer reliable barometers of value. It is that they are no longer fulfilling their entire modern raison d'etre—to assist in the efficient and rational allocation of capital—and too often are facilitating the exact opposite: channeling big money to stupid ends amid frenzied speculation, as we saw in the dot-com bubble. The social-media "bubblette" of 2011–2012, in which companies like Facebook, Zynga, and their ilk were bid up way beyond reason, is a more recent example. Yes, Morgan Stanley grossly mispriced the Facebook offering; but the whole episode revealed deeper flaws in a system that is often anything but rational and efficient.

Letting equity markets operate like this is unacceptable in an era of global hypercompetitiveness, when the developed nations need capital formation to happen as productively as possible. We can't have modern equivalents of the Dutch tulip-bulb mania of the 1630s (the recent Bitcoin phenomenon comes to mind in this respect) when we're up against countries like China. We can't afford the gross misallocation of resources that results when economic value is disconnected from intrinsic value. Growing economies like China's can misallocate resources and get bailed out by growth everywhere else, but we are no longer in that world.

True conservatism would dictate curtailing such speculation in an environment in which rising global competitors aren't squandering their national wealth in so foolish a manner but instead are plowing it systematically into the foundations of long-term national prosperity. Sure, there is plenty of speculation (some of it not all that rational) in the nascent equity markets of emerging nations. But those markets are puny relative to their impact on emerging societies. For example, the combined equity market capitalization of all of the BRIC nations, with a population of 3 billion, is only $7 trillion, while that of the advanced nations, with a population of 800 million, is $36 trillion—19 times larger on a per-capita basis. And that's ignoring the fact that a lot of capital invested in equities on the BRICs' exchanges is from developed-world investors.

And talking about misallocation of wealth: there is no "creativity" to the destruction of capital that occurs when somebody like Mark

Pincus, CEO of the social-gaming company Zynga, sells shares to "greater fools" willing to buy them at $12 a share when they are, at this writing, worth about $3.39—less than a latte at Starbucks. What economic purposes were served by this episode? The answer, unfortunately, is none. Had the world been deprived of Zygna's principal "product," an online game called FarmVille, in which users spend real money on "virtual" assets, the intrinsic value of which is zero, I would argue that we'd all have been better off. Meanwhile, the Chinese are building non-virtual airports, high-speed rail lines, and all forms of energy infrastructure.

While the essence of capitalism is found in markets, in earlier times we learned how to manage markets so as to minimize irrational speculation. And then we forgot what we learned. While it is difficult to put the genie back into the bottle—I cannot, for example, foresee the re-mutualization of the world's now-public equities exchanges—we can reregulate the operations of the secondary markets. And we can try to tamp down the speculation that encourages overallocation, in primary markets, of capital to enterprises that have little intrinsic value to offer.

So what, exactly, needs to be done?

A bunch of things. We need to seriously discourage high-frequency trading operations—and ideally, disconnect those HFT computers. We need to toughen disclosure rules and increase corporate transparency so that all market participants are playing with good information. We need management compensation structures that tie management to ownership and make sure that they hold on to that ownership for the duration of their involvement with the enterprises they are managing (and when they cash out upon departure, remain liable for bad acts committed with their knowledge during their tenure). Finally, we must reinstate in full the so-called uptick rule that prohibits short selling of equities other than on an uptick in prices. These and other sensible solutions can both reduce the ill effects of money manager capitalism and reorient investment behavior toward that which will produce longer-term benefit, growth, and employment.

Ultimately, it is hard to imagine any set of regulations that would fully rein in money managers. It is largely up to investors, and fiduciaries for investors, to recognize the darker side of the incentives they have bestowed upon the managers of their money—and to appreciate the misalignment of interests. More broadly, policy can do only so much to squelch market behavior that produces economic volatility and a gross misallocation of resources. The owners of the "money" itself—individual investors, public and private pension funds (and their beneficiaries), endowments, insurance companies, and the like—eventually need to wake up and smell the coffee—or rather the burning, empty pot that remains each time the coffee is siphoned off by misincetivized managers, leaving little more than the grounds for their investors.

In March 2013, I wrote an op-ed for *The Wall Street Journal* regarding the futility of attempting to regulate senior-executive compensation through shareholder "say-on-pay" laws (binding or otherwise).[12] I am of that opinion because in a money manager capitalist environment, the question is, to what extent have professional money managers (clearly a very-well-compensated bunch) been co-opted into crony networks with the management of companies they are investing in? I would argue, to a very significant degree. And so I believe that until that link is broken by those who allocate capital to such managers, the problem will remain unresolved. Handing say-on-pay to money managers already so co-opted is merely akin to moving deck chairs around on the *Titanic*.

This is not an indictment of all money managers. There are plenty of responsible managers who have significant amounts of their own capital (and preferably *all* their own capital) exposed side by side with their investors. And in cases where their own capital is substantial as a percentage of the assets and base management fees they receive are not so egregious, I think there is good reason to invest with seasoned professionals. But where the opposite is true, the model is flawed and must be avoided by investors.

RAISE SAVINGS RATES
TO REPAIR THE HOUSEHOLD BALANCE SHEET

Given the concerns raised throughout this book about deflation and sluggish growth, the nations of the developed world need to focus strong attention on rebuilding household balance sheets.

Why? For three reasons: first, to lessen the pressure on governments to support those without savings when they are no longer able to earn; second, to reduce risk to households and enable them to be more confident about making other economic decisions, like buying a house or starting a small business with their own, as opposed to borrowed, capital; and three, to rebalance the consumption versus savings equation relative to the emerging nations. It's time for emerging nations to increase domestic consumption and for people in rich countries to do more to build up their nest eggs. The developed world must generate a higher rate of savings to cover internal investments rather than to continuously rely on capital inflows initiated at the whim of offshore investors. Furthermore, economies that invest more of their incomes tend to grow at faster rates. Consumption-driven economies therefore tend to crowd out investment spending, and that is not something that should be perpetuated in the age of oversupply.

To that end I propose that all developed nations with low savings rates enact a five-year tax holiday on interest paid to individuals—and only to individuals—up to the first 3 percent per annum on insured accounts, high-investment-grade bonds, and government/government agency bonds.

Promotion of savings, and risk-free/low-risk investment, is critical in a time of global imbalances, low inflation, and sluggish growth in the developed world. And when, in the longer term, global imbalances are moderated, the developed world's households should be self-supporting, with strong balance sheets and a substantial ability to invest in future growth.

As important as encouraging savings, the United States and other rich countries need to discourage *dissaving*.

Shortly after the elimination of credit card interest deductibility in the United States in 1986, a new industry was born that offered second home mortgages on homes and provided consumers with cash for consumption—together with the ability to deduct that interest because of its connection to mortgage debt. This ultimately led to the development of the home equity line of credit (HELOC) industry, which took the matter full circle by linking interest-deductible debt to a revolving credit line. The HELOC phenomenon facilitated hundreds of billions of dollars in withdrawals of home equity during the bubble in U.S. residential real estate, and contributed enormously to the net dissaving by American households. While a case can be made for keeping the home mortgage interest deduction in a modified form, there is absolutely no purpose to the deductibility of interest paid on general purpose HELOC lines. There might be some rationale for deductibility with respect to interest on HELOC debt taken out to start a business and to pay education or health-related expenses, but general deductibility merely promotes net dissaving and overconsumption. It's past time to bring that party to an end.

BREAKING THE ADDICTION TO CHEAP MONEY

With the dramatic recovery in financial markets since the spring of 2009, one might view the emergency monetary actions of recent years—including $5 trillion in aggregate quantitative and credit easing by the Federal Reserve, the European Central Bank, the Bank of England, and the Bank of Japan, together with the adoption of zero, or near zero, interest rate policies (ZIRP)—as a resounding success. And I would argue that they have been—or, at least, were—wildly successful in terms of saving the world's economies and financial system from outright global depression.

Yet we've also seen how the global supply glut has sorely tested the ability to turn this ocean of excess liquidity into real economic growth. It has turned out that monetary easing is great at inducing risk taking and not so great at creating new productive capacity in an environment in which there is no demand for such additional capacity. Meanwhile, ZIRP has levied an effective tax on savers while boosting the profits of banks as they borrow money for free, then turn around and lend to consumers at double-digit interest rates.

Monetary policy that favors cheap money has become like a drug that no longer delivers the big highs but remains highly addictive.

So how do we end this dependency? The happy story would be that eventually the onslaught of liquidity will push capital into risk beyond secondary financial markets—that is, into the creation of new plants and equipment, new real estate, and, ultimately, more jobs—in a restarting of developed-world economies that could be described as monetary Keynesianism: priming the pump through money "printing," not fiscal spending. That would be the economic equivalent of the trick of pulling the tablecloth off the table without disturbing the settings: the enormous indebtedness incurred during the credit bubble would be rendered harmless through the resumption of growth and inflation. A happy ending indeed!

But not, I am afraid, a likely one. It is more likely that the excess liquidity will continue to create intermittent bubbles in financial assets—periodically pushing things like interest rates and energy costs higher and, as we've seen in repeated post-recession minicycles to date, squashing recoveries in things like housing and consumer spending as mortgages become more expensive and gasoline and home heating oil siphon off other consumer discretionary spending. While the U.S. consumer has been responsive to the wealth effect attendant to the liquidity induced rallies in equity markets (mostly perceived, inasmuch as most consumers don't directly own shares), expansion in real consumption is ultimately tied to incomes, and if median real wages continue to decline, whatever boost in consumption seen from time to time will prove ephemeral.

If this is again the outcome of the present round of quantitative easing in the United States, then it is about time to stop hoping for happy endings and concede that a new supply and demand dynamic for labor is unlikely to emerge in a world with too great a supply of labor and capital.

For years, the central bankers of the developed world have voiced their concerns that monetary stimulus has its inherent limitations in a world where central banks are getting no help from—or are hindered by—the holders of the fiscal purse strings of governments. Furthermore, monetary easing has routinely worked at cross-purposes with austerity policies that suck money out of a number of the developed world's economies. That doesn't make a lot of sense.

But a changed approach has already materialized in Japan in 2013. Until recently, the Bank of Japan had essentially told leaders of government that it would support inflation targeting with additional easing, but it wanted to see the government move first on the fiscal side. With the installation of Haruhiko Kuroda as governor of the BOJ in March 2013, however, things changed dramatically and the bank adopted a program of quantitative easing several times more aggressive than that of the Federal Reserve relative to the size of the Japanese economy.

This triggers a conundrum: For the opponents of extraordinary monetary actions have been right, even as they have been fundamentally wrong. They have been clearly wrong about extraordinary monetary action—in the present climate—triggering runaway inflation or "bond strikes." But they are right in that excessive easing must not continue ad infinitum. But contrary to the thinking of the "austerians," however, in my opinion the reason rests in the moral hazard involved in giving the fiscal elements of government an excuse not to act in a similarly stimulatory manner. It is apparent that this is not going to change until the moral hazard is removed. So I favor seeing the Fed, the European Central Bank, and the Bank of England sending the same message the Bank of Japan used to send and has now abandoned as well: we are winding down the easing until we see the rest of government do what is necessary to help transmit the excess liquidity into the real economy.

For too long, debates about economic policy and financial regulation have revolved around a false choice between growth and stability. And, for thirty years, roughly up until the financial crisis, the apostles of greater risk and supposedly faster growth won the day—with disastrous results.

Despite the harsh lessons of the crisis, this debate is far from over, with left and right endlessly gridlocked over the question of whether government's hand should be heavier or lighter. That familiar ideological fault line, I've suggested, misses a bigger point. Stability and growth are not opposite ends of a spectrum. Rather, stability is a prerequisite for steady growth. We have now had two major financial meltdowns since the late 1990s that derailed growth, both precipitated in part by grossly irresponsible risk taking and other kinds of imprudent behavior. And, obviously, growth is more likely to occur when investors put their money into useful things, as opposed to putting it into the next bubble.

In any case, in the age of oversupply, we don't need to worry so much about limiting risk in ways that constrain capital formation and investment since there is, and will continue to be, plenty of cheap money around for those engaged in productive economic activities. In contrast, the inescapable lesson of recent history is that ensuring stability in a complex and fragile global economy must be a *much* higher priority. Every political leader needs to embrace this priority before the system once again goes off the rails. That includes conservatives who, if they are true to their values, should favor policies that will produce a stable system wherein executives and traders are maximally incentivized to behave prudently and responsibly.

CHAPTER 11

UNDERWATER NO MORE

How to Finally Put
the Great Credit Bubble Behind Us

A ny number of politicians and pundits can't stop talking about public debt. But today's big piles of private debt are in many ways more troubling, and anyone interested in creating more economic growth and stability has to confront the fact that many of today's private debts simply cannot be paid back.

The big hope, of course, has been that the legacy debts of the go-go years would disappear as the economy rebounded and asset prices rose. Just give it time, the logic went, and underwater homes and office buildings would rise from beneath the waves as the usual kind of cyclical recovery took hold.

Well, that's not going to happen.

Yes, there has been some firming of home prices and legacy mortgage-backed securities are trading at higher prices than during the years immediately following the Great Recession.

But let's face it, the developed world is not going to be able to inflate itself all of the way out of legacy indebtedness, for all the reasons discussed in this book. And what that means is that we need to finally get serious about restructuring the debts of households and financial institutions.

Why is this so important? Because today's huge private burden—with U.S. household debt still at 105 percent of household income (having peaked at 130 percent in 2007)—is a major drag on the economy.[1] In fact, other than underemployment, there is no greater dampener on consumption than too much debt. If you're making a $2,000 payment every month on an underwater home that you couldn't afford in the first place, chances are you don't have a lot of walking-around money. You'd be able to spend more on goods and services if someone waved a magic wand and suddenly you were only paying $1,200 a month on a mortgage that reflected your home's true value.

The private-debt overhang differs from one developed country to the next, concentrated to varying degrees from one region to the next among households, businesses, and financial institutions. But the common thread for all developed nations is the inability to grow or inflate themselves out of legacy indebtedness. Other solutions are required, and it is foolish to follow the experience of the Japanese, who waited a dozen years from the end of their bubble in late 1989 to tackle their unresolved overhang. It is time to take the losses and move on.

I know, of course, that this is easier said than done. Few issues have proven more nettlesome for the Obama administration than tackling the problem of underwater homes and helping people avoid foreclosure and renegotiate their mortgages. While the administration has been famously timid and slow in this crucial area, it's also true that the magnitude and complexity of the problem is daunting—with millions of U.S. homes underwater and a byzantine maze of paperwork behind many of those troubled mortgages.

The deeper problem, though, is that "resolving" legacy debt means that somebody is going to lose a lot of money. And when it comes to devalued U.S. homes, that somebody is the banking system as well as investors in private mortgage-backed securities and, of course, the U.S. taxpayer as de facto guarantor of mortgage-backed securities issued with the guarantee of newly government-owned Fannie Mae and Freddie Mac, and the FHA.

But if political courage is one obvious ingredient to resolve the legacy-debt overhang, we also need new approaches.

THE DEBT CALCULUS

One of the most underappreciated consequences of cheap-money policies is the superlow cost to financial institutions of holding underwater or distressed assets (loans and securities). As a result, it makes more sense for institutions to bet on the future recovery in asset values than to cut losses and liquidate those assets. Meanwhile, the lack of other appealing places to invest capital nowadays is all the more reason to hang on to "legacy" assets (those still on the books from pre-crisis days) and hope—however fantastically—they someday will be worth more money. There's just not a big downside to this strategy. Why clean up a toxic-waste site when, just maybe, it will clean itself up?

So, for example, if a lender holds a large pile of $100 billion in underperforming investments on its books that, let's say, it has marked down to $80 billion, but can't be sold in quantity without depressing their value to $60 billion, it has an incentive to wait to sell. But that incentive is offset by its cost of carrying the assets until they recover in value or can at least be sold for what they are being carried at ($80 billion) to avoid further losses. If the bank's cost of capital to carry the assets is, say, 2 percent, then each year that the assets are generating 2 percent in income, the bank can hold the assets indefinitely at almost no net cost other than the overhead to manage them.

Even if the assets aren't paying much at all, the bank can hold the assets for a decade at a 2 percent cost of funds and avoid the day of reckoning with a $60 billion valuation. An institution is certainly going to hold on to an asset if it believes that there is a decent chance markets will recover and the asset will rise in value.

But let's look at what would happen if we didn't live in the age of ZIRP, with banks borrowing money for nearly free. Let's say a bank's cost of funds is 6 percent per annum (which would be more normal in a growing, healthy, non-ZIRP economy) and the loan is paying nothing. Well, the bank could hold the assets for three years at an aggregate cost of 18 percent and end up with almost double the $20 billion loss it would take today by selling if values did not improve. That's quite an incentive to cut losses and liquidate today.

This is yet another dark side of aggressive monetary easing. It's an aspect no one talks about, but it has a big effect on the real economy. Not only are we buried under a pile of household debt that puts a huge drag on growth, but we are buried under debts that banks don't have any incentive to resolve as long as money is so cheap. The only way out of the mess is to true it up—to take the loss and settle accounts, with the debtor losing what he has to lose and the creditor recovering only what is there today to recover, and freeing the debtor from the remaining burden. This is what happens in corporate bankruptcies. No hand-wringing about moral hazard and other such canards, just cut the most equitable arrangement available and move on.

But in the case of mortgage debt in the United States and some countries in Europe, and in the case of the sovereign debt of the GIIPS of the Eurozone, there has been no resolution, no moving on. And the reasons are actually quite simple. In the United States, individuals cannot discharge mortgage debt in bankruptcy—a sop to the mortgage-lending industry. And in the Eurozone we have highly leveraged banks operating amid the continued fear of an entire currency (and political regimes) falling to pieces, a fear that apparently is held by currency-oppressed debtors as much as it is their creditors, perhaps arising out of the horrible experience of a Europe at war. But none of these reasons are good reasons for inaction and stagnation.

I'm no stranger to this problem of the debt overhang. Robert Hockett, Nouriel Roubini, and I tried to tackle the challenge in "The Way Forward" in October 2011.[2] More recently, I've worked with government policy makers on a hands-on way to resolve the problem of underwater homes. So here, let me lay out the plan we proposed in "The Way Forward"—steps that are still needed today, with some updates.

In setting the context of the debt challenge in "The Way Forward," we argued that, as a practical matter, there are only four solutions to an unsustainable debt problem:

> One. Strong economic growth can make debt sustainable; but growth in advanced economies will remain anemic as long as there is a need to delever.
>
> Two. Net debt can be reduced by increasing savings; but Keynes's paradox of thrift suggests that if consumers and governments simultaneously spend less and save more, the

resulting recession and contraction of GDP will simply render the original debt unsustainable again. A macroeconomy cannot "save its way out of recession."

Three. Unexpected inflation can wipe out the real value of private and public debts and avoid debt deflation. But inflation can also result in substantial collateral damage and, in any case, is nearly impossible to engineer when an economy is in a deflationary liquidity trap, as is the case today.

Four. If an economy cannot (i) grow, (ii) save, or (iii) inflate itself out of an excessive debt problem, then the only solution remaining is (iv) debt restructuring: reduction and/or conversion into equity. This is widely recognized to be true for businesses but it is just as true for governments, households, and banks and other financial institutions.

In order to avoid a sustained period of debt deflation because of a massive debt overhang, it is imperative to trim back, refinance, and restructure the overhang itself. That is the only way to avoid multiple decades of a debt-deflationary slump such as Japan has endured since the early 1990s. Moreover, in cases involving a credit-fueled asset price bubble that was no more foreseen by debtors than by creditors, equitable burden sharing is as fair as it is necessary.

A creditor's interest lies in maximizing recovery on loans that are not otherwise fully collectible. In other words, banks and other financial institutions that hold mortgage and other impaired loans would like to maximize the net present values of loans that cannot fully perform. Debtors, for their part, seek to eliminate as much of the burden as possible. The problem, however, is that multiple creditors of individual debtors notoriously face collective-action problems of their own when it comes to designing workable arrangements that will benefit all while maximizing value. That is precisely why the United States, like other developed nations, has a bankruptcy code. Unfortunately, the U.S. Bankruptcy Code is weak where real estate is concerned: mortgaged primary residences are generally excluded from bankruptcy courts' consideration and intervention. Recent proposals in Congress to amend the bankruptcy code accordingly warrant careful consideration.

While that decision is pending, however, we offer complementary and much more streamlined measures of our own.

Regardless of the relative benefit of debtor/creditor settlement and how that benefit might be most efficiently obtained, one overriding fact remains. Creditors must recognize some loss of capital connected to restructurings. But some banks and other financial institutions may not have adequately provided for that eventuality and/or for the amount of the loss involved. This is the case for financial institutions in the United States and Europe that hold loan portfolio assets involving households, commercial real estate owners, and certain sovereign nations that are unable to repay or even service their debts, given economic conditions over the foreseeable future.

Not a heck of a lot has changed since we published "The Way Forward" in the fall of 2011.

After setting the context, the report then laid out a plan for the resolution of the mortgage overhang in the United States—which today is still massive, with nearly 20 percent of mortgaged homes remaining underwater and some five million borrowers in default or seriously delinquent. But we prefaced our plan with the caveat that our proposals were drafted with an eye toward minimizing possible moral hazard, noting: "That risk is undeniably present, in potential at least, in both (a) any offer of settlement of a debt for less than the amount owed and (b) any regulatory forbearance with respect to delayed recognition of losses. We have therefore carefully crafted our proposals to avoid the prospect of any "free lunch," while also weighing the risk of moral hazard against the relative macroeconomic benefits and costs of debt reduction. Under our proposals, the parties to the suggested remediation must work for whatever benefit they are afforded, either by forgoing certain other rights or by agreeing to a conservative regime of financial, legal, and/or accounting requirements." Our plan was—we believed and continue to believe—fair, equitable, and in the best interest of all parties. Yet neither it, nor anything like it, was attempted. We suggested a three-part approach:

First, we proposed bridge loan assistance for mortgagors in temporary distress. A sizable fraction of mortgagors now facing difficulty in remaining current on mortgage debt payments are distressed only temporarily, through no fault of their own but simply because they are underemployed in the current recession. Their mortgages are not underwater and their capacity to pay is not permanently impaired. Because most mortgagors are found to be in default after as little as sixty days' delinquency on mortgage payments, foreclosure on these borrowers' loans is needlessly costly to lenders and tragic for borrowers.

Furthermore, federal programs like the Home Affordable Modification Program (HAMP) and the Home Affordable Refinance Program (HARP), which cost the government many thousands of dollars per mortgage to administer and induce lenders to forgo portions of what they are owed, are much more expensive than necessary when employed on behalf of this class of mortgagors. All that these people need are temporary bridge loans. But, of course, under current economic conditions, they can't get such loans. Private lenders are leery about "throwing good money after bad." Bridge loan assistance programs, which afford temporary payment assistance to distressed mortgagors—typically for no more than twenty-four to thirty-six months—have accordingly proved very effective and virtually cost-free in the few states that have tried them.

A noteworthy case in point is Pennsylvania's Home Emergency Mortgage Assistance Program (HEMAP), on the books since 1983, which dramatically outperforms the federal HAMP and HARP programs. Other states, such as Connecticut, Delaware, and Nevada, have instituted counterpart programs of their own. There is no reason not to adopt such a program at the national level for those current HAMP and HARP beneficiaries who require only temporary bridge loan assistance.

Second, we proposed reducing the principal on certain mortgages where home owners are underwater. These mortgages comprise a big part of today's debt overhang and are a drag on the housing market and the economy broadly. The only real solution here is to bring outstanding loan balances more closely into line with home values.

A host of studies demonstrates that unless principal reductions meaningfully reduce loan amounts to a level at or quite near the value of underlying home collateral, and unless payments are affordable, loan modifications are ultimately more likely to fail than to succeed. One challenge to principal reductions to date, however, has been the perceived moral hazard entailed by partial debt forgiveness. So in order to minimize the potential for moral hazard that might be occasioned by affording borrowers "something for nothing," we proposed that lender debt forgiveness should be coupled with equivalent cooperation from borrowers. In other words, principal reduction will be required to be earned in the form of proven loan performance on restructured mortgage loans.

We called this idea contingent principal reduction. To add an additional layer of prudence to the plan, we proposed that contingent principal reduction plans should be limited to homes with mortgages that are deeply underwater—that is, with first and second mortgages combined that exceed 110 percent of the value thereof. A 10 percent underwater measure is both simply administrable and appropriately in sync with what research shows to be realistic repayability.

Finally, we put forward new ideas around deed surrender and the right to rent. As noted above, a third subclass of borrowers will inevitably have suffered such extreme economic dislocation and/or deflation in the value of their homes that the degree of loan principal reduction required to stabilize loans and avoid enormous losses renders the contingent principal reduction plan infeasible. These are the people who should have never bought their homes in the first place and could do so only because lenders were making loans to anyone with a pulse.

The way to address this third segment of the debt overhang problem, we argued, is to keep them in their homes but shift from mortgage to rent payments.

This idea drew on a *New York Times* op-ed I published in October 2008 proposing what I called the Freedom Recovery Plan, which laid out a plan for home owners to voluntarily surrender the deeds to their homes in exchange for the right to rent them back from their lenders for a period of five years.[3] The leased homes would then be sold by the lenders to investors; and I laid out a slew of tax and regulatory policy suggestions to help banks cope with the losses and to give incentives to investors in such homes. The focus of this and other similar plans was to keep people in their homes.

Ironically, a robust single-family rental investment market developed in the United States beginning in 2012, but it focused on throwing people out of their homes through foreclosure and finding new tenants to occupy them. So far, that market has absorbed perhaps a hundred thousand or so liquidated foreclosures. But there are literally millions more to come, as noted above. Must we continue to throw millions of people out of their homes, with all of the attendant social and civic disruption this entails? Of course not.

Unfortunately, the first Obama administration did not see things the way I (and others) saw them. In late 2012 and early 2013 there was some greater recognition by the federal government of the need for a solution to the debt overhang, initially from the Federal Reserve Bank and subsequently from the Treasury and the White House. A good deal of this new attention was instigated by the activities of a rump coalition organized by a company I advised, Mortgage Resolution Partners (MRP) in San Francisco. MRP developed a strategy to permit local governments to seize underwater mortgages within their borders and force the issue of principal write-downs. Not surprisingly, the mortgage industry became highly incensed at this notion, accusing MRP of everything from unconstitutional to "communist" behavior. The matter has still not been resolved, but there has been some support from regulators in Washington and, with the problem still severe in any number of cities and counties, despite interim improvements in home prices, the local government-led resolution of the 10 million underwater mortgages still outstanding in the United States remains an option very much on the table.

EUROZONE DEBT

As for the problems in the Eurozone, I have covered much already on the need for a combination of far more substantial debt reductions or term extensions for the peripheral nations. I have also already noted that some nations may need to leave the zone in order to achieve rebalancing relative to the core nations (or, as is increasingly more accurate, relative to Germany). Such an outcome, or anything with similar effect, will invariably fall squarely on the shoulders of the creditor nations of Europe and greatly impact the broader European banking system.

That system is, I am afraid, at the present time a bit of a sham. Large banks throughout the core of the Eurozone are undercapitalized and some of them may prove to be insolvent. And that is to say nothing of the banks of the periphery which, absent accounting and cross-your-heart-and-pray valuation chicanery, are pretty much insolvent across the board. On top of problems in the private banking system are the imbalances in the EMU's central banking system. The Eurozone has been keeping cash flowing among its nations' banks through the TARGET2 system of national central bank debits and credits, clearing through the European Central Bank. As one can imagine, the Bundesbank is owed a lot of money and its internal balance sheet would be seriously exposed if the Eurozone splinters at some point.

None of this is sustainable over the long haul and European growth is stymied by wave after wave of debt crises followed by temporary fixes, while the underlying legacy of the European credit bubble—the debt in the periphery and the imbalances between the periphery and the core—continues to go unresolved. The wealthy nations of Europe know that, as presently capitalized, their banks (private and central) cannot absorb further losses. In Spain and elsewhere, banks are sitting on hundreds of billions of euros of underwater real estate and household debt that they have not adequately provisioned for or written down.

Again, the prognosis is not favorable in Europe for growth that is anywhere near sufficient to resolve these problems through inflation and attrition. And such growth as is occurring in the Eurozone is occurring in the wrong places—in the creditor and not the debtor nations. It is a nightmare.

The governments of Europe and their central bank, the ECB, seem bereft of solutions that can actually end the pain. All they have been doing with their alphabet soup of initiatives is to toss around the credit problem with the bizarre outcome of seeing near-defaulting nations severally (but not jointly, mind you) guarantee rescue facilities that are set up to bear the credit risk they themselves are experiencing. The litany of initiatives in the Eurozone, even the July 2012 promise by ECB head Mario Draghi to "do whatever it takes" to save the euro, can have no real chance at success if all that is happening is hoping for growth that won't come and praying that a recession won't intervene and set off even deeper panic.

And all this in a world awash in capital. There are responsible and prudent things that can be done, however. Europe's stronger private financial institutions should be raising piles of equity—"whatever it takes"—to shore themselves up against the prospect of additional losses. Germany's best bet right now is to take advantage of its respected credit before something changes to alter the status quo, to jointly guarantee with all the other creditworthy Eurozone nations (and the poor ones, too, but that's just for show) Eurobonds to be issued not only to grant relief to those countries in the periphery that cannot refinance existing debt (other than at economy-crushing interest rates) but also to establish a present-day "Marshall Plan" to rebuild the periphery and to provide financing to their own companies seeking to take advantage of doing business in cheaper areas of the Eurozone.

Finally, and most important, Europe needs a short-term disaggregation plan—of the type suggested by myself and others over the past two years—pursuant to which the debtor nations beset with massive underemployment and failing economies would withdraw from the Eurozone proper and adopt a "euro B" currency, administered by the ECB, with a pegged exchange into the existing euro, "euro A." Such a plan would set that peg at "whatever it takes" to make those economies competitive again (starting, perhaps, around 70 percent of the euro A), and then gradually adjusting the peg over time as imbalances are rectified by a relocation of production and jobs to the presently distressed nations. Debts of the distressed nations would become payable in euro B, which would provide de facto debt relief, while creditors receiving the euro B in payment would be rooting for growth in the periphery and the upgrading of the peg over time. And when the euro B is back to parity with the euro A, we can finally put the whole comedy of errors behind us and Europe can finally embrace a monetary *and fiscal* transfer union without the threat of future imbalances.

Yes, Germany will lose the benefit of a mercantilism it should not have benefited from in the first place had the EMU been more than a premature monetary union. But they will also benefit—as will all other nations—from dramatically increased consumption by their presently moribund cousins and will leg into the mutually responsible union that appeals so much to the German sense of right and wrong. And instead of financing consumption in the periphery (as they were, leading up to the crisis), they will be financing investment in the periphery that their own firms will reap rewards from. They will be doing much as Japanese companies did with investments in the emerging nations of

Asia—transferring production to lower-wage nations and reaping the benefits.

Nobody likes to lose money. And nobody wants to admit that underwater assets won't eventually recover their value as good times return. So don't expect the overhang to go away by itself. We need brave and creative public policies to deal with these debt issues. Equally important, we need to move this problem to the front burner and push political leaders to give it the time and political capital it requires.

Resolving the legacy debts of the boom years is a bit like clearing minefields after a war. Too often, as we know, armies never get around to demining and leave buried explosives set to go off for years to come, making real security uncertain for anyone nearby.

If we just try to move on, the legacy debts will keep holding us back. Better to deal with this challenge now, and endure sharp pain, than to endure years of persistent low-level pain and eventually have to tear off the bandage anyway. Just ask the Japanese.

CHAPTER 12

REBUILD AND REFORM

A Strategy for Restoring Growth

I believe in the power of free markets and the private sector to solve big problems, spearhead prosperity, and make the world a better place. If I didn't, I would not have spent the past few decades as an investment banker working with a wide range of companies.

But markets can't solve all our problems in every situation. And there are moments when the private sector is incapable of jump-starting prosperity by itself. We are in one of those moments now.

The beauty of the market is the way that it channels and harnesses the power of an endless array of individual actors to produce astonishing innovation and wealth. Sometimes, though, what we actually need to tackle a big challenge is a planned and collective effort. This is the case today when it comes to restoring economic growth in the United States and other developed nations.

Yes, I know that the word "collective" is associated with socialism and is highly charged in some circles. But, go ahead, bring it on! I am neither a socialist nor a utopian idealist of any color. I am a pragmatic realist who has devoted much of his career to finding novel solutions to financial challenges, and I've done so only by thinking outside the box. And thinking outside the box is exactly what is needed to overcome the deep systemic problems of today's global economy.

To be sure, there's been a lot of outside-the-box thinking already since the crisis began. We've had eye-popping bailouts, government takeovers of private companies, and unprecedented actions by central banks. And while the most dramatic steps have been in the sphere of monetary policy, policy makers have also pushed the envelope in the fiscal realm—enacting the largest fiscal stimulus ever in the United States and channeling vast new resources to the renewable-energy sector, as Michael Grunwald detailed in his book *The New New Deal*.[1]

I favored many of those steps. Ultimately, though, these actions have not addressed the underlying cause of our problems—the rise of oversupply and the policy failures that accompanied that trend. We have succeeded in treating some of the symptoms while hoping that the disease will run its course swiftly, or will at least go into remission for a time.

Even in cases of serious illness, there are periods of hope when the patient rallies and it seems there may be a chance to avoid surgery or other dramatic interventions. Too often, though, the patient not only remains encumbered by the disease, he also remains vulnerable to new illnesses by virtue of his weakened state.

And so it is with the developed economies of the world five years after the financial crisis. We have treated the obvious symptoms, done our best to ignore others, and remain vulnerable to many more. If it's not a Eurozone meltdown, then it's a slowdown in the emerging markets, causing them to stimulate more production in an overproducing world. If it's not a dysfunctional government or a fiscal cliff (or one of its many equivalents) then it's a once-in-a-century storm knocking out the east coast of the United States. And let's not even speak of another dramatic terrorist strike on a large developed nation. We all know—we all feel—that we remain vulnerable in our present state to any number of challenges—and that we have few tools left with which to meet them.

Remaining vulnerable should not be acceptable, especially when we actually have tools available to treat the disease of insufficient aggregate demand in a world of oversupply of labor, productive capacity, and capital.

That some of the solutions I will describe in the pages ahead make use of collective action should be of no greater concern to readers than would the use of our most powerful collective agency—our military forces—in times of war. For make no mistake: the outcomes of today's global economic competition will determine the developed world's level of prosperity, and ultimately our freedom of action as citizens, as much as any war would. And one reason this competition has turned so fierce is because emerging nations—especially China—have employed an aggressive form of state-guided capitalism. They believe deeply in collective action and that government can and should play a big role in setting long-term geoeconomic strategy.

Of course, using the muscular collective capacity of government to tackle huge and historic challenges is hardly a foreign notion to the nations of the advanced world. We may have forgotten some of the details and methods, but the record is extensive. During the eighteenth and nineteenth centuries, Europe's governments accumulated empires within which private interests could thrive. The United States harnessed state power to open and manage vast territories and build railroads and other infrastructure to unite a nation. Japan's government coordinated its industry to recover from World War II and become the wildly thriving "Japan Inc." of the 1970s and 1980s.

We have acted in bold, collective ways before. We can do so again in the face of a challenge—the emergence of two billion new, eager, and ambitious capitalist workers into competition with workers of the advanced nations—that easily equals many of the big challenges of the past.

Whether doing nothing will result in decades of slow stagnation/deflation, as it has in Japan, or will precipitate a new, acute crisis makes little difference. We find ourselves "fighting the last war" with ordnance that is appropriate to stimulating supply but not to dealing with our present oversupply in the face of insufficient demand. Our economic artillery is bogged down in muddy fears of government spending, fears of the markets, and by scolds calling for very harmful forms of government austerity at a time when taking pragmatic, collective action is the only option available to us that will do more good than harm.

So what, exactly, should we be doing? In the pages that follow, I discuss three big and bold tasks we need to undertake. And fast.

PUTTING EXCESS LABOR BACK TO WORK

By 2013, the developed world began to recognize the folly of austerity policy. The Japanese elected a pro-stimulus government and protests and elections in Europe rejected contractionary government policies. In the United States, which never really pursued austerity, a series of budget battles—while at times threatening broad cuts—has resulted in relatively harmless contraction. For all the hyperventilating over automatic sequestration cuts, these cuts—$85 billion a year—are relatively minor in the context of the $16 trillion U.S. economy.

But recognizing the false promises of austerity policy is not the same as the adoption of expansionary policy that may involve additional government spending. To reach the economic escape velocity needed to rebalance the advanced economies—both vis-à-vis the emerging economies, with respect to trade, and within the developed nations themselves, with respect to the diffusion of wealth and income—there is simply no other engine more powerful than a collectively ignited engine with government in the lead.

In the age of oversupply, the prospects are dim for the private sector investing in job-creating new capacity. Sure, some service jobs will be created to sell and implement technologies that create better ways of getting things done, but other jobs will be destroyed by those same technologies. The problem, as I have said throughout this book, is insufficient aggregate demand relative to an overabundance of supply. Human labor is presently the world's most overabundant resource—just look at the two billion not-yet-urbanized peoples of the emerging world and the low employment-to-population ratios in the advanced nations.

Yet when it comes to revitalization of infrastructure, advanced nations are lagging and threaten to fall behind their new competitors. And infrastructure development and redevelopment is both a massive employer and—given that I drive on bridges that are a hundred years old as things stand today—represent long-term investment in the productive future of nations. With money as cheap as it is, and secondary benefits abounding from the domestic sourcing of materials, a full-blown redevelopment program in advanced nations is called for.

So it is without reservation that I repeat the exhortation Robert Hockett, Nouriel Roubini, and I made in "The Way Forward" in 2011 to undertake a historic investment in infrastructure. The plan we laid out focused on the United States, but similar programs are appropriate for other developed regions.

Specifically, we called for a $1.2 trillion, five-year public investment program targeting high-return investment in energy, transportation, education, research and technology development, and water-treatment infrastructure. Today, two years later, that level of spending still makes sense—all the more so because the highest and most persistent U.S. unemployment is among construction workers, at least 15 percent of whom remain jobless years after the crash of the housing sector, according to the Bureau of Labor Statistics.

Meanwhile, it is no secret that U.S. public infrastructure is in shambles and is rapidly deteriorating. You can see this everywhere, certainly in the state of New York, where I live. According to the American Society of Civil Engineers (ASCE), New York has more than 2,000 bridges that are structurally deficient, and its roads and highways are so beat up that motorists spend $4.5 billion a year in extra vehicle repairs and operating costs resulting simply from road use. The state's drinking water and waste treatment systems are also falling apart, and the ASCE estimates that $50 billion needs to be spent on these systems over the next 20 years. Neighboring New Jersey is in some ways even worse off.[2]

All told, the ASCE estimates that the United States must spend $2.2 trillion on infrastructure over the next five years to meet the country's most basic infrastructure needs. But that is less than half the money that is currently budgeted, which leaves an approximately $1.2 trillion shortfall. These repairs and improvements need to be done eventually. Why not now?

A multiyear program to upgrade infrastructure would not only put armies of people to work, but would also make the economy more productive and efficient in the long term. For instance, reviving the new rail tunnel under the Hudson River that was abandoned in 2010 would not only create thousands of jobs, but also save millions of hours in commuting time in coming decades and ensure greater labor mobility between employment opportunities in New York City and northern New Jersey—to say nothing of cutting emissions from the thousands of automobiles and buses currently making the trip.

Money spent on infrastructure has well-known multiplier effects on the economy. The Congressional Budget Office has estimated that every dollar of infrastructure spending generates a $1.60 increase in GDP on average.[3] Some critical transportation and energy projects have even larger multiplier effects. Even better, though, is that infrastructure spending *directly* creates jobs, as opposed to tax cuts or other cash transfers where the multiplier effects on job growth are entirely indirect. Also, such spending can be directed to places where unemployment is highest. New Jersey, with badly deteriorating infrastructure and an unemployment rate over 9 percent—among the highest in the nation—would be a great target of such spending. Over the course of five years, a national $1.2 trillion infrastructure program would create more than five million jobs.

Another major benefit of a big new infrastructure program is that it would increase U.S. competitiveness. According to reports by the World Economic Forum and other groups, the United States lags behind more than a dozen other countries in the quality of its infrastructure. A variety of infrastructure bottlenecks—traffic-choked roads, clogged ports, an antiquated air transportation system, and an unreliable electrical grid—are costing our economy billions in lost income and growth.[4] The Department of Transportation, for example, reports that freight bottlenecks cost the American economy $200 billion a year—the equivalent of more than 1 percent of GDP. And the Federal Aviation Administration estimates that air traffic delays cost the economy $32.9 billion a year. Perhaps even more worrying, there is growing evidence that uncertainties about the future reliability of our energy, water, and transportation systems are creating obstacles to investment in some parts of the country and thus impeding new business investment. The American Society of Civil Engineers estimates that the economic cost of infrastructure deficiencies will rapidly escalate in coming decades.

All this stands in stark contrast with the behavior of top U.S. competitors. China, for example, invests 9 percent of GDP per annum in public infrastructure, while the United States spends well less than 3 percent. China understands that public infrastructure investment makes private investment more efficient and more competitive globally by eliminating many of the bottlenecks mentioned above and by lowering the cost of transportation, electricity, and other core business expenses.

Infrastructure investment is also essential to the development of new growth industries. For instance, fully developing America's wind and solar potential—a big creator of jobs already—requires an expensive overhaul of the U.S. electrical grid.

A crash program to upgrade U.S. infrastructure in coming years wouldn't just produce a variety of economic benefits, it would also save money over the long term. Deteriorating infrastructure is subject to "cost acceleration" wherein repair or replacement costs grow over time. A project that costs $5 million or $6 million to repair now may cost upwards of $30 million to repair merely two years from now. Since most of these projects will need to be undertaken at some point, the question is literally not whether but when. Not to undertake them now would be to leave money on the table. Combine this consideration with the fact that labor and capital may never be cheaper than they are now, with interest rates at historic lows and unemployment of construction workers near an all-time high.

The detailed plan I put forward with Hockett and Roubini gave considerable attention to the efficiency of such an investment program. Among analysts of economic stimulus, a major concern is over what is known as "leakage." Leakage occurs when stimulus is overly broad (monetary stimulus fits into this category) and it benefits those outside of the country that is doing the economic stimulating. Another form of leakage is tax breaks to corporations and individuals, to the extent that the breaks, in the case of tax breaks to multinational companies, result in non-domestic investment or expansion or, in the case of tax breaks to individuals, either end up in the pockets of the wealthy (who have little propensity to add to their consumption) or increase domestic consumption of foreign-made goods.

We felt it was critical in 2011—and I continue to feel it is even more critical today—that fiscal stimulus in the age of oversupply be (a) directed primarily at increasing domestic employment as opposed to merely stimulating the theoretical economic activity that would, in another era, have led to job creation, and (b) as economically efficient as possible, in both limiting overhead and procuring goods and labor at market clearing (not subsidized) prices, notwithstanding that such procurement is being done exclusively domestically. Both things are not only logical, but very achievable.

Our 2011 plan emphasized high-return strategic investments in energy, transportation, and communications to eliminate economic bottlenecks and restore productivity, complemented by labor-intensive investments in energy efficiency (retrofitting homes, offices, and public buildings) to maximize job creation. As well, it called for the establishment of a national infrastructure bank, the expanded use of existing public-purpose credit facilities, and the use of existing bond issuance authority in order to maximize investment at the lowest possible cost to the taxpayer.

And there is more. We also proposed tapping private-capital markets additionally through issuance of reconstruction bonds by an agency established to fund and operate major public works programs constructed under the auspices of the Directorate of Civil Works of the U.S. Army Corps of Engineers (USACE), mostly through private-sector contracting. The USACE is already the world's largest construction project manager and has capabilities that exceed those of any individual private firm. While the USACE subcontracts a good deal of work to the private sector, it represents a nationally available existing overhead that does not require duplication by or within the private sector to implement an infrastructure plan.

So our plan called for the expansion of the Directorate of Civil Works of the USACE to act as project manager and general contractor of last resort in order to limit private-sector overbidding and labor union dominance—to exhort both labor and private businesses to either build at a fair price, or risk having the Army Corps build it themselves.

"The Way Forward" also advocated the streamlining and the speeding up of the environmental impact review process and the suspension of Davis-Bacon Act–era wage laws, which currently impact federally sponsored construction projects and those of many states as well. These important suggestions were not well received by many progressives, but are among the necessary elements of a targeted program aimed at the reemployment of millions with taxpayer support. To do otherwise would be unconscionable from the standpoint of governments' responsibilities to their taxpaying citizens.

Finally, our plan called for offering multinational businesses the opportunity to fully repatriate profits from abroad with no additional taxation on a dollar-for-dollar basis for all investments in the above-mentioned reconstruction bonds. Over a trillion dollars of unutilized private-sector corporate cash is "stranded" in offshore subsidiaries and affiliates, for tax purposes. Much is made of giving corporations tax breaks on repatriating these funds, as though doing so would definitely see those funds invested domestically. But recent history has told us that excess corporate cash is far more likely to find its way into dividends or stock buybacks for shareholders and acquisitions of smaller businesses by larger corporations (the latter of which often sees a reduction in jobs). But allowing companies a full tax break in exchange for long-term investment in infrastructure redevelopment at today's prevailing low interest rates would be a winner for all.

Hockett, Roubini, and I estimated that the proposed five-year $1.2 trillion program would produce the following returns on investment:

- A 7 percent total uplift in GDP during each year the program is in effect (i.e., it would boost the current prevailing GDP level of about $15 trillion to around $16 trillion).
- An additional 5.52 million jobs over the five-year program, many of which would result in new-skills training for lesser-skilled workers.
- Productivity and efficiency gains as improved infrastructure reduces travel times as well as cost and frequency of remedial maintenance, resulting in increased flow rates for people, products, power, and information throughout the economy.
- Substantially lower private and public costs and a higher quality of life, including less pollution, lower energy costs, faster commute times, fewer traffic casualties, cleaner drinking water, and better educational facilities.
- The expansion of public capital (assets) and higher future tax revenues due to the economy's increased economic growth potential.
- Reduction of the long-term federal government deficit because of higher tax revenues and lower government income-support program costs that result from higher economic growth and lower unemployment.

Yes, this would be a huge undertaking, and a costly one. But these are unique times. Five years after the financial crisis, the developed world has been unable to grow or inflate its way beyond the debilitating legacy of the Great Credit Bubble. The answer is not yet more attempts to induce demand through even more debilitating credit extension. It is through bold, direct efforts to employ the millions of Americans (and Europeans) who now sit at home idly; to create jobs that are productive for the economy and society. Now is the time for such investment, when the cost of public borrowing to create jobs is absurdly low and fixed for long terms.

If developed nations can dramatically increase labor utilization, and hence aggregate demand, they can stabilize the deflationary forces presently bearing down on wages from both global and post-bubble factors. The plain fact is that creating millions of jobs by borrowing cheaply to fund positive-return investments in public infrastructure is the least costly way of increasing aggregate demand within the borders of developed nations. Period.

And with an increase in aggregate demand, the pattern of reliance on credit-induced overconsumption by each employed individual can finally be reversed, making room for an increase in household savings and stability and slowing the insidious pace of wealth and income polarization.

As I have noted previously, the private sector can't, won't, and shouldn't be the driver of such mass labor reutilization. That would be asking far too much of private interests in an age of oversupply. I certainly would not do it with my own money. It is not in the interest of the private sector to underwrite the costs of public goods, other than indirectly by paying taxes to a government that can furnish such goods at the lowest possible capital costs. Yes, businesses do make their own investments in physical and operational infrastructure, but the scale of such investments is nothing compared to, say, rebuilding the thousands of bridges in the United States that are now in serious disrepair. Anyway, asking the private sector to risk capital to build "public goods" that will equally benefit all citizens of a given area is simply not realistic. The private market can do many things well. Rebuilding the nation's crumbling infrastructure is not one of them.

REMOVING OBSTACLES TO GLOBAL COMPETITIVENESS

It ever there was a time to reevaluate the competitiveness of our developed economies, that time is now.

Beyond major new investments in infrastructure—a key foundation of prosperity—there are four ways the developed world can make itself more competitive with emerging nations, other than the more painful route of wage and price deflation. First and second, the United States needs to reform its education and health-care sectors. Third, continental Europe and Japan need to become more business-friendly, removing obstacles to entrepreneurship and reducing the overprotection of labor. And fourth, the entire developed world needs to reduce its energy costs over the long term and turn this sector into a driver of growth and innovation.

Let's start with the problems of higher education and health care in the United States. In an earlier chapter I discussed the student-debt dilemma and the burden it is placing on young adults, many of whom can't find the jobs they need to handle their student-debt burdens—or which justify taking on such debt in the first place.

But this problem is about more than the impact on individuals: it's about competitiveness. In both higher education and health care, two giant and crucial sectors, normal market conditions aren't in place and we have deeply distorted pricing mechanisms. That's because a huge part of the tab for medical care is picked up by third-party payers—government and insurance companies—and something similar is true in higher education, with government heavily subsidizing the cost of college, and easy credit allowing students to kick their share of the actual costs of college down the line.

The United States has made important strides recently in confronting runaway health-care spending, with the Patient Protection and Affordable Care Act already slowing the rise in Medicare costs and a slew of experiments promulgated under that law possibly holding the key to far better cost containment in the future. But fundamental problems remain and make the U.S. health-care sector so costly that it undermines our competitiveness. Any number of actors in the U.S. health-care system—doctors, hospitals, insurance companies, drug and device makers—have strong financial incentives to develop better and costlier products and services and to get Americans to spend ever more on health care. Americans, meanwhile, have few disincentives to not keep voraciously consuming medical care—and wanting better care—since somebody else is typically picking up the tab.

Higher education is an even less hopeful story. We have seen student-loan debt just about double from $507 billion in 2007, at the beginning of the Great Recession, to over $1 trillion today. This is an unsustainable and dangerous trend.

The perverse functioning of the health-care and education sectors is both inefficient and a barrier to greater U.S. competitiveness. The sheer level of wasted wealth is mind-boggling, with a recent study by the Institute of Medicine estimating that thirty cents of every health-care dollar spent in the United States goes for unneeded procedures, excessive overhead, and other forms of waste.[5] That's hundreds of billions of dollars of national wealth that the United States is basically pouring down the drain every year. You don't see our leading competitors throwing away that kind of money.

The overspending on health care in the United States, now 17 percent of GDP, is particularly problematic at this moment of stalled growth, in that it channels money away from the pockets of those most likely to consume and toward those more likely to stash money away in stock portfolios and college savings accounts: hospital and insurance executives, shareholders of pharmaceutical companies, and other medical specialists.

From November 2007 to November 2012 the U.S. Consumer Price Index (CPI) grew at an average annual rate of 1.9 percent. Health care in the United States grew by 3.5 percent per annum (17 percent during the period) and higher-education tuition and fees grew by a whopping 5.8 percent per annum (29 percent during the period). Taken together, health care and higher education accounted for a full 0.3 percent of the 1.9 percent average annual increase in the overall CPI (meaning that the average annual CPI growth would have been only 1.6 percent during that period if health care and higher education were removed from the calculus).

There can be very little reason for these prices to continue rising but for the fact that there seems to be little resistance to increased costs on the demand side. I believe that this is due to a substantial bifurcation of user and payer. And addressing this disconnect must be a major focus of reform. Fortunately, efforts at such reform are moving ahead in both health care and higher education.

For example, there is a growing movement to push the U.S. health-care system away from today's fee-for-service system, whereby doctors have a financial incentive to provide more costly care. As the National Commission for Physician Payment Reform stated: "Physicians are paid more to perform more procedures and order more tests, instead of better overall care. . . . Physicians and patients continue to utilize high tech interventions that may or may not be necessary."

In early 2013, the commission released a report recommending that "over time, payers should largely eliminate stand-alone fee-for-service payment to medical practices because of its inherent inefficiencies and problematic financial incentives."[6] The Affordable Care Act helps move things in this direction in different ways, including by starting to channel more public health-care spending through programs such as Accountable Care Organizations (ACOs) and Patient-Centered Medical Homes, both of which do hinge on a fee-for-service model and instead reward providers who offer good health-care results at low costs.

Even if the United States can contain health-care costs through efforts like this, it will still be spending far more than its competitors on health care in coming years—in many cases twice as much a percentage of GDP. Ultimately, to be globally competitive, the United States will have to revisit the question of large-scale health-care reform and explore ways to offer quality universal care at a much lower cost. The United States remains the only major industrialized nation without some kind of universal national health-care regime.

At the very least, the United States should attempt to find consensus on a truly universal form of basic health care, taking advantage of the enormous purchasing and price-setting power of an expanded version of Medicare to ensure all of its citizens have access to basic medical services. This needn't be an overly costly program—to an extent, unnecessary/elective care has already begun to slow in the United States, so expanding the Affordable Care Act (the so-called Obamacare) to have premiums paid through the existing U.S. social-insurance infrastructure, and expanding Medicare to provide cradle-to-grave checkups and basic care for all Americans should really be a no-brainer.[7] It is simply inefficient for private-sector insurers to attempt to provide that coverage at a profit (and in many states, private basic care insurance and major medical insurance are not severable and must be bought as a package for that reason). The United States should then mandate that private insurers make available—and consumers either purchase voluntarily or are taxed to purchase on their behalf—stand-alone major medical coverage offering various levels of health-care security, from run-of-the-mill coverage for accidents and acute disease during working years all the way through coverage that incorporates all available treatments for extending life.

Sad as it may be to have to say this, if a person wants the option of receiving, for example, a heart transplant at age seventy-one (as former vice president Dick Cheney did in 2012), they would have to invest in coverage that would extend them that privilege. If they are content to exit life in a dignified manner if disease strikes at old age (30 percent of Medicare expenses occur during the final year of life), then they should have the option of paying less. Many people have signed "do not resuscitate" orders requiring medical professionals to allow a natural death in the event of, for example, heart stoppage. Why should those signing such standing orders pay the same for catastrophic or end-of-life health care as those who aren't so inclined? The United States and several other advanced nations provide the best health care available in the world but the inability of all to afford access to life-extending treatments should not be a reason that collective resources should not be marshaled in the United States to provide basic care to all citizens. The economic reasons for doing so are very hard to dispute. Relieving employees and employers of the need to carry basic insurance from the private sector, and having the cost of such care spread over the largest possible coverage pool (that is to say, everyone) will make the United States far more competitive with the rest of the world.

It may be wishful thinking to believe that what should happen in U.S. health care can actually be effectuated on a national level. The United States has some serious regional political differences that may make it impossible to accomplish what needs to be done. Well, the truth is that the United States needn't wait for the federal government to achieve consensus on this issue. Any state, or even a large municipality that has been granted taxing power by a state, could institute a strong single-payer regime that manages the risk of their entire population. From a competitiveness standpoint, I believe that would make any state adopting such a plan (health-care industry lobbyists be damned) extraordinarily attractive to employers because overall health-care costs would fall in that state or municipality. And perhaps that's the way this needs to happen—as have so many changes in the history of the United States. Eventually, states without such plans will be forced to come around.

I wish I had more time to cover the subject of health care in the United States, but this book is on global macroeconomics and, unfortunately, U.S. health-care problems are just a small part of the overall competitiveness problem faced by the advanced nations in the age of oversupply. But before leaving this subject I'd recommend taking a look at an excellent article—more of a twenty-six-thousand-word manifesto, really—by Steven Brill for *Time* in March 2013 entitled "Bitter Pill: Why Medical Bills Are Killing Us." I wish I could do justice to the topic here as well as Brill did in that piece, but I will leave you with his conclusion:

> We've created a secure, prosperous island [the health-care industry] in an economy that is suffering under the weight of the riches those on the island extract. And we've allowed those on the island and their lobbyists and allies to control the debate, diverting us from what Gerard Anderson, a healthcare economist at the Johns Hopkins Bloomberg School of Public Health says is the obvious and only issue: 'All the prices are too damn high.'[8]

The United States simply cannot afford to support Brill's islanders in the style to which they have become accustomed and also be globally competitive with other nations that provide health care to their populations (and good health care, mind you) far more efficiently.

Back to the issue of higher education: Americans now owe more in student loans than in credit card debt. (Indeed, outstanding credit card debt actually fell—through repayment and default—by around 15 percent). The number of student-loan borrowers, and average amounts outstanding therefrom, have risen by one-half and one-third, respectively, over the same period. There are more than 37 million Americans with student loan debt. Many of them are holding balances well into their working lives:

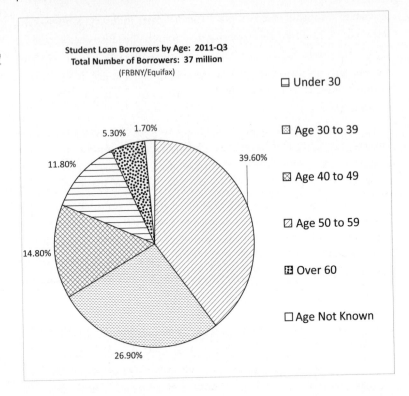

Student Loan Borrowers by Age: 2011-Q3
Total Number of Borrowers: 37 million
(FRBNY/Equifax)

- ☐ Under 30
- ▨ Age 30 to 39
- ⊠ Age 40 to 49
- ▧ Age 50 to 59
- ⊞ Over 60
- ☐ Age Not Known

There is every reason to think that the student debt balloon will keep inflating, as the huge millennial generation continues to pour into college. This balloon, moreover, bears a growing resemblance to the real estate bubble—especially as we learn more about the aggressive marketing practices of for-profit colleges. Just as the mortgage industry vacuumed in every potential borrower with a pulse, regardless of their creditworthiness, so too is the for-profit college industry pushing a higher education to anyone literate enough to sign the documents for a student loan. Dropout rates are extremely high at many colleges, with students who were unprepared for college walking away with plenty of debt but no degree. Like the unscrupulous mortgage brokers who got their commissions even if a home owner eventually defaulted, the for-profit colleges and student-loan companies have made a killing even as dropout rates have soared. Clearly, government grants to students, guarantees for student loans, and other subsidies have helped to inflate this latest balloon. Moral hazard goes to college, in effect. And with student-loan defaults mushrooming, government will pay out a growing fortune on borrowing backed up by federal guarantees. Reforming the two giant sectors of health care and higher education will take time. Meanwhile, the good news is that jobs in both sectors can't be outsourced and are relatively immune from direct competition.

Now let's turn to the question of how to unleash the power of business in Europe and Japan.

While continental Europe and Japan have fostered relatively harmonious societies with high living standards and less inequality than the United States or the United Kingdom, there are significant competitiveness issues to be addressed. I am willing to accept that cultures valuing internal harmony should treat their workers honorably. In this sense I am more impressed with Japanese labor statutes, which are not anywhere as detailed as those in the European Union. What one does as a matter of conscience or by cultural imperative is not for me to question.

But I do question the guild-like business licensing laws and extensive permit processes that can be found both in Japan and in certain countries of the European Union. They are anticompetitive and are in place to protect the established over the establishing. And such laws are just the tip of a bureaucratic iceberg.

Perhaps the best illustration of overregulation of businesses in Europe was written by my colleague, the Eurozone economics expert Megan Greene. Writing for Bloomberg about Greece in March 2012, she noted:

> One example of the bureaucracy involved in running an enterprise in Greece is a new bookstore-cafe I visited recently in Athens. The owner had spent almost a year jumping through the hoops required to open her business, now a month old. I ordered a coffee at the cafe and the waitress walked immediately over to the bar across the street to pick one up. Despite months of trying, the owner had been unable to get a license to make coffee on the premises. Shortly after, I watched a customer get turned away when she tried to purchase a book. It was 6:05 p.m., and it is illegal to sell books after 6 p.m. in Athens. I was in a bookstore-cafe that could neither make coffee nor sell books.[9]

I would submit that Greece has plenty of other problems with competitiveness and that eliminating these types of restrictions should be an obvious first step. But this is not just a problem for Greece; it prevails throughout much of the European Union and Japan.

As it happens, there are any number of proposals sitting on the shelves in both Europe and Japan for making those places more business friendly by clearing away red tape and aiding entrepreneurs. For instance, the EU recently published the "Entrepreneurship Action Plan," which includes detailed recommendations for how member states can foster start-ups through changes in tax codes, regulations, bankruptcy laws, and other steps to encourage hospitable "ecosystems" for new businesses.[10]

In recent years, various European countries have pushed forward with labor reforms intended to make it easier to hire and fire workers, and the Eurozone crisis has accelerated these efforts, particularly in southern Europe. Even French socialist president François Hollande has pledged to reform the rigid labor laws in that country, although he hasn't made much progress yet in creating the kind of flexible labor markets that employers in the United States take for granted.

Ensuring stable and moderate energy costs is another key challenge for the developed countries. High energy costs are a natural enemy of growth, because more money spent on electricity and fuel bills means less money going to produce goods and services. And spikes in energy prices—which can come in the wake of international crises—can derail or slow growth at crucial moments. Also, of course, imports of oil from energy-exporting countries contribute to trade deficits with those countries.

The good news here is the discovery of enormous reserves of shale gas (natural gas) throughout the North American continent and the perfection of technologies to extract it. As my Century Foundation cofellow, Charles R. Morris, wrote recently in his 2013 book, *Comeback: America's New Economic Boom,* this is a very big deal. Estimates by the U.S. Energy Information Administration (EIA) have run from "technically recoverable resources" of shale gas ranging from 141 trillion cubic feet to as high as 750 trillion cubic feet. According to Morris, the Bureau of Economic Geology at the University of Texas at Austin came up with a number about midway between the optimistic and pessimistic EIA assessments—approximately 450 trillion cubic feet. That's about 80 billion barrels of oil or about eight years' worth of the current oil production of Saudi Arabia.[11]

Morris has estimated that the cost of shale gas at the wellhead is currently about one-third to one-half the cost of energy-equivalent crude oil.

And if Europe can figure out a way to work around its own population density and legal issues, it is likely to be able to locate and exploit large reserves of shale gas as well (with similar promise elsewhere in the world). In any event, natural gas liquefaction technology is far enough along to permit the development of the infrastructure to extract and transport shale gas, which allows for the export of this surplus (although Morris cautions against focusing on export potential in the United States—something with which I agree). And the infrastructure to replace oil-consuming machinery (including autos) with natural-gas-burning engines will involve highly stimulative expenditures and employment for years.

More good news is that the natural-gas industry has been challenged by high levels of local concern about environmental issues surrounding contaminants from shale gas extraction—and this time, rather than spending all their time fighting with authorities and local populations, the industry has made some progress in the development of "fracking" (hydraulic fracturing) technologies that many of their former critics now concede are safe and responsible. Morris noted to me, however, that in implementing safe technologies, "the industry has so far done a poor job of it, and they need to raise their game a lot. There are no obstacles to their doing so except that they still mostly think like wildcatters."[12] I have every confidence this will change as economies of scale in the extraction industry are recognized and costs come down a bit.

Secondary benefits arising from the development of a far cheaper energy source will be the repatriation of a variety of industries (chemicals, steel production, and many other manufactures that are more energy-intensive than labor-intensive) away from the emerging nations and back to many of the present net energy-importing nations. Moreover, the burning of natural gas is by far cleaner environmentally than burning coal or oil. Already the shift to natural gas is reducing greenhouse gas emissions by the United States.

All of this, as Morris also points out, will require intelligent government policy. And I would contend that every opportunity to accelerate the process should be among our highest priorities. If President Kennedy in May 1961 could call for sending men 240,000 miles to the moon (and returning them, of course) within the decade of the 1960s and have the United States accomplish that feat a mere eight years later, certainly the development of an environmentally safe natural-gas industry can be similarly accelerated via collectively pragmatic policies.

Perhaps the most obvious of those policies would be the establishment of infrastructure to distribute and sell natural gas for use in motor vehicles. The technology for such use already exists. The United States already has a robust natural-gas pipeline system to move inventories around the nation. The problem is in the "last mile," to borrow a term from telecommunications. A national program to finance the retrofitting of every gas station in the country, with equipment made in the United States and installed by U.S. workers, would be at the top of my list for taking advantage of the opportunity to gain massive competitive advantage from this new bounty. To expect such investment to occur through economic parthenogenesis on an accelerated time frame is folly, and is also not how the United States has traditionally undertaken the introduction of major changes to its transportation infrastructure—from railroads to the Interstate Highway System to the Internet—all of which were jump-started by government infrastructure programs.

Ultimately, though, natural gas is best seen as a bridge to a carbon-free future in which a range of renewable energy technologies finally reach their potential and free developed countries from unreliable energy imports from some of the most volatile regions of the world.

Is this a pipe dream? Hardly. Germany has already made remarkable progress in shifting to non-carbon renewable energy, with a quarter of all its energy now generated by such sources, up from 6 percent in 2000. Germany has moved this quickly by enacting feed-in tariffs that mandate that electric-grid operators must buy a growing share of their power from renewable energy sources. Germany has spent heavily on scientific research into clean-energy technologies. Sweden is even further ahead of Germany in this area, now getting nearly half of its energy from renewable sources. Both countries are not only on the path to energy interdependence with stable prices, but have also created large job growth in their renewable-energy sectors. These are promising trends as the developed world looks for every possible opportunity to reduce its account deficits with emerging nations and generate jobs at home.

The United States has lagged in this shift to renewables, but it's not too late to catch up. Indeed, signs abound that the United States is getting more serious on this front. California now gets a fifth of its energy from renewable sources and is on track to up that to one third by 2020. Like Germany, it has used feed-in tariffs to speed progress and ensure a reliable market for producers of renewable energy.

Much more can be done, obviously, to accelerate renewable energy use in the United States. Feed-in tariffs are spreading to different states and municipalities, and new business models have emerged to speed up the residential use of solar power, with more companies offering to install panels on homes without any cost to home owners. In recent years, "green" jobs have been one of the fastest-growing sectors of employment in the United States.

Armies of policy wonks, politicians, and pundits are engaged in unending debate about the proper role of government. In truth, of course, there is no fixed answer to this question. The proper scope of collective action very much depends on the times. Some moments require a massive mobilization of resources (and willpower) through the public sector. Others call for a more limited government that clearly takes a backseat to a dynamic private sector. Probably even the most ardent New Dealers of the 1930s couldn't have imagined the size and power of the federal government at the height of World War II. And it made perfect sense, after that war, for Washington to again become a sleepy city under Dwight Eisenhower.

Today is one of those moments when we need bold and innovative governments—not powered by ideology nor permanent, but pragmatic, with a laser-like focus on bolstering economic demand in the short term and improving competitiveness over the longer term.

We have tackled this kind of challenge before. We can do so again.

CHAPTER 13

GOOD DEBT, BAD DEBT

Dealing with Deficits

After reading the last chapter, anyone who has read this far and is worried about deficits will surely hear alarm bells ringing.

Yes, it's true: I'm proposing that the U.S. government borrow more money to get the economy going again. Certain large European nations need to borrow, too. A new and much bigger push to juice up demand with public spending is not my only solution to the current mess, but it's a big one. And I'm well aware that any new pile of debt will be added to an already towering pile of debt that the United States and other developed countries have accumulated over the past few decades.

Is such borrowing really prudent? In a word, yes. The United States, particularly, can borrow trillions more without destabilizing its economy. What's more, I don't see any other choice if we want ultimately to avoid even bigger deficits down the line amid an endless slump, declining competitiveness, and a rapidly aging population.

To be sure, the United States eventually needs to tame its public-debt problem. But first it needs to fix its economy. So hear me out as I explain why bigger deficits are manageable until sufficient economic growth is obtained.

When we wrote "The Way Forward" in 2011, long-term borrowing rates had declined substantially from where they were at the beginning of that year. In the United States, the rates on 10-year and 30-year Treasury bonds declined by an average of 1.5 percent (or 150 basis points, as we in finance say) from the beginning of that year through the fall. Not long after we published the paper, the economists J. Bradford DeLong of the University of California at Berkeley, and Larry Summers of Harvard University (the same Larry Summers who counseled President Obama not to go overboard on fiscal stimulus in early 2009), authored a technical economics paper for the Brookings Institution on the issue of intensive infrastructure spending, "Fiscal Policy in a Depressed Economy."[1] Their principal finding was that "when interest rates are constrained by the zero nominal lower bound, discretionary fiscal policy can be highly efficacious as a stabilization policy tool. Indeed, under what we defend as plausible assumptions of temporary expansionary fiscal policies may well reduce long-run debt-financing burdens."

In more understandable language, DeLong and Summers argued that infrastructure spending would actually reduce future deficits by taking advantage of cheap money and labor to do now what would need to be done in any event at a later date. They demonstrated conclusively that the economic effects of additional employment, the increase in primary and secondary demand, and the increased productivity that would result from a large government-led infrastructure program would far outweigh the financing costs of shifting infrastructure work forward in time.

At various times since "The Way Forward" was published in 2011, and DeLong and Summers published their papers, interest rates have fallen even further. In late 2012 the 10-year U.S. Treasury bond was trading at a near historic low, in a range to yield between 1.5 percent and 2.0 percent, and the 30-year bond in a range to yield between 2.5 percent and 3.0 percent. Bond rates have spiked from time to time since then but the ten-year rate has generally remained below 2.5 percent through this writing. Across the Atlantic, UK gilts (long-dated bonds) have traded a few hundredths of a percentage point higher than U.S. Treasuries, and German Bunds (government bonds) a few tenths of a percentage point lower. They are all joining Japanese government bond (JGB) yields, which trade between half a percent and 1 percent, on average, lower still and for 14 years haven't traded at a yield north of 2 percent.

In short, money for public investment is cheap. As cheap as it will probably ever be.

And for those fans of the private sector who abjure government borrowing of any sort (because of fear of higher taxes in the future to pay it off) and who fear government "crowding out" private-sector access to cheap capital, I would say that, first, government acceleration of eventually needed infrastructure spending through borrowing does not increase future tax rates. Quite the contrary. If the cost of money to a government is low enough and the near-term benefits of employment-induced economic growth are significant enough, future tax rates will be *lower* than they would have been if costly infrastructure repairs are put off to a future time—when money is more expensive and the infrastructure problems have worsened.

Second, the notion of government crowding capital availability to the private sector at this point in history is a near impossibility, given the global capital glut we are experiencing. The problem in developed countries is not that there is a shortage of available capital, it is that there is a shortage of profitable opportunities for new investment given the global capacity glut in the tradable sectors (i.e., the making of things and provision of services that do not need to be made or provided locally). There is therefore nothing compelling the transmission of the oceans of capital sloshing around the world into dependable investments apart from the debt of hard-currency sovereigns and the periodic refinancing of the world's largest multinational companies' balance sheets.

And in that last statement rests the proof of the pudding. U.S. corporate bond issuance has exploded since the Great Recession. As of September 2012, U.S. corporations were on pace to have issued an average of $1.1 trillion of debt per annum for the three years from 2010 through 2012. This is an amount 55 percent higher than the average of $700 billion per annum for the bubbling decade of 1997 through 2006.

And why have America's corporations been borrowing at such a rapid clip? It certainly can't be because of enormous growth in either the domestic or global economies—global growth is slow and developed-world growth is anemic. And given the surfeit of cash on corporate balance sheets, it certainly does not appear that corporations are in need of liquidity. The answer, of course, is that businesses with access to global capital markets are "doin' the gettin' while the gettin' is good." They know cheap money when they see it and are grabbing it while they can. Why then shouldn't the governments of the people of the developed world, which can borrow even more cheaply than private businesses, do likewise?

Some say that the safe-haven government-bond markets are evidence of the impact of quantitative easing on the part of central banks, that rates are this low only because central banks are buying bonds. But this is not borne out by the facts. Germany, for example—or, rather, the European Central Bank—is not doing any quantitative easing at all, and in the United States during the periods of actual quantitative easing known as QE1, QE2, and QE3, bond yields did not fall but actually, net of fluctuations, rose in a misguided anticipation of emerging inflation.

No, as discussed throughout this book, bonds are trading at levels that reflect the vast oversupply of global capital and the disinflationary pressures on the developed world of other global imbalances and a continuing debt overhang. The surplus nations are essentially begging us to take their money and do something useful with it to repair global demand—and we can do exactly that by putting our own houses in order so to speak, thus benefiting our nations, our peoples, and the world's markets by doing that which will boost demand in the short to medium term and make us more productive and competitive in the long run.

Brad DeLong has argued that governments essentially have a moral obligation to borrow to build infrastructure under these circumstances because, through growth, such actions will ultimately reduce government debt-to-GDP ratios. He noted in October 2012: "For any credit-worthy sovereign—or for anybody who can borrow on the credit of any credit-worthy sovereign—it is fiscal expansion now that reduces the effective debt, and fiscal austerity that increases it."[2]

THE WEALTH OF NATIONS

Fears about too much public debt tend to get entwined with anxiety about today's high levels of private debt. But these are very different issues. I have devoted many pages of this book to describing the truly alarming rise of private debt in the United States and other advanced countries. Too many households borrowed too much money, often to make up for stagnating or falling incomes. And too many banks, corporations, and other financial players also gorged on debt.

In effect, China and other surplus nations gave the deficit nations a credit card with no limit, and we went nuts. That was bad. It was also bad that the U.S. government needlessly racked up trillions in public debt starting under Reagan and George W. Bush simply because politicians found that offering Americans a free lunch was a great way to get elected. After all, who doesn't like low taxes and plenty of services?

It was equally bad that the core nations of the Eurozone stuffed the periphery nations full of loans to further their consumption of core exports and to finance extensive social-welfare systems with money they could not repay and could not print themselves. For a while, mercantilism paid well, kept core economies growing, and kept their unemployment low. Today, that has been substantially reversed.

However, none of this means that taking on more public debt right now is a bad thing if incurred for the right purposes. Government deficits are not the same as private-sector deficits to the extent that they are incurred in the same currency issued by the government incurring them. When households and private-sector businesses incur more debt than they can handle, they must go bankrupt and often restructure their debts. The results can be pretty ugly.

But governments issuing debt in their own currencies, of course, cannot go bankrupt for liquidity reasons because they can merely print whatever additional monetary resources are needed to service their debt (either directly, in the absence of a central bank, or by monetization of existing treasury debt, in the presence of one). The opposite, of course, is the problem that plagues the overly indebted countries of the Eurozone: they borrowed in a currency they don't print and therefore face severe illiquidity problems.

But here's a thought regarding sovereign debt that few seem to pay much attention to. As much as hard-currency-printing countries can never be insolvent from a liquidity standpoint, it is equally true that a developed-world country would be extremely unlikely to become insolvent by virtue of an excess of liabilities over assets. Even Japan, which has the highest debt ratios in the world, leveraged itself to the hilt during its bubble, and is still arguably underwater in much of its corporate and financial sector, is a long way from having debt that exceeds the total value of all its assets.

224

It is very easy to measure the liabilities (debts) of a government, and we hear endless scary reports about just how big those liabilities are, both in the short term and looking decades ahead over the horizon. But what about the assets of a national government, or a nation as a whole? How does one establish the base—the wealth of nations, as it were—that essentially backs the "full faith and credit" promise of governments to pay their debts?

Before answering these questions with some numbers, let's establish a basic premise that is necessary to grasp those numbers. While the age of absolute monarchies may be long gone in the developed world, today's modern democratic governments have, in many ways, just as much "sovereign" power as the kings of old had. The power of these governments is the final power in each of our lands. And among those final powers are the right to tax and the right of eminent domain.

The parliaments and congresses of the developed world possess the right—given internal consensus within those bodies—to tax income and property as is necessary to cover the expenses of government, including the payment of interest on, and the principal amount of, government debt. Moreover, for fair and just compensation (measured in the currency of the realm—a critical point) all governments in the developed world have the power to take possession of all property within their respective borders to the extent that there is a fairly broadly defined public purpose in their doing so. In other words, governments have access, at least in theory, to *all* the wealth of their nations.

That is the sometimes forgotten definition of sovereignty, for economic purposes: ultimate control over the means of exchange (money), the power to tax, the ultimate right of ownership for legitimate public purposes, and—of course—the so-called police power to enforce all of the above, together with other laws and regulations of the state. I realize that these statements, while true, must be highly disturbing to my more libertarian friends. But modern constitutional governments evolved, among other reasons, to have the capacity to ensure stability and tranquility via collective action, if necessary . . . and specifically at times in which private interests are unable to work things out on their own. Yes, America's founding fathers were rebelling against an autocrat, but they certainly understood that a government of, by, and for the people would at times need to lead and muster collective responses to both internal and external challenges.

This is so important that I want to emphasize it further by reference to a whole school of economic thought known as Modern Monetary Theory (MMT). There is an excellent primer on the subject by L. Randall Wray of the University of Missouri at Kansas City titled *Modern Money Theory: A Primer on Macroeconomics for Sovereign Monetary Systems*. Wray, together with his UMKC colleague Stephanie Kelton and others such as James K. Galbraith of the University of Texas at Austin (the son of the renowned economist John Kenneth Galbraith), have formed the vanguard of MMT.[3]

MMT correctly points out that the value of fiat currency derives from the issuing government's power to tax and the fact that the currency itself is accepted in payment of such taxes. Wray notes that it is often felt that currency is accepted for payment of purchases, wages, or debts mainly because of the notion that other people and institutions (both in the issuing country or, as in the case of the U.S. dollar, abroad) are also likely to accept it. This mistaken notion—or, as Wray puts it, "greater fool" analysis—would also give rise to the idea that a change in such sentiment is also a possibility—that we might awaken one day with the major currency-issuing nations printing "unpopular" fiat notes that no one would want. This is not, the MMTers would posit, even a possibility in the case of a large economy of a wealthy country that issues its own currency. In theory, currency issuance could be limitless (as could government spending) as long as the amount of currency in issuance is correctly sized to the measure of the issuing economy and its flows, with the only variable being the currency's relative value versus that of currencies of which there is lesser supply. In other words, it is a matter of degree of value, not acceptance, with an offset to devaluation being ultimately found in the economic growth that occurs as a result of increased spending. It relates to the cost of money to a degree, but not to the ability of the government of a large nation to raise money or pay its debts in its own currency.

Now, I have some problems with MMT theory when it comes to its potential multilateral impacts (on both developed-world and emerging-world trading partners) during the period in between which the spending is telegraphed/begun and the point at which it has produced the desired growth (which I obviously believe it will). Too much such money creation would be highly destabilizing and induce potential emergency actions to thwart it by countries either dependent on the issuing country for exports or which compete with the issuing country's exports on price. So I believe the amount of money creation and resulting spending that is viable is not—as a practical matter—limitless. Neither do many MMTers; they would say for reasons of government and nongovernment budgetary discipline as well as destabilization of global currencies. I am just a bit more wary about the latter.

And clearly the taxing that would be required to support limitless amounts of debt would be deleterious to private-sector risk taking after a point—a point from which we are still rather far away, however. I don't know if the developed world, even with its enormous "buffer stock" of labor (an MMT term) acting as a bulwark against runaway inflation, can aspire to the guarantees of full employment that the MMTers believe would be possible using the government as employer of last resort. But it is clear to me that we can do a lot better than we are and that considerably more government debt issuance to spur growth, relative to national assets and the power to tax both those assets and flows, is possible in the United States, Japan, and the United Kingdom (and the Eurozone if its members could ever get their acts together and issue Eurobonds, jointly and severally).

What are those national assets that developed-world governments have the right to tax and, in exchange for fiat money, take possession of? And how do they relate to outstanding debts and government deficits?

There are several ways of calculating national wealth. Net private-sector wealth is one. Tallying up all the financial assets of all players in an economy is another. A more inclusive approach measures both financial and non-financial wealth to account for the value of assets such as natural resources (land and extractable commodities) and human labor.

It is important to note that within any nation, one party's liability is another party's asset (for example, if you own a home with a mortgage, your mortgage is your liability but is an asset of your lender; or if you buy a Treasury bond, it is a liability of your government but is most assuredly your asset). So whether that of a government or the private sector, the debt of a nation needs to be evaluated in consideration of the overall value of an economy, not merely its output.

Let's get more concrete here by looking at the wealth of the United States, which we can then compare to all the frightful liabilities we are always hearing about. More specifically, let's examine three different estimates of total U.S. wealth.

The first estimate is from Allianz Global Wealth Report, and is a total of all private wealth. According to Allianz, the United States was worth $43 trillion in 2011.[4]

A second, much bigger, estimate comes from the 2012 Inclusive Wealth Report published by United Nations University International Human Dimensions Programme. That organization, which takes into account nonfinancial assets such as oil deposits, pegs U.S. net worth at $118 trillion.[5]

Finally, there is an even bigger number—$164 trillion—which is the Federal Reserve's estimate of total U.S. financial assets.[6] There is lots of double counting in that number, but any way you measure it, the United States is a very wealthy nation.

MANAGEABLE U.S. DEBTS

Given the United States' aggregate assets, total public-sector debts are far less significant than politicians, the media, and the "fix the debt" crowd of debt-scolding economists and business leaders would have us believe.

In proper context, America's supposed ocean of red ink looks more like a lake.

In November 2012, the total debt owed by the U.S. Treasury was $16.4 trillion. But this number is misleading. Of that $16.4 trillion, $4.8 trillion was owned by and/or owed to other government agencies (mostly the Social Security trust funds, which—like other divisions of government—need to know they have sufficient funding down the line but don't need it today) and another $1.7 trillion was held by the Federal Reserve Bank (which is "owned," for all intents and purposes, by the U.S. Treasury).

So that takes total U.S. debt that is owed to private interests down to $9.9 trillion. And here's the last point: only $5.5 trillion of that amount is owed to those outside of the United States; and of that amount, $3.9 trillion is owed to foreign governments and central banks of (mostly) trade surplus countries. The remaining $4.4 trillion is assets of parties in the United States (mostly in the private sector) and a part of overall U.S. nongovernmental wealth.

So to recap: The U.S. government, which controls its own currency and presides over a nation worth somewhere between $43 trillion and $164 trillion, owes a mere $5.5 trillion to parties outside its borders.

And Jan Hatzius of Goldman Sachs projected in early 2013 that in his reasonable (midpoint) forecast, using real GDP growth averaging less than 3 percent for 2013 and 2014 (which may prove a bit high), the U.S. budget deficit will—if nothing further is done—fall on its own accord to below 3 percent of GDP ($500 billion). Even if growth is more sluggish, this doesn't really sound so scary to me, yet budget deficits at the time of Hatzius's report were a source of endless hand-wringing and shrill warnings. Worse, hysteria about the debt led politicians to effectively tie their own hands in dealing with the worst economic slump since the Great Depression.

What the fearmongers say is that the party can't go on forever and that global capital markets will eventually exact a terrible retribution on the U.S. government for its profligate ways (the same is said about the governments of the UK and Japan). Yet such retribution would seem to make very little sense at all. And according to those same capital markets, it's not happening: the market value of U.S. government debt is near all-time highs and interest rates are at historic lows.

The U.S. government has borrowed more money more rapidly since the financial crisis hit in 2008 than at any time in its history, save the World War II years. From the time that Lehman Brothers crashed, in September 2008, to the beginning of 2013, the U.S. government borrowed $6.8 trillion, including both intragovernment debt and that held by the public.[7] That is roughly $4.3 billion a day. It's $179 million an hour. Or $3 million a minute.

To be sure, this borrowing binge provoked panic in plenty of places. Senators and presidential candidates decried the binge. A boyish Congressman rose from obscurity to become the vice-presidential nominee of his party by warning that the debt would lead to ruin. A powerful grassroots movement, the Tea Party, rose up to stop the borrowing and began knocking off establishment Republicans deemed insufficiently hawkish on the deficit. A billionaire, Peter G. Peterson, began spending an ever-larger chunk of his fortune to sound the alarm about the deficit. A national commission was formed to find a solution. The U.S. government almost shut down following a showdown over the budget ceiling.

Yet capital markets basically just yawned as the United States borrowed $179 million an hour. Every time the United States auctioned off Treasuries, there were plenty of buyers. Indeed, things went in exactly the opposite direction that deficit hawks might have imagined. So many people wanted to buy U.S. debt that U.S. borrowing costs fell to record lows. Whether or not this phenomenon proves what many economists believe—that government bond interest rates, in countries with large economies and sovereign currencies, are a policy matter engineered by central banks and are not, as free-marketers take as gospel, established by market forces—makes little difference to me. Either way, the global capital glut is such that we can expect to be saddled with the beneficiaries of low rates for some time to come.

Debt crisis? What debt crisis?

Now, concluding that we are not in a debt crisis is not the same as suggesting that a country can simply print money willy-nilly to finance all government expenditures and not worry about revenue at all. For there are three other key factors in this mix: the relative values of currencies, the connection between a devalued currency and inflation, and the adverse impact on overall economic growth when a bloated debt burden forces taxes higher in order to service that debt (and the multilateral issues about which I have spoken earlier in this chapter).

In normal times, all of these would raise valid concerns for economies engaged in high levels of deficit spending and debt accumulation. These are not, as I have repeated throughout this book, normal times. The normal good effects of deficit spending are not occurring as usual. However, neither are the normal bad effects.

As Keynes taught, deficit spending is generally just what the doctor ordered to recover from a recession—especially one accompanied by a private debt overhang. When nominal growth and inflation both slow, fiscal (and monetary) stimulus is more than called for and is normally successful in reviving commerce and consumption. Inflation, which hopefully results, devalues the debt previously incurred and devalues the currency, which makes exports more competitive. But again, nothing is "normal" this time around.

As I've noted throughout, in the present supply-induced demand deficiency, the mechanisms that would normally transmit monetary stimulus to reverse disinflation are not functioning. Moreover, the forms of deficit spending that are occurring in most developed nations are of the wrong type. As with monetary actions, much deficit spending has been focused on subsidizing existing programs and government operations, rather than instituting new spending aimed directly at job creation, and thereby stimulating sustainable growth.

Ordinarily, flooding an economy with excess money (which is what happens when a government deficit-spends—they create/print money that does not have a source in economic output; no one "earned" it) would serve both to fuel domestic inflation and devalue the currency. These are conventional supply-and-demand functions, as excess cash is delinked from boosted output, causing prices to rise; and as the supply of cash makes the currency less valuable (because there is so much of it) exports, in turn, become more expensive.

Yet this hasn't happened. And such adverse effects, along with some kind of debt crisis, are extremely unlikely to occur in the absence of substantial rebalancing of the global economy. There's simply too much cheap money and cheap labor floating around. The chances of markets sustaining higher interest rates for any meaningful period of time, amid a capital glut, are *slim to none*. The likelihood of sustainable inflation in a globally oversupplied labor market featuring dramatic wage imbalances is similarly small. The likelihood of deficits leading to meaningful currency devaluation within/among developed nations when all are trying the same thing at once is *zero*, for what I hope by now are obvious reasons.

Allow me to dispatch one other phantom threat associated with heavy public borrowing, which is that high debt-to-GDP levels stunt economic growth. This is a supply-side concept that extrapolates deficits into debt, debt into higher interest rates, higher interest rates into lower investment (and higher savings), all of the foregoing into stagflation (low growth with inflation), and inflation to a weaker dollar.

All that sure sounds bad. And during stronger economic times, irresponsible deficit spending should have exactly many of these results.

But things work differently in weaker times. We know this because we have a fair amount of evidence from past episodes in which deficit spending was extensively utilized amid slow economic growth. There just isn't strong evidence that more borrowing leads to higher interest rates, less investment, and stagnating growth. Correlations between high levels of sovereign debt and anemic economic growth would appear to be awash in false positives, noted most directly in the International Monetary Fund's October 2012 World Economic Outlook, in which the authors wrote:

> Our analysis is not meant to dispute the notion that, all else equal, higher levels of debt may lead to higher real interest rates. Rather it highlights that there is no simple relationship between debt and growth. In fact, our subsequent analysis emphasizes that there are many factors that matter for a country's growth and debt performance. Moreover, there is no single threshold for debt ratios that can delineate the "bad" from the "good."[8]

Note the language: "*may* lead to higher real interest rates." As present conditions amply demonstrate, it also may *not*. And the "may" remains "won't" until the developed world's output gap is closed considerably. Until then, higher levels of deficit spending will translate to increasing output, not to inflating prices for existing output.

It can't be emphasized enough just how cheap it has been for the U.S. government to borrow in recent years. In fact, borrowing costs are so low that the United States spent less money last year servicing its debt, as a percentage of GDP, than it did in 1979—before the first great borrowing binge under President Reagan. America's interest costs are lower today as a percentage of GDP, with $16 trillion in debt, than when the national debt was a mere $845 billion.

Again: what debt crisis?

EUROPEAN DEBT

The Eurozone presents an entirely different conundrum when it comes to deficits and debt.

The signatories to the Maastricht Treaty on European Union (TEU) in 1992 took steps to advance their union and create a common currency under a set of provisions that have since become their worst nightmare. One problem lies with the basic notion of having a currency union without also having a fiscal union—that is, sharing currency but not sharing budgeting power. Add to that the same global phenomena that drove credit bubbles throughout the developed world during the first decade of the euro's existence and you're just asking for trouble.

So here we are, four years after the debt crisis was "revealed" in Europe, with the Eurozone stuck in the mud fiscally and destabilizing capital markets everywhere with unending hints of an even bigger meltdown. To boot, the Eurozone is not generating sufficient growth to help raise global demand and mitigate the problem of oversupply.

The Eurozone's disconnection of its monetary authority from the fiscal realms of each constituent nation, along with the uncoordinated regulation of its banking system has created massive imbalances internal to the zone itself. Worse yet, Europe's leaders haven't aggressively used the monetary tools they do have to offset fiscal shortcomings—through the direct purchase of sovereign debt by the European Central Bank. On top of that is the inability inherent in a shared currency to adjust the value of that currency between surplus/creditor nations and deficit/debtor nations. All this helps explain why Europe has leaned so heavily on the austerity route.

So, yes, unlike the United States, the individual nations of the Eurozone really do have a serious and enduring debt and deficit problem. But it's a problem that can be solved—*if* the wealthy surplus/creditor nations, Germany first and foremost, are willing politically to endure such a remedy.

DEMOCRACY AND DEBT

One last point before we leave the topic of deficits: bold new borrowing to increase demand and spur growth would be consistent with the public's view that fixing the economy is more important than reducing deficits.

Poll after poll over the past few years has found that while many Americans are worried about deficits and the national debt, creating jobs and improving the economy has been a higher priority for the public. For example, a June 2010 NBC News/Wall Street Journal poll found that 33 percent of Americans named job creation and economic growth as their top priority; 15 percent named "deficit and government spending." A FOX News/Opinion Dynamics poll that same month found a similar spread, with 32 percent naming jobs as a top priority compared to only 12 percent that named the deficit.

Two other polls in the preelection summer of 2010 found much smaller spreads, but a series of polls in the fall of 2010 all found the public much more concerned about jobs than the deficit—often by huge margins. For example, a CBS News poll after the November 2010 election, which swept many Tea Party–backed candidates into Congress, asked this question: "Of all the problems facing this country today, which one do you most want the new Congress to concentrate on first when it begins in January?" Fifty-four percent of respondents named the economy and jobs. Just four percent named the deficit and national debt.

Most polls throughout 2011 and 2012 found that the public remained focused on jobs and the economy over the deficit by two-to-one margins or more, although some—most notably by Gallup—have shown much smaller margins. A CBS News/New York Times poll in September 2012 found that 37 percent of respondents named jobs and the economy as the top issue that they would vote on in this election and just 4 percent named the budget deficit and national debt. A Bloomberg poll the same month found 43 percent identifying jobs and the economy as the most important issue facing the country with 14 percent naming the federal deficit. Polls by the Pew Research Center have found similar trends. Finally, exit polls after the 2012 election showed that job creation remained a priority over deficit reduction.[9]

Also, when given the direct choice between spending money to invest in infrastructure/public-sector hiring, for, say, teachers and firemen versus cutting spending to reduce the deficit, Americans routinely say they'd rather preserve jobs or create jobs than cut the deficit. In one poll, for example, 52 percent said that we should be spending money, while only 43 percent said that we should cut spending for deficit reduction.[10]

Sure, the Tea Party talked a lot about deficits when it emerged in 2009/2010, but there was never evidence that the movement was mainly focused on deficits—as opposed to other issues like taxes and health care—or that they spoke for a majority of Americans who favored austerity.

As I discussed earlier, Americans don't spend a lot of time worrying about debt, either their own or the government's. While that is

234

normally a bad thing, it's actually helpful during an economic crisis, when political leaders need to borrow a lot of money fast to restart growth.

No, what's standing in the way of smart public investment right now are the economically powerful, not the masses. In many cases these same people sat by quietly during the Bush years as the United States needlessly piled up trillions of dollars in new debt in order to enjoy the benefits of near-record low tax rates. Now, when the United States really does need to borrow, they have suddenly become converts to fiscal discipline.

Maybe it's naive to expect more from ideological conservatives. But surely the more sober business leaders pushing for austerity, like Pete Peterson, should know better. If you're a corporate CEO, or once were, you know how important demand is for driving growth and you know, or should know, that cutting government spending reduces demand. As well, as a CEO, you should know a thing or two about global capital markets and be familiar with how those markets have shown an insatiable appetite for U.S government debt that is unlikely to abate for many years to come—putting the lie to foolish predictions of a debt crisis.

Business leaders should be leading the charge for more borrowing to recharge growth, not jumping aboard an austerity push by politicians who don't know the first thing about macroeconomics.

The sheer amount of money that the United States has been borrowing, along with the sources of some of that money (e.g., China), certainly looks alarming to anyone not well-read in economics. And the very idea of Keynesianism may seem inherently suspect in many parts of the United States. Yet despite all this, ordinary Americans get the simple idea that government needs to step in to create demand during a slump.

It's time for our leaders to catch up with the people.

CHAPTER 14

A GLOBAL SYSTEM THAT WORKS
Managing Multilateralism

Perhaps the most formidable economic challenge today lies in the area outside the borders of any one nation or region. Present-day imbalances are global in nature and can no longer be resolved by any one power, or even by two or three. Indeed, there is enormous risk today of unilateral or bilateral actions (between the United States and the Eurozone, for example) being viewed by players left out of such actions as economically threatening or even hostile, leading to economic countermeasures, trade wars, or worse. The issue is compounded by the complexity of the relationship among and between developed nations on the one hand and emerging ones on the other. It is hard to imagine moving beyond a global economy that is just getting by, and therefore at material risk of new and deeper crisis, without a more open dialogue among the Group of 20 (G-20) nations and proactive steps toward mutual accommodation.

We are fortunate, I suppose, in one respect. All nations are put at risk by a slumping developed-world economy. Whether a country exports consumer products, steel, or natural resources, it is now coping with the downsides of global stagnation and overproduction. No one is immune. There is thus enormous commonality of interest if nations can find the right way to open a dialogue with one another.

Both surplus and debtor nations have understood that it is to no one's benefit to attempt to aggressively advance their singular interests at the expense of their trading partners. We're all in this together, our interests are intertwined in a flat world, and we're dealing with more economic interdependence than ever before. And thus far, at least, we have more or less avoided the "beggar thy neighbor" strategies that went awry in previous slumps, either out of wisdom or the good fortune of their ineffectiveness. That said, we are a long way from a harmonious, cooperative global trading environment and I fear that the recent actions of the Bank of Japan to weaken the yen (despite the BOJ's protestation that its monetary policy is not meant to target the value of the currency) is heading the global economy in a very challenging direction.

It is tempting, for simplicity's sake, to view our problems in a more limited scope: the United States versus China; the core Eurozone nations versus the Eurozone periphery; Japan versus the rest of Asia. But we are well beyond that.

And if the complexity of the dilemma before us is not enough, there is another. Keynes's greatest contribution to the study of macroeconomics may be one for which he is perhaps least remembered—the study and resolution of trade imbalances between nations. His views on how to resolve global trade imbalances in a world of fiat currencies were never fully implemented—and were often objected to. But they fully presaged the possibility of out-of-control imbalances of enormous size. But what he could never have realistically contemplated was the magnitude of the underlying cause of today's imbalance: three billion people from emerging low-wage nations rapidly joining the global economy.

This Great Rejoining is far from over. Tens, if not hundreds, of millions of low-wage workers and trillions of dollars of new capital will flow into the global economy in the next decade. If the world doesn't work together to find a better way to manage this change, we can count on new crises to come.

Three key multilateral issues need to be dealt with in order to achieve global stability:

The situation in the Eurozone will continue to plague the global economy until it either self-stabilizes or a solution is found. I do not believe that it will self-stabilize, so let's discuss several proactive alternatives. A multilateral effort is going to require give-and-take across the board, and the European situation is at a stalemate. Other regions, I believe, would be willing to aid a European solution if it were part and parcel of moving the entire global economy forward. But no outside power is currently interested in assisting because the remedies that have been attempted to date have been decidedly lacking.

On a similar note, regionally, China is at a crossroads in terms of its internal rebalancing from an oversaving and overinvesting nation (with a national savings rate—not to be confused with the personal savings rate—in 2011 equal to a whopping 51 percent of GDP) to one in which consumption plays a greater role. The same is true, to a lesser extent, of the other ELOWASEENS. The table below contrasts the ELOWAS-EENS' national savings rates with those of the major advanced regions:

ELOWASEENS		ADVANCED NATIONS	
Qatar	54.47%	Japan	21.93%
China	51.04%	Canada	20.01%
Kuwait	48.70%	Eurozone	19.80%
Singapore	44.37%	United Kingdom	12.92%
Saudi Arabia	43.04%	United States	12.88%
Libya	42.92%		
Malaysia	33.67%		
South Korea	32.42%		
Thailand	30.00%		
Russia	28.63%		
Nigeria	28.35%		
Venezuela	26.85%		

Source: International Monetary Fund (latest of 2011 or 2010 as available)

Finally, part of any G-20 grand bargain needs to include banking reform. At the beginning of the financial crisis, in 2007, Warren Buffett was widely quoted as observing, "It's only when the tide goes out that you learn who's been swimming naked." As it turned out, the parade of nude bathers was quite long and included banks, investment banks, insurance companies, government-sponsored enterprises, and, in the case of the European periphery, entire countries.

Some were swept out to sea with the tide, but a sizable number have since obtained swimwear and are walking the boardwalk as though nothing ever happened. The fact is that many financial institutions today look pretty dismal under their cover-ups. Moreover, there is a substantial difference among regions of the developed world in terms of what constitutes a strong financial institution. Given the enormous interdependence of global financial institutions, having multiple standards means that the entire international financial system is as vulnerable as the weakest of those standards—which in the case of Eurozone banks is very weak indeed.

Resolving these interlocking problems, trade imbalances, ELOWASEEN underconsumption, the resolution of the Eurozone crisis, and the fortification of the global banking system will require a new level of global economic cooperation. And, to a certain extent, it is reasonable to assume that the emerging surplus and energy-exporting members of the G-20 will want to be assured that progress is being made across the board on stabilizing the economies and financial systems of the developed world (to assure both global stability and the strength of the emerging members' principal markets) in order to make the concessions required of the surplus nations, particularly with regard to trade and internal consumption issues.

Since 1971, and growing massively with the enormous buildup of the ELOWASEEN trade surplus from the late 1990s forward, the U.S. dollar has acted as the global reserve currency. Today, some 62 percent of all foreign reserves are held in U.S. dollars. In the private sector, many of our most liquid commodities and the largest share of global financial and other assets are denominated and traded in dollars. Why is this a problem for the United States? Well, on the one hand, I suppose it's not. The United States enjoys the many benefits of the "exorbitant privilege" of being the issuer of the world's currency: enormous demand for both the currency itself (maintaining its global purchasing power) and for debt issued by the U.S. government and its agencies (keeping the cost of borrowing low, and today absurdly so).

But there is a dark side to all of this—the so-called Triffin dilemma, after the economist Robert Triffin—that posits that the issuer of the global reserve currency must, as a mathematical matter, be willing to run trade/current account deficits in order to supply the rest of the world with (in the present case) the dollars it wishes to hold. Thought of another way, if the global economic players were indifferent as to the issuer of the currency in which they held their reserves, they would take payment for those goods in any currency, there would be fewer dollars spent by Americans for foreign goods, less demand for the dollar, and correspondingly more balanced national trade accounts. The paradox to all of this is that, eventually, an economy that is running large and persistent trade deficits should become viewed as unstable and therefore should diminish the demand for and strength of the reserve currency.

But again, here's where the magnitude issue comes into play. Global wage imbalances are so substantial between developed and emerging nations, and oversupply is so substantial relative to demand, that the emerging nations continue to seek U.S. demand, and correspondingly hold dollar reserves to avoid appreciation in their own currencies without worrying too much about long-term stability issues. In a very material sense, they have to. The principal goal of the emerging nations is to increase employment and the size of their middle classes as rapidly as possible. And given the numbers of people who have yet to be urbanized and/or are in poverty in the emerging world, they have a long way to go and cannot afford to lose any share of global demand. So the instability concern takes a backseat to the growth imperative.

Put another way, this crazy system—with all its obvious dangers—works just fine for China and other export powerhouses. They want the United States—the largest consumer market in the world—to keep buying more goods and borrowing more of their surplus cash.

But this cycle can't go on forever. Growth inevitably must slow in an age of too much supply and too little demand. And the debt overhang in the developed nations slows growth even further. These phenomena, combined with the United States being the issuer of the global reserve currency, are deeply distorting the global picture. Because we see not only massive issuance of dollars to fulfill demand, but we also see enormous *hoarding* of dollars rather than the investment of dollars in the country of their issuance. In fact, what we see instead is huge demand to lend money to the U.S. government, *which is not at all the same thing as investing in the U.S. real economy*, encouraging U.S. government deficits (because it is so cheap to finance them, among other reasons) in addition to the trade deficits already mentioned.

In today's world we see a condition that I refer to as "triple hoarding" of U.S. dollars in (i) the over $3.5 trillion held in foreign currency reserves; (ii) the nearly $2 trillion in excess domestic liquid assets held by nonfinancial U.S. corporations (together with perhaps another $3 trillion held in liquid form by U.S. business interests outside of the United States) and (iii) the trillions of dollars of uninvested household wealth, 75 percent of which is held by the top 10 percent of households. And I don't blame any of the foregoing holders for not investing their money in new capacity. As discussed throughout this book, there is nothing very sensible for them to invest in, given the oversupply. Similar points can be raised with respect to the world's secondary reserve currencies, the euro and the yen, but the numbers are of course far smaller.

This leaves the developed world with a dilemma even worse than Triffin's. Either allow the pricing mechanism to clear the market of excess (which would mean further wage, price, and asset deflation in the developed world) or find some other way of getting excess reserves invested into their real economies. And that, of course, is what this entire book has been about!

Repairing all of the problems addressed here is an ambitious agenda, to say the least. It will require an overhaul of the global economic and financial system of no lesser scope than that of the 1944 Bretton Woods Agreement, which established a new such order for the post–World War II era, or the de facto Bretton Woods II understanding that has prevailed since the United States terminated the dollar's gold convertibility in 1971 and most major world currencies became free-floating.

A Bretton Woods III plan, addressing all of the foregoing issues, is very much overdue, so in this chapter I lay out what I believe needs to be done in that regard.

Toward the end of World War II, in July 1944, the financial policy leaders of the soon-to-be victorious Allied Powers gathered together at the Mount Washington Hotel in Bretton Woods, New Hampshire. While what was then called the United Nations Monetary and Financial Conference took place in the nation that financially dominated the world, the Bretton Woods Conference (as the meeting was subsequently called) was actually dominated by a Briton, John Maynard Keynes.

Keynes may have been the greatest economic mind at Bretton Woods, but he was far from the most politically powerful one. He came to the conference with the most comprehensive plan ever seen (to this day) for the management of global currencies and trade in what was then a world as economically imbalanced as it has ever been (until the present age). What he left with was a package of half measures that acknowledged and stabilized existing problems but did little to reverse them or prevent their recurrence in the future.

Nevertheless, Bretton Woods saw many unprecedented developments, among them the delinking of other currencies from gold (chiefly because at that time the United States pretty much had all the gold in monetary circulation, or effectively owned it as a creditor of other nations) and, unsurprisingly, the linking of the dollar to gold and the rest of the world's currencies to the dollar. The International Monetary Fund and the International Bank for Reconstruction and Development—the predecessor of The World Bank—sprang from the Bretton Woods Conference as well. Overall, a litany of multilateral economic issues that arose from fifteen years of depression and war were addressed and, to an extent, resolved.

But that was not Keynes's plan going into the conference. Much has been written of the political machinations and details of the conference. No need to go into that here, other than to say that broader attempts at instituting global policy that would address the enormous economic imbalances that had arisen from the earliest glimmers of globalization—albeit one that excluded most of the globe—were watered down. Such efforts could have been of great use later, when the rest of the globe, following the collapse of international communism, joined the party in force.

No surprise again, the primary objector to broader economic integration was the world's biggest (and basically only) creditor at the time, the United States.

The so-called Bretton Woods System was not fully implemented until 1958 and, as a practical matter existed in full flower for fewer than two decades. It ultimately collapsed when the burden borne by the United States in tying the dollar to gold (thus restricting credit growth) became too great to bear—thus, in 1971, ushering in the era of fully fiat global currencies and by 1980 the explosion of global credit that has been with us ever since.

What emerged from Bretton Woods was, at best, a temporary fix that seemed like the right thing to do as the war was coming to a close. Or, more accurately and by default, it represented the highest degree of coordination that global economic powers were capable of at the time.

But, again, it was not what Keynes put on the table—which, to a large extent, except among academic economists, has been long forgotten. In fact, what Keynes was most concerned about was resolving *ongoing international account imbalances*. He wanted not only to rebalance the post-depression and post-war imbalances that existed among a few of the developed nations of that day, but also to create an environment in which extraordinary external surpluses and deficits could be dealt with without economic conflict and crisis. That the world's largest creditor/surplus nation at that time has today become the world's most indebted/deficit nation should be testament to the wisdom of Keynes with regard to his proposals at Bretton Woods.

What Keynes suggested was an incredibly well-thought-out plan for the creation of a global central bank for central banks. But unlike the European Central Bank (arguably, the closest thing we have to a regional super-central bank), Keynes's International Clearing Union (ICU) would have required a relatively continuous trueing up of large trade imbalances among fully sovereign independent currency-issuing nations.

Keynes's proposal offers much guidance and insight with regard to today's situation. So without getting too far into the plumbing, consider what Keynes suggested:

- The creation of an inter-central-bank "currency" unit that all global currencies could be marked against and that transactions among central banks (i.e. trade) would clear through. Note that this is not a global currency in that it was not meant to be used within the nations of the ICU, only as a means of exchange among their central banks. But based on what Keynes had in mind for using the ICU currency unit (which he called the bancor)—to stabilize global trade and credit—it was more than a means of exchange at the central-bank level or merely a call on the credit of the constituent central banks. What Keynes was proposing was really more of a fully convertible reference unit, similar to the far more limited special drawing rights (SDR) maintained by the IMF (which itself grew from Keynes's original plan).

- In a nod to the gold standard, which could not possibly have been reinstituted at the time because the supply of global gold was so disproportionately concentrated in the United States, Keynes used the notion of a global reference currency as a means to ensure the global exchange-rate stability that is key to avoiding crises in trade. Anchoring the dollar to gold, and other currencies to the dollar, was a reasonable compromise until, of course, the pressures on the United States that resulted from having an overly strong currency and a growing balance of payments/trade deficit (as its products were too expensive for foreign buyers) became too much to endure and the United States took itself off gold. An elastic global reference currency, given the balance of what Keynes proposed, would not cause the same problems as those created by tying the global money supply, and therefore credit, to an always limited supply of the "barbarous relic."

- While the global reference currency unit—bancor—would itself constitute fiat money (as is any currency today issued by a central bank without a peg to anything else, as most are) Keynes proposed that member nations would subscribe to bancor in an amount necessary to handle their respective volumes of global trade (i.e., a bancor money supply sufficient to clear aggregate cross-border trade).

- The relative value of each member state's currency to every other one and, therefore, to bancor, would be based on relative purchasing price parity (PPP), the well-understood method of determining relative value based on the cost of a similar basket of goods and services in each nation. While PPP analysis is performed regularly today by international institutions such as the World Bank, there is some controversy in computational methods which, safe to say, were far less robust in Keynes's time and may, as a practical matter, have been the best reason for having rejected his ICU at the time (putting aside political issues). Today, however, PPP modeling methods are far more powerful and are worthy of renewed attention by governments and academia.

- Limiting bancor to a country's current level of trade ignored the obvious fact that economies grow at different speeds by virtue of endogenous circumstances. Today, for example, China is growing at a rate far faster than that of advanced nations owing, in part, to the enormous number of people it adds to the nonfarming, urbanized labor force each year. As growth varies, so does the demand for money. So Keynes assumed that his ICU would need to extend credit—create bancor—much as central banks create money today in order to keep their respective domestic economies running smoothly. But to avoid the massive current account and trade imbalances we see today, Keynes's ICU would have capped the amount of "overdraft" credit to a fixed percentage of each deficit nation's aggregate cross-border trade. So nations could still choose to run modest deficits, but as no nation would be issuing the reserve currency (the bancor) and capital-to-finance deficits would be limited by the foregoing credit cap, wannabe deficit nations would eventually need to kick up internal production relative to demand, as opposed to filling that demand from abroad. I hope readers can by now intuitively understand what that would mean in terms of maintaining a respectable level of employment in nations (the United States being the present-day example) that would otherwise run enormous, destabilizing deficits.

As is certainly the case today, and as Keynes realized in the 1940s (and earlier), enormous trade imbalances are always accompanied by—if not caused by—currency-exchange rigidities, sometimes circumstantial, often intentional. As discussed throughout this book, other than protectionism, devaluation is the oldest trick in the book to help deficit nations to get their houses in order again. It is certainly more popular than deflation (or even dropping interest rates to nearly nothing in an attempt to fight off deflation). But as much as deficit nations might wish to devalue their currencies in order to regain economic vigor, surplus nations are seldom interested in seeing their currency appreciate— thus hurting exports and slowing their economies. So Keynes structured his ICU to include mandatory currency devaluation/appreciation formulas that would permit some leeway—after all, temporary surpluses and deficits occur all the time, and no country has a zero current account balance—but would crack down hard on countries that maintained vast surpluses. Why? Because Keynes believed that, de facto, such countries were engaging in mercantilism to the detriment of their trading partners.

Since no mercantilist nation would ever voluntarily permit its currency to appreciate merely to balance trade, Keynes's ICU did it for them—requiring surplus/creditor nations that had accumulated an average annual surplus equal to 50 percent of "overdraft" credit to not only

appreciate their currency but to pay an annual "fine" on that surplus (even at lower amounts than 50 percent) at a rate of up to 10 percent thereof per annum. This would essentially place a penalty on the hoard-   245
ing inherent in running persistent surpluses or would, in other words, force hefty amounts of the savings being accumulated out of the pockets of those doing the hoarding. The opposite was prescribed in the case of nations running persistent deficits. They would have to depreciate their currencies if they hit the foregoing target of 50 percent and would, of course, pay interest to the ICU on the amount of the actual overdraft being carried. Nations failing to comply would be drummed out of the ICU and lose clearing privileges, thus damaging their ability to trade.

Some of the most cogent analysis of Keynes's proposals at Bretton Woods can be found in an as-yet unpublished (at this writing) academic article by my Century Foundation cofellow and writing partner, Professor Robert Hockett of Cornell University, titled "Bretton Woods 1.0: A Constructive Retrieval." In his article, Hockett sums up Keynes's intentions well, as follows:

> What Keynes hoped to accomplish with the Clearing Union plan, then, was to prevent global hoarding and the loss of domestic credit-money control that this tended to foment, and thereby to safeguard national control of domestic financial conditions and underwrite balanced, hence sustainable, growth worldwide. That would in turn give rise to a reciprocal reinforcement dynamic between liberal global trading arrangements on the one hand, and stable full-employment growth . . . within national economies on the other.

So why have I spent so much ink writing about a seventy-year-old proposal? Simply because the global financial crisis of 2007–2009 was nothing less than the first moment in modern history when international economic imbalances grew to a point comparable to the situation at the end of World War II—to the point at which the global economy literally began to shut itself down.

But this time, instead of rethinking the past couple of decades and coming up with solutions aimed at real underlying problems, the leaders of today's largest economies (the G-20 nations) settled for making emergency monetary actions nearly permanent and took an every-man-for-himself approach to trade and currency issues. Had they been able to, any one of the major trading nations would have gladly beggared its neighbors by attempting to devalue its currency. But in the age of oversupply, with everyone attempting mercantilist currency devaluation at once, the result is that all go begging, so the G-20 nations made halfhearted pledges not to do what they couldn't do anyway (although, in early 2013, Japan again went on a mission to talk the yen down). Moreover, in today's environment, demands for surplus/creditor nations to allow their currencies to appreciate against the currencies of their deficit/debtor trading partners fall on deaf ears. In short, nothing changes.

And yet there can be no doubt that the Chinese, for example, would vastly prefer stronger trading partners and more robust demand. They and others with vast (or potential) capacity would gladly finance a "Marshall Plan" of employment-oriented infrastructure redevelopment for their best customers (with their trading partners' own currencies, of course). Instead of hoarding gold today, surplus nations hoard dollars and euros, so there is plenty to invest.

Furthermore, the Chinese have expressed their view repeatedly that the U.S. dollar cannot be the world's reserve currency forever. As Dr. Ken Courtis, the former vice chairman of Goldman Sachs Asia cited previously, noted to me: the Chinese are not inclined to allow their currency to be both freely exchangeable and freely floating in a world in which global monetary policy is dominated by decisions made in Washington from the standpoint of what is good for America.[1] Some may criticize the foregoing view, given claims—mostly true—that the yuan is kept deliberately undervalued by the Chinese government for mercantilist reasons. But can we really expect that to change, or for the Chinese to move beyond mercantilism, until the world's second-largest economy is offered a reasonable and stable currency exchange, a controlled market economy, and a balance-of-payments environment in which to compete on a truly level playing field?

Courtis has also pointed out that the Chinese would react well to a grand bargain that afforded them access—at market prices—to America's new energy bounty, which I discussed in chapter 12.[2] A grand bargain between the developed and emerging nations will doubtlessly involve a variety of economic and political concessions by both sides, and will be as complex as one might imagine; but the need for such an accord is unavoidable.

It can be said that the age of oversupply resulted from the absence of a cross-border monetary, currency, and balance-of-payments architecture commensurate with the massive explosion in global trade over the past two decades. In order to achieve the balanced and sustainable global growth to which Hockett refers above, we need to do what we should have done when we essentially stumbled haphazardly into the postsocialist era. How can bringing half the world's population suddenly into competition with a developed world one-fifth its size in population call for anything less than the level of coordination required after the Great Depression and World War II?

We need to commit to such cooperation now—belatedly, but in earnest. A modernized ICU-type architecture would be a good place to start. In the long run, market forces will whittle down the imbalances discussed in this book. But as Keynes himself wrote in 1923, "The long run is a misleading guide to current affairs. In the long run we are all dead. Economists set themselves too easy, too useless a task if in tempestuous seasons they can only tell us that when the storm is past the ocean is flat again."

What we need today is a way of getting out of the present global slump that is based on both endogenous demand creation within countries—through reemployment-oriented investment policy in advanced nations—and more aggressive efforts to increase consumption by workers and businesses in emerging nations. That can happen only within a balanced system of global trade and a stable currency environment. The sooner we recognize this, the better. The faster we act, the more responsible our governments will be toward the populations of both emerging and advanced nations.

Just as I was completing this book, in March 2013, the former president of the European Central Bank, Jean-Claude Trichet, penned an op-ed for *The New York Times* in which he both acknowledged the global nature of the problems affecting the advanced economies and suggested, with respect to the Eurozone, that imbalances could be resolved only through the implementation of a system of monitoring macroeconomic imbalances and competitiveness within the zone, among other remedies.[3] While I was heartened to see his reference to a global problem, I was dismayed that he thought "global" was chiefly a Euro-American measurement. Similarly, efforts to merely monitor imbalances in trade are relatively worthless without an agreed-upon method for resolving them.

Some may argue that the problems are too complex to be resolved and the best we can do is to wait them out. If we were able to do that, policy makers would be saved from having to make some very tough decisions. But economic, political, and social pressures arising during this age of oversupply are not likely to grant us that luxury. It is long past time to sit down and lay out a new economic playing field that is conducive to more evenly shared growth.

CHAPTER 15

IN PURSUIT OF PRAGMATISM

Tear Down This Ideological Wall

I n the second quarters of three successive calendar years—2010, 2011, and 2012—improvements in the U.S. economy that generated hopes for economic rebirth were dashed by what seemed to have been economic "forces of gravity" that mysteriously pulled glimmering positive trend lines downward just as the crocuses of spring were pushing up through the earth's soil.

In each of those years, for example, the rate of growth in aggregate U.S. payrolls spiked and then declined, resulting in hand-wringing for much of the balance of the year. Hourly wage growth attempted to turn positive on a "real" (inflation adjusted) basis, only to be dragged back into the same pattern of stagnation or decline that has been characteristic of each of the last dozen years, save for the years of the Great Recession, when the United States experienced deflation and real wages rose as a result.

And in the autumn of each of those years, people from every school of economic thinking (myself included) penned white papers, articles, and op-eds in a cacophonous chorus prescribing—in the aggregate—a bipolar set of solutions to help the economies of the United States and the rest of the developed world achieve escape velocity from a pattern of perennial slump. There are always other factors at play when growth stalls, the "if onlys" that distract: If only Europe wasn't going to hell in a handbasket. If only the United States had a government that could achieve consensus on matters of extreme importance. If only consumers would click their collective heels together and believe enough in economic recovery to go out and "do what they're supposed to do."

Late 2012 and early 2013 saw the strongest push yet toward recovery in the United States as employment, the housing sector, and other economic indices showed the renewed vigor seen in the first quarter of prior years, even as Europe fell further into recession and Japan languished (although Japan showed some glimmers of hope with a 1.5 percent expansion in nominal GDP, despite continuing deflation, during the first quarter of 2013). And it is possible that growth in one region of the developed world or another (but unlikely in all at once) may sustain a decent pace for a few quarters here and there. But the fundamentals underlying the global economy will not alter substantially for years, maybe decades.

While the mutual animosity among those who govern the advanced nations generates headlines, the reality is that such belligerence is made possible largely by the absence of agreement among members of the economics profession as to what should be done to address those underlying fundamentals. It is made worse by temporizing with the "if onlys"—which are not causes, but rather symptoms of the underlying problems.

And yet, there are many aspects of present conditions that are pretty clear—clear to all but the most ideologically hemmed-in:

- That demand for goods and services by consumers in the developed world remains muted is axiomatic.

- That companies—while seeing the record profits that are the spoils of the survivors in a world of substantial industry consolidation—are seeing little reason to invest in the expansion of physical and human assets amid flat demand, is unsurprising.

- That consumers are once again taking on new debt (and have failed to meaningfully deleverage and save) in the absence of wages that afford them any margin with which to avoid further dissaving, is a fact of life which, in the United States at least, is over a dozen years' duration.

▪ And that countries, particularly in the Eurozone, that have attempted to afford their citizens a measure of personal financial security are coming face-to-face with the realities of massive indebtedness and (together with the pension funds of many U.S. private-sector companies) enormous, unfunded future liabilities that may prove impossible to meet, has led to the specter of dysfunctional governments unwilling to choose among unpopular and painful alternatives.

Save for a few nations of the developed world blessed with small populations relative to their enormous, exportable natural resources, the industrialized nations have encountered a wall standing between them and renewed growth.

Rather than experiencing a "depression"—a word that implies a depth difficult to dig out of—the people of the developed nations, only about 11 percent of the world's population but holding over 50 percent of the globe's financial assets, are under siege in lush countries, behind high economic walls that limit growth even while they contain a multiplicity of portals that enable those outside to freely interact and trade with the constrained but wealthy inhabitants within.

The wealth of the nations of the developed world has—shockingly—proven less and less an engine for economic growth and dominance in recent years. Instead, that wealth is more and more the target of poaching by emerging nations with enormous populations that are now able to compete with many sectors of the world's most advanced economies. The high living standards of the rich countries have also become a liability as their governments and populations alike have overborrowed to maintain those standards.

The developed world has implemented bailouts, bail-ins, zero interest rate policies, liquidity gluts, tax cuts, and small amounts of deficit stimulus—and, in many countries, the damaging diet of austerity prescribed for demand-deprived economies. As the years mount, our central banks and political leaders caution patience, try in vain to produce expectations of future inflation, and commit to financial repression for years into the future.

The results have been decidedly underwhelming.

The developed world has descended into a waiting game punctuated by intermittent (mostly monetary) stimulus-induced economic activity and periods of relapse as the underlying economic disease remains largely undiagnosed, misunderstood, and inadequately treated—much in the way a doctor treating the wrong illness can cause his or her patient's health to rally temporarily as a veiled core problem continues to worsen.

The argument—exhortation, really—that I have made in this book is that we sorely need new thinking to move the developed world back onto a sustainable macroeconomic-policy track. And this is within our ability to execute, even in today's disturbing political environment. I am convinced that the majority of responsible policy makers—on both sides of the debate—as well as the common citizens of our industrialized democracies, can be made to understand that the challenge facing us is largely outside the framework of the philosophical and economic disputes that divide us. At least that is my fervent hope and my reason for writing *The Age of Oversupply.*

Historically, the ideological divisions of the sort we see today across the developed world have not been dominant, even in the sharply divided and highly pluralistic United States. As Edward Luce noted in his 2012 book, *Time to Start Thinking,* economic *progressivism* was a traditional part of the Republican Party's history in the development of the United States, just as it has been for the Democrats. He wrote:

> In the 1860s Abraham Lincoln unleashed a series of investments that was to unify the continent into a single national economy—from the railroads to public universities. In the early 1900s Teddy Roosevelt, another Republican, broke up the oil monopolies, introduced regulation of workplace conditions, and set up the first national parks to preserve the American wilderness. Dwight Eisenhower, their fellow party alumnus, responded to the Soviet launch of Sputnik in 1957 with massive investments in public education, science, and road building. In a classic of unintended consequences, Ike also created the research agency that went on to develop the Internet [DARPA].

As I have noted, government is the agent that all individuals depend upon to accomplish big things that are beyond the capacity of either the market or civil society. We rely on government to exercise our collective will for change. And so it is time to ask what each of us can do to help our governments get with a new program and stop merely beating government over the head for the foolishness of the past. Governments don't make bad policy decisions on their own (any more than guns kill on their own). People elect governments that make bad policy—and they often do so because they want to believe in whatever political message requires the least in terms of sacrifice and the most in terms of immediate gratification. So the era of blaming government must come to a rapid close or we will go nowhere—and get there fast.

The need for collective action today is no less great than it would be in a time of war or natural disaster. Today we are confronting a global economic emergency that is a near-disaster for all but the most wealthy among us. Faced with a challenge like this, it is necessary to find common ground. That's not easy, I know. Even the supposedly monolithic 1 percent tend to be divided among different schools of economic thought. Add to that the highly imperfect nature of the union in the Eurozone, which clearly is unable to view itself as a collective beyond the shared colors of its common currency. All in all, it's extremely difficult to get affluent nations united on matters of money.

But the beauty of the present crisis is that there is actually an exogenous, underlying, real enemy (to use that word very loosely) that those setting policy in advanced nations—whether rich or poor—can rally to confront. *So regardless of whether you share my views on the supply-anchored economic policies of the 1980s and 1990s, the emerging of the post-socialist nations into the global free-market economy effectively changed everything.* I therefore can look my staunchest opponent in the economic debate straight in the eye and say, quite sincerely, "There are many things about which you were right some thirty years ago, but the facts on the global ground started changing radically about fifteen years ago and none of us saw it coming, or correctly interpreted its impact (save perhaps the few anti-globalization voices out there who were totally ignored), until it was long past too late to avoid the present state of affairs." No one, and nearly everyone, was wrong.

The developed world is facing nations that are acting in their own short- and medium-term (if not long-term) best interests by pursuing one version or another of state/oligarchic mercantilist capitalism. We can hardly blame them for doing so, but we do have the power to make it far less easy for them to do well as mercantilists. And, for the most part, we have been doing precisely the opposite and need to approach the challenge differently. What we need our governments to do is to begin responding to a real threat to our future, not with malice or rashness but with equanimity.

As former Intel chief Andy Grove once said: "We are in the middle of an economic war for global supremacy. We shouldn't be carrying on as though it's business as usual."

It would be nice to be able to coddle our private sector under the protective umbrella of tariffs and other trade restrictions as an incentive for them to spend, expand, and employ. But after decades of advocating free trade, acting as steward of the World Trade Organization, and enabling our emerging trading partners to achieve geopolitical and military strength and influence, there is simply no going back. I would hardly want to be the American president who calls the president of China and tells him, "Oh, you know that globalization stuff we've been advocating all these years? Well, it didn't work out so well for us, so . . ." There are clearly multilateral commercial agreements and future understandings that can limit governmental subsidies to businesses in surplus nations, but at the end of the day, rapidly increasing employment in emerging nations will continue to be their governments' chief priority for decades.

Policy makers have gone to extremes to try to reflate the economies of the United States and Europe. The Japanese have been trying desperately to do so for two decades, and at this writing they seem prepared to try again. The advanced nations have been futilely fighting the enormous deflationary pressures bearing down upon them from the global excess of supply relative to aggregate demand and from the continuing debt overhang that burdens their household and/or governmental sectors (depending on the individual nation). Not only is massive liquidity-pumping by the developed world's central banks not flowing into the real economy (the production and consumption of goods, services, and capital assets), but it has at times served to inflate commodities and other money "substitutes" to which liquidity flows when there is nothing reasonably productive to invest in. That has proven to be counterproductive. Each time oil and foodstuffs have increased in price in a given developed nation, fragile recoveries have been snuffed out; there is no ability for wages to track upward on a real basis—there is simply too much labor elsewhere.

And attempts at currency devaluation—which would help achieve reflation and make developed-world production more competitive (and others' less so)—have likewise failed. In this environment of oversupply, every distressed nation will attempt devaluation, and everyone can't devalue simultaneously. Anyway, there has never been a currency that devalues when its purchasing power is being held steady or is rising because of deflationary forces.

Without targeted collective action to offset these forces, I am afraid that the natural economic outcome is inevitably similar to what we have seen in Japan: the economy deflates to restore competitiveness and the debt overhang, unless extinguished consensually, simply becomes intractable because paying off debt with a more expensive currency, which is what comes along with deflation, is that much more difficult.

This book has laid out an appropriate set of actions to avoid that fate. Some of them will be viewed by many as distasteful. The fact that things have come to this—that we failed to appropriately regulate our financial markets and pursued policies that weakened us as we chased a purloined prosperity—is pitiable. Unfortunately, the United States drifted too far from a classic American ethos best described as "conservatism with progressive characteristics" (a nod to Beijing's "capitalism with Chinese characteristics"), and much of the developed world drifted right along with the United States. That ethos had once been embraced by both American political parties, although to different degrees, and, more broadly, had been the hallmark of the advanced world.

It's time to recover that balance and bust through the ideological walls that stand between the developed world and its renewed prosperity.

As President Ronald Reagan said in a very different, although curiously related, context, it is time to "tear down this wall" and free ourselves from the tyranny of a debate over issues that have long since been eclipsed by a different reality. When the age of global socialism came to an end in places like Berlin and Tiananmen Square, a new age dawned that no one really saw coming and must now be fully and finally confronted—*The Age of Oversupply.*

ACKNOWLEDGMENTS

I am humbled that a leading publisher, Penguin Portfolio, would ask a guy who has made his living mostly as an investment banker to write a book on the greatest macroeconomic challenges of our time. I suppose therefore that my thanks should go first to The Century Foundation, the oldest continuously operating think tank in the United States, for having named me a Fellow in Economics. Century's recognition provided gravitas to the musings of this banker, who realized in 2007 that his misgivings about U.S. and global economic and financial behavior over the prior decade were destined to rise to a level far beyond mere curiosity and chagrin. I am indebted to Janice Nittoli and Greg Anrig, president and vice president of Century, respectively, for having faith in me and what I had to say, and for encouraging me to pursue this project. I am especially grateful to Charles R. Morris, also a Century Fellow, who was kind enough to introduce me to that fine institution, and thankful as well to my other Fellows and the staff at Century, especially my analyst, Ben Landy, and our communications director, Derek Newton.

To find a publisher, however, most new writers need the help of a literary agent, and I have a terrific one in Andrew Stuart. So, armed with agent and publisher, there remained only one obstacle to seeing this book completed—I was not a writer. While I have learned a bit about the craft since, this book would not be in your hands (or on your screen) without the help of David Callahan, a superb writer with many books under his belt. David is a former Fellow of The Century Foundation and is currently cofounder and Senior Fellow at Demos, a New York–based research and policy center. David's voice, in support of the progressive views we share, comes through in several sections of *The Age of Oversupply.*

Thank you to Adrian Zackheim, president of the Portfolio imprint at Penguin, for giving me this extraordinary opportunity; to my brilliant editor, Niki Papadopoulos; and to their colleagues. You have all been incredibly supportive.

In 2007, when I first started writing and speaking in earnest on the coming financial crisis, there were few in academia, business, government, or even the media who were ready to play the part of the child in Hans Christian Andersen's "The Emperor's New Clothes" and proclaim the nakedness of what appeared to be a prosperous global economy. While it took me a bit longer than others to get there, I was fortunate to befriend two individuals, more prescient than myself, who were instrumental and encouraging as they helped me advance my thinking: Professor Nouriel Roubini of New York University and Dean Baker of the Center for Economic Policy Research.

It was to Nouriel Roubini that I originally pitched my underlying thesis of postsocialist global oversupply and who then asked me to be an early blogger on what became the respected economics site EconoMonitor.com, where I joined excellent bloggers from around the world. As for Dean Baker, I remember sending him e-mails in the summer of 2007 containing questions such as "Am I crazy or . . . ?" Unfortunately for the state of global finance, neither of us was crazy.

In 2011, Nouriel Roubini was kind enough to collaborate with me and Professor Robert C. Hockett of Cornell University Law School to write the New America Foundation white paper "The Way Forward: Moving from the Post-Bubble, Post-Bust Economy to Renewed Growth and Competitiveness," which is cited numerous times in this book. Bob Hockett and I were fortunate to meet at a Levy Institute Hyman P. Minsky Conference during the global financial crisis and became fast friends—Bob is one of the smartest people in law, history, and economics that I have ever met and is a walking definition of the word "polymath." We continue to collaborate regularly.

"The Way Forward" would not have been written (and this book's appearance would have been unlikely) but for the sponsorship of the Economic Growth Program of the New America Foundation, led by Sherle Schwenninger. New America has been a great supporter of my work and I would like to single out one of its board members, Pulitzer Prize winner Liaquat Ahamed (*The Lords of Finance*), who has more knowledge about financial history in his fingertip than I will ever have and who has been greatly encouraging to me in ways he probably doesn't fully appreciate.

In 2010 Sherle Schwenninger and a small group of economists and market participants, including me, formed New America's World Economic Roundtable, which has since grown to provide a forum for macroeconomic discussion and thought in New York and hosts speakers from around the world. The roundtable has also served as a brain trust/ sounding board for my ideas over the years, and I would like to acknowledge my fellow founders and participants who have views on all sides of the debate, especially Peter Atwater, Eric Best, Steven Blitz, Robert Brusca, Jonathan Carmel, Cameron Cowan, Lincoln Ellis, Constance Hunter, Jay Pelosky, and Peter Tchir.

My thanks go out as well to Professor L. Randall Wray of the Levy Institute and the University of Missouri at Kansas City, who brought me into his circle of Modern Monetary Theorists and other macroeconomists of great experience and note.

Others with whom I have exchanged ideas and compared notes since the financial crisis deserve a tip of the hat for helping me focus my views, including Sallie Krawcheck, Megan Greene, Barry Ritholz, Josh Rosner, and Chris Whalen. My thanks too to my fellow fourteen members of the small but venerable International Club of Business Economists, from whom I have learned much.

No insights, economic or otherwise, gain currency without some opportunity to express them to an audience larger than friends and family. This book would not have been possible without the attention paid to my views beginning half a dozen years ago by people in the media, many of whom I am today honored to call friends. For listening to and spreading what I had to say early on, I thank, at *The New York Times*, Joe Nocera, Binya Applebaum, Vikas Bajaj, and Andrew Ross Sorkin, as well as the op-ed staff; at *The Wall Street Journal*, Justin

Lahart, Aaron Lucchetti, Damian Paletta, Nick Timiraos, Rolfe Winkler, Alan Zibel, and Gregory Zuckerman; at the *Financial Times*, Gillian Tett and Martin Wolf; at Bloomberg, Joe Brusuelas, Peter Coy, Sara Eisen, the inimitable Pimm Fox, Kathleen Hays, Tom Keane, Bradley Keoun, Michael McKee, Matt Miller, and Yalman Onaran; at CNBC, Maria Bartiromo, Nick Dunn, and David Faber; at Reuters, Dan Wilchins and Mark White; and elsewhere, Henry Blodget, Astrid Doerner, Jesse Eisinger, Mark Gongloff, Paul La Monica, Steve Schaeffer, and Aaron Task. While you were all just doing your jobs, you provided encouragement and gave me the ability to gauge reaction to my thinking.

In late 2008, I got a call from the documentarian Charles Ferguson, who enlisted me in the team of far greater minds who helped him create the Oscar-winning documentary *Inside Job*, on the history of the global financial crisis. The film premiered to great acclaim in 2010 and afforded me both significant exposure for my views on global oversupply as well as the ability to cross "Appear in Academy Award–Winning Movie" off my so-called bucket list. For both, Charles, I am very appreciative.

I am also very appreciative of the encouragement offered by my partners and staff at Westwood Capital, LLC—the investment banking firm I founded in 1995. They both dealt with a very stretched partner while I was writing this book, and have for years had to listen to me to me drone an in macroeconomic detail, when asking me about almost anything other than perhaps the weather.

Finally, I would like to thank my father and mother, who taught me to question that which, though it may come from the mouths or pens of authorities and experts, makes little sense. If there is anything the events of the last decade have taught us, it is that my parents were right and that there is danger in not questioning that which seems too perfect. I have dedicated *The Age of Oversupply* to them and to my four children, who have had to put up with a father who wears too many other hats in addition to his favorite one, the one that says "Dad." Thank you for your patience with me.

NOTES

PREFACE TO THE PAPERBACK EDITION

1. "Credit and Liquidity Programs and the Balance Sheet," Federal Reserve Board of Governors website, http://federalreserve.gov/monetarypolicy/bst_recenttrends.htm.
2. "S&P 500 Stock Price Index (SP500)," Federal Reserve Economic Data (FRED), Federal Reserve Bank of St. Louis website, http://research.stlouisfed.org/fred2/series/SP500.
3. "S&P Case-Shiller 20-City Home Price Index (SPCS20RNSA)," Federal Reserve Economic Data (FRED), Federal Reserve Bank of St. Louis website, http://research.stlouisfed.org/fred2/series/SPCS20RNSA.
4. "Negative Equity Rate Falls at Fastest Pace Ever in Q3," Zillow.com, November 20, 2013, www.zillow.com/blog/2013-11-20/negative-equity-rate-falls-at-fastest-pace-ever-in-q3.
5. "Consumer Credit—G. 19," Federal Reserve Bank Board of Governors website, http://federalreserve.gov/releases/g19/current/default.htm.
6. "Consumer Price Index—December 3013," Table A, Bureau of Labor Statistics, January 16, 2014, http://www.bls.gov/news.release/pdf/cpi.pdf.
7. "Consumer Price Index—December 3013," Table 7, Bureau of Labor Statistics, January 16, 2014, http://www.bls.gov/news.release/pdf/cpi.pdf.
8. Ibid.
9. "Daily Treasury Yield Curve Rates," U.S. Department of the Treasury website, http://www.treasury.gov/resource-center/data-chart-center/interest-rates/Pages/TextView.aspx?data=yieldYear&year=2013.
10. From the phrase, "You can't catch a falling knife without getting hurt."

11. Under President Bill Clinton.
12. Under President Barack Obama.
13. November 8, 2013.
14. Not a phrase of his own coinage—but one which had lost currency in macroeconomic circles of late.
15. Unofficial Transcript—"Larry Summers Remarks IMF Annual Research Conference," November 8, 2013, http://www.fulcrumasset.com/files/summersstagnation.pdf.

INTRODUCTION: THE ENDLESS SLUMP

1. Gideon Rachman, "The Making of a German Europe," *Financial Times*, March 23, 2013.

CHAPTER ONE: THE RISE OF OVERSUPPLY

1. Lester Thurow, *Head to Head: The Coming Economic Battle Among Japan, Europe, and America* (New York: William Morrow, 1992).
2. Francis Fukuyama, *The End of History and the Last Man* (New York: Free Press, 1992).
3. Richard Dobbs et al., "The World at Work: Jobs, Pay, and Skills for 3.5 Billion People," McKinsey Global Institute, January 2012.
4. "Social Security with Chinese Characteristics," *The Economist*, April 11, 2012.
5. Benjamin Carlson, "In China, College Education Comes at a Price," *Global Post*, August 6, 2012.
6. Geeta Anad, "India Graduates Millions, But Too Few Are Fit to Hire," *Wall Street Journal*, April 5, 2011.
7. "Emerging vs. Developed Countries' GDP Growth Rates 1986 to 2015," *Real World Economics Review* blog, March 24, 2011.
8. "Power Shift," *The Economist*, August 4, 2011.
9. "China Foreign Exchange Reserves," Trading Economics website.
10. "Gross Domestic Savings (% of GDP), Trading Economics website.
11. Ibid.
12. James Fallows, "The $1.4 Trillion Question," *The Atlantic*, January 1, 2008.
13. "Health Expenditure, Total (% of GDP)," The World Bank website.
14. "Total Reserves (Includes Gold, Current U.S. $)," The World Bank website.
15. "Gross Domestic Savings (% of GDP), The World Bank website.
16. "Global Shadow Banking Monitoring Report 2012," Financial Stability Board, November 11, 2012.
17. "A World Awash in Money," Bain & Company website, November 14, 2012.

18. "Mortgage Debt Outstanding by Type of Property and Holder: 1990 to 2010," U.S. Census Bureau website.

19. Heather Timmons, "Trouble at Fannie Mae and Freddie Mac Stirs Concern Abroad," *New York Times*, July 21, 2008.

20. "Major Foreign Holders of Treasury Securities," U.S. Department of Treasury website.

21. Ibid.

22. "State and Local Governments—Indebtedness: 1990 to 2008," U.S. Census Bureau website.

23. Shahien Nasiripour, "Joseph Cassano, Ex-AIG Exec, Is Unapologetic, Blames Auditors for Losses," *Huffington Post*, June 30, 2010.

24. "Global Shadow Banking Monitoring Report 2012."

25. Jinyoung Kim, "Past and Future of the Labor Force in Emerging Asian Economies," Asian Development Bank website, September 2010.

26. Ibid.

27. Richard Dobbs et al., "The World at Work."

28. "Education Indicators in Focus," Organization for Economic Co-operation and Development website, May 2012.

29. "Currency Composition of Official Foreign Exchange Reserves," International Monetary Fund website.

30. "A World Awash in Money."

CHAPTER TWO: OUT OF BALANCE

1. Jonathan Woetzel et al., "Preparing for China's Urban Billion," McKinsey Global Institute, February 2009.

2. "Major Foreign Holders of Treasury Securities," U.S. Treasury Department website.

3. "Income and Poverty Rate at 1990s Level," *New York Times*, September 13, 2011.

4. Author's analysis, based on data from "Current Account Balance (BoP, Current US $)," World Bank website.

5. Author's analysis, based on data from "Current Account Balance (BoP, Current US $)."

6. Ibid.

7. Ibid.

CHAPTER THREE: MAKING THE WORST OF IT

1. "U.S. Domestic Debt as a Percentage of GDP," Charting the Economy, http://chartingtheeconomy.com, June 25, 2009.

2. Daniel Yergin and Joseph Stanislaw, *The Commanding Heights: The Battle Between Government and the Marketplace That Is Remaking the Modern World* (New York: Simon and Schuster, 1998).

3. "U.S. Savings Rate's Deterioration Since 1980," Seeking Alpha, http://seekingalpha.com, March 22, 2009.

4. "Sold Out: How Wall Street and Washington Betrayed America," Essential Information and the Consumer Education Foundation website, March 4, 2009.

5. Matthew Sherman, "A Short History of Financial Deregulation in the United States," Center for Economic and Policy Research website, July 2009.

6. See for example Robert B. Reich, "Making Industrial Policy," *Foreign Affairs*, Spring 1982.

7. Timothy Noah, *The Great Divergence: America's Growing Inequality Crisis and What We Can Do About It* (New York: Bloomsbury Press, 2012).

CHAPTER FOUR: LET THEM EAT DEBT

1. Thomas Frank, *What's the Matter with Kansas? How Conservatives Won the Heart of America* (New York: Metropolitan Books, 2004).

2. "Remarks by Chairman Alan Greenspan," Federal Reserve Board, April 8, 2005.

3. Jennifer Wheary and Tamara Draut, "Who Pays? The Winners and Losers of Credit Card Deregulation," Demos website, August 1, 2007.

4. "Historical Data: Consumer Credit Outstanding," The Federal Reserve website.

5. "Debt Nation," PBS NewsHour, April 18, 2001.

6. "Historical Data: Consumer Credit Outstanding."

7. "The Garn–St. Germain Depository Institutions Act of 1982," Federal Deposit Insurance Corporation website.

8. "America's Debt Overhang: Growth, Austerity, and Other Policy Choices," New America Foundation website, September 2009.

9. Elizabeth Warren and Amelia Warren Tyagi, *The Two-Income Trap: Why Middle-Class Mothers and Fathers Are Going Broke* (New York: Basic Books, 2003).

10. "Trends in the Distribution of Household Income," Congressional Budget Office website, October 2011.

11. Thomas Piketty and Emmanuel Saez, "The Evolution of Top Incomes: A Historical and International Perspective," *AEA Papers and Proceedings* 96 (2006): 200–205.

12. "U.S. Trade in Goods and Services—Balance of Payments," U.S. Census Bureau website, February 13, 2013.

13. Peter Kilborn, "Japan Invests Huge Sums Abroad, Much of It in U.S. Treasury Bonds," *New York Times*, March 11, 1985.

14. Rakesh Kochhar, "A Recovery No Better Than the Recession: Median Household Income, 2007 to 2011," Pew Research Center website, September 12, 2012.

15. Neil Irwin and Dan Eggen, "Economy Made Few Gains in Bush Years," *Washington Post*, January 12, 2009.

16. "The Low-Wage Recovery and Growing Inequality," National Employment Law Project website, August 2012.
17. "Trends in the Distribution of Household Income."
18. Robert E. Scott, "Growing U.S. Trade Deficit with China Cost 2.8 Million Jobs Between 2001 and 2010," Economic Policy Institute website, September 10, 2011.
19. Justin R. Pierce and Peter K. Schott, "The Surprisingly Swift Decline of U.S. Manufacturing Employment," The National Bureau of Economic Research website, December 2012.
20. "Growing U.S. Trade Deficit with China."
21. "Foreign Trade: Trade in Goods with China," U.S. Census Bureau website.
22. All figures from "Foreign Trade: Trade in Goods with China."
23. "Historical Data: Consumer Credit Outstanding."
24. "Credit Cards: Holders, Number, Spending, and Debt, 2000 and 2009, and Projections, 2012," U.S. Census Bureau website.
25. Brett Weiss, "$1,000 a Day: Credit Card Solicitations in America," Bankruptcy Law Network.
26. "The Plastic Safety Net: The Reality Behind Debt in America," Demos website, October 12, 2005.
27. Cindy Zeldin and Mark Rukavina, "Borrowing to Stay Healthy: How Credit Card Debt Is Related to Medical Expenses," Demos website, January 16, 2007.
28. Mark Kantrowitz, "Total College Debt Now Exceeds Total Credit Card Debt," Fast Web, August 11, 2010, http:// www.fastweb.com/financial -aid/articles/2589-total-college-debt-now-exceeds-total-credit-card-debt.
29. "Flow of Funds Accounts of the United States," Federal Reserve website, March 7, 2013.
30. "Refinance Activities Reports," Freddie Mac, http://www.freddiemac .com/news/finance/refi_archives.htm.
31. Bill McBride, "Q3 2012: Mortgage Equity Withdrawal Strong," Calculated Risk, December 10, 2012, http://www.calculatedriskblog .com/2012/12/q3-2012-mortgage-equity-withdrawal.html.
32. Alan Greenspan and James Kennedy, "Sources and Uses of Equity Extracted from Homes," Federal Reserve website, March 2007.
33. "Household Sector Debt as a Percent of GDP," Economagic.com, http:// www.economagic.com/em-cgi/data.exe/var/togdp-householdsectordebt.
34. John Gittelsohn, "U.S. 'Underwater' Homes Increase to 28 Percent, Zillow Says," Bloomberg, May 9, 2011.

CHAPTER FIVE: NATIONS IN NEUTRAL

1. "Employment Situation Summary," Bureau of Labor Statistics, April 5, 2013, http://www.bls.gov/news.release/empsit.nr0.htm.
2. "Table A-15. Alternative Measures of Labor Utilization," Bureau of Labor Statistics, April 5, 2013, http://www.bls.gov/news.release/empsit.t15.htm

3. "Alternative Unemployment Charts," John Williams' Shadow Government Statistics, http://www.shadowstats.com/alternate_data/unemployment-charts.

4. "Euro Area Unemployment at 11.8%," Eurostate News Release, November 2012, http://epp.eurostat.ec.europa.eu/cache/ITY_PUBLIC/3-08012013-BP/EN/3-08012013-BP-EN.PDF.

5. "Euro Area Unemployment at 11.8%."

6. "A Year of More: The High Cost of Long-Term Unemployment," The Pew Charitable Trusts website, May 2012.

7. Rand Ghayad and William Dickens, "What Can We Learn by Disaggregating the Unemployment-Vacancy Relationship?" Federal Reserve of Boston website, October 2012.

8. "A New Jobs Program for People Trapped in Unemployment," CBS News, February 19, 2012.

9. Katherine Bindley, "Long-Term Unemployment Worse Than a Criminal Record When It Comes to Job Placement: Survey," *Huffington Post*, September 18, 2012.

10. Arthur Delaney, "Unemployed Face Discrimination Just One Month After Losing Their Jobs, Report Says," *Huffington Post*, July 30, 2012.

11. Jeff Teitz, "The Sharp, Sudden Decline of America's Middle Class," *Rolling Stone*, June 25, 2012.

12. "Output Gap in Percent of Potential GDP," World Economic Outlook, International Monetary Fund, http://www.econstats.com/weo/V009.htm.

13. "Budget and Economic Outlook: An Update," Congressional Budget Office website, August 24, 2011.

14. "Output Gap in Percent of Potential GDP."

15. Laurence M. Ball, "Hysteresis in Unemployment: Old and New Evidence," National Bureau of Economic Research website, March 2009.

16. "Failure to Act: The Economic Impact of Current Investment Trends in Airports, Inland Waterways, and Marine Ports Infrastructure," American Society of Civil Engineers website, September 2012.

17. Paul Krugman, *End This Depression Now!* (New York: W.W. Norton & Company, 2012).

CHAPTER SIX: THE EMPTY TOOLBOX

1. Eli Saslow, " 'Jobs Day': Monthly Release Employment Data an Economic, Political Obsession," *Washington Post*, March 9, 2012.

2. Michael Greenstone and Adam Looney, "The Role of Fiscal Stimulus in the Ongoing Recovery," Brookings Institution website, July 6, 2012.

3. Josh Bivens and Heidi Shierholz, "Three Years into Recovery, Just How Much Has State and Local Austerity Hurt Job Growth?" Economic Policy Institute website, July 6, 2012.

4. Heidi Shierholz, "The Unemployment Rate Is Hugely Underestimating Slack in the Labor Market," Economic Policy Institute website, April 5, 2013.

5. "Breakdown of Funds Paid Out by Category," Recovery.gov, http://www.recovery.gov/Transparency/fundingoverview/Pages/fundingbreakdown.aspx.

6. Daniel Alpert, Robert Hockett, and Nouriel Roubini, "The Way Forward: Moving from the Post-Bubble, Post-Bust Economy to Renewed Growth and Competitiveness," The New America Foundation, October 10, 2011.

7. Paul Krugman, "Earth to Ben Bernanke," *New York Times*, April 24, 2012.

8. Molly Ball, "Romney Unveils 59-Point Jobs Plan," *Politico*, September 6, 2011.

9. James Sherk and Salim Furth, "Heritage Employment Report: March Job Market Goes Out Like a Lamb," Heritage Foundation website, April 5, 2013.

10. "Out of Keynes's Shadow," *The Economist*, February 12, 2009.

11. Joshua Cooper Ramo, "The Three Marketeers," *Time*, February 15, 1999.

CHAPTER SEVEN: THE DETOUR ECONOMY

1. "Japan Interest Rate," Trading Economics, http://www.tradingeconomics.com/japan/interest-rate.

2. Reference is to the speech made on August 15, 1945, by former Japanese emperor Hirohito when he asked his subjects to tolerate the American occupation of Japan after its defeat in World War II.

3. Conversation with author, April 11, 2013.

4. Alexandra Harney, "Without Babies, Can Japan Survive?" *New York Times*, December 15, 2012.

5. "Eurozone Recession to Deepen in 2013: Capital Economics," FXstreet, January 10, 2013, http://www.fxstreet.com/news/forex-news/article.aspx?storyid=53dd8bde-1b4b-4ab4-8022-39f2513e3755.

6. Charles Roxburgh et al., "Debt and Deleveraging: Uneven Progress on the Path to Growth," McKinsey Global Institute website, January 2012.

CHAPTER EIGHT: BAD VALUES

1. Walter Hickey and Grace Wyler, "Here's Everything We Know About Mitt Romney's Economic Plan," *Business Insider*, October 4, 2012.

2. Léon Walras, *Elements of Pure Economics* (New York: Routledge, 2010).

3. Julian Hebron, "Shiller: Everyone's Too Optimistic on Housing," StockTwits.com, February 6, 2013; and Lauren Lyster, "This is Housing Bubble 2.0: David Stockman," Daily Ticker, Yahoo! Finance, February 4, 2013.

4. Jared Bernstein, "Inflation and the Output Gap," On the Economy website, August 28, 2012, http://jaredbernsteinblog.com/inflation-and-the-output-gap/

5. Jann Swanson, "Shadow Inventory on the Rise After 2012 Foreclosure Legislation," *Mortgage News Daily*, March 28, 2013.

CHAPTER NINE: BLIND SPOTS

1. Daniel Alpert, Robert Hockett, and Nouriel Roubini, "The Way Forward: Moving from the Post-Bubble, Post-Bust Economy to Renewed Growth and Competitiveness," The New America Foundation, October 10, 2011, 4.
2. Shawn Tully, "The 2011 Fortune 500: The Big Boys Rack Up Record-Setting Profits," *CNNMoney website*, May 7, 2012.
3. "Cumulative Change in Total Economy Productivity and Real Hourly Compensation of Production/ Nonsupervisory Workers, 1948–2011," State of Working America, http://stateofworkingamerica.org/chart/swa -wages-figure-4u-change-total-economy/
4. Chrystia Freeland, *Plutocrats: The Rise of the New Global Super-Rich and the Fall of Everyone Else* (New York: Penguin Press, 2012).
5. Ross Eisenbrey, "America's Genius Glut," *New York Times*, February 7, 2013.
6. Holly Ellyatt, "Depression, Suicide Rise as Euro Debt Crisis Intensifies," CNBC, September 4, 2012.
7. Mark Howarth, "Shock 15% Rise in Suicides Since the Recession as Unemployment and Bankruptcy Take Their Toll," *Daily Mail*, May 25, 2012.
8. Alan Hall, "Suicides in Greece Rise by a Third as Financial Crisis Takes Its Toll," *Daily Mail*, August 15, 2012.
9. Mari Yamaguchi, "Japan Suicide Rate Still Among the World's Highest Due to Low Job Prospects," *Huffington Post*, March 3, 2011.
10. http://www.nytimes.com/2013/05/03/health/suicide-rate-rises -sharply-in-us.html?_r=0.
11. Mark Follman, Gavin Aronsen, and Deanna Pan, "A Guide to Mass Shootings in America," *Mother Jones*, February 27, 2013.
12. Tamara Draut, *Strapped: Why America's 20- and 30-Somethings Can't Get Ahead* (New York: Doubleday, 2006).
13. Steven Erlanger, "Young, Educated, and Jobless in France," *New York Times*, December 2, 2012.
14. Edward N. Wolff and Maury Gittleman, "Inheritances and the Distribution of Wealth, or, Whatever Happened to the Great Inheritance Boom?" European Central Bank Working Paper No. 1300, February 14, 2011.
15. Susan Saulny, "After Recession, More Young Adults Are Living on Street," *New York Times*, December 18, 2012.

CHAPTER TEN: THE STABILITY IMPERATIVE

1. "Statement on Signing the Omnibus Budget Reconciliation Act of 1990, November 5, 1990," The American Presidency Project, http://www .presidency.ucsb.edu/ws/index.php?pid=19000.

2. Richard Grant, "How Reagan Was Compromised," *Forbes*, September 2, 2012.

3. Douglas Martin, "Richard Darman, Veteran White House Deal Maker, Dead at 64," *New York Times,* January 27, 2008.

4. Yalman Onaran, "U.S. Banks Bigger Than GDP as Accounting Rift Masks Risk," Bloomberg, February 19, 2013.

5. Anat Admati and Martin Hellwig, "Must Financial Reform Await Another Crisis?" Bloomberg, February 5, 2013.

6. Sallie Krawcheck, "Four Ways to Fix Banks," *Harvard Business Review*, June 2012.

7. Hyman P. Minsky, *Stabilizing an Unstable Economy* (New Haven: Yale University Press, 1986).

8. L. Randall Wray, "Minsky's Money Manager Capitalism and the Global Financial Crisis," Levy Economics Institute of Bard College, March 2011.

9. Simon Lack, *The Hedge Fund Mirage: The Illusion of Big Money and Why It's Too Good to Be True* (New York: Wiley, 2012).

10. John Maynard Keynes, *The General Theory of Employment, Interest, and Money* (New York: Harcourt, Brace, and World, 1965).

11. Lynn Stout, *The Shareholder Value Myth: How Putting Shareholders First Harms Investors, Corporations, and the Public* (San Francisco: Berrett-Koehler Publishers, 2012).

12. Daniel Alpert, "The Swiss Miss on Executive Pay," *Wall Street Journal*, March 17, 2013.

CHAPTER ELEVEN: UNDERWATER NO MORE

1. "UPDATE 2—U.S. Household Debt Burden Eases in Second Quarter," Reuters, September 16, 2011.

2. Daniel Alpert, Robert Hockett, and Nouriel Roubini, "The Way Forward: Moving from the Post-Bubble, Post-Bust Economy to Renewed Growth and Competitiveness," The New America Foundation, October 10, 2011.

3. Joe Nocera, "The Freedom Recovery Plan," *New York Times*, October 17, 2008.

CHAPTER TWELVE: REBUILD AND REFORM

1. Michael Grunwald, *The New New Deal: The Hidden Story of Change in the Obama Era* (New York: Simon and Schuster, 2012).

2. "2013 Report Card for America's Infrastructure," American Society of Civil Engineers website.

3. "Policies for Increasing Economic Growth and Employment in 2012 and 2013," Congressional Budget Office website, November 15, 2011.

4. "Failure to Act: The Economic Impact of Current Investment Trends in Airports, Inland Waterways, and Marine Ports Infrastructure," American Society of Civil Engineers website, September 2012.

5. Annie Lowrey, "Study of U.S. Health Care System Finds Opportunity to Improve," *New York Times*, September 11, 2012.

6. "Report of the National Commission on Physician Payment Report," National Commission on Physician Payment Reform website, March 2013.

7. Annie Lowrey, "Slower Growth of Health Costs Eases Budget Deficit," *New York Times*, February 11, 2013.

8. Steven Brill, "Bitter Pill: Why Medical Bills Are Killing Us," *Time*, March 4, 2013.

9. Megan Greene, "Greece Will Suffer Less If It Leaves Euro Now," Bloomberg, March 11, 2012.

10. "Entrepreneurship Action Plan," EUbusiness, January 9, 2013, http://www.eubusiness.com/topics/sme/entrepreneurship.

11. Charles R. Morris, *Comeback: America's New Economic Boom* (New York: PublicAffairs, 2013).

12. E-mail to the author, April 9, 2013.

CHAPTER THIRTEEN: GOOD DEBT, BAD DEBT

1. J. Bradford DeLong and Lawrence H. Summers, "Fiscal Policy in a Depressed Economy," Brookings Institution website, Spring 2012.

2. L. Bradford DeLong, "Increased Government Purchases Right Now Are Self-Funding," Brad DeLong, October 11, 2012, http://delong.typepad.com/sdj/2012/10/increased-government-purchases-right-now-are-self-funding.html.

3. L. Randall Wray, *Modern Money Theory: A Primer on Macroeconomics for Sovereign Monetary Systems* (New York: Palgrave Macmillan, 2012).

4. "Allianz Global Wealth Report 2011," Allianz website, September 14, 2011.

5. "Inclusive Wealth Report 2012," International Human Dimensions Programme on Global Environmental Change website.

6. "Flow of Funds Accounts of the United States," Federal Reserve website, March 7, 2013.

7. "The Debt to the Penny and Who Holds It," Treasury Direct, http://www.treasurydirect.gov/NP/BPDLogin?application=np.

8. "World Economic Outlook," International Monetary Fund website, October 2012.

9. "Problems and Priorities," PollingReport.com website.

10. "The Real Election and Mandate," Democracycorps.com, November 8, 2012.

CHAPTER FOURTEEN: A GLOBAL SYSTEM THAT WORKS

1. Conversation with the author, November 20, 2012.

2. Ibid.

3. Jean-Claude Trichet, "The Euro Zone and the Global Crisis," *New York Times*, March 15, 2013.

INDEX